D0169969

Whatever Happened To Baseball?

Jeff Potter

Copyright © 2008 Jeff Potter
All rights reserved.

ISBN: 978-14196-9882-8

Inquiries or orders may be sent to the author at:
2407 Killarney Terrace
Odenton, Md. 21113
potterbaseball@yahoo.com

Photo on page 19 from the book, *Baseball, An Illustrated History* by Geoffrey
C. Ward and Ken Burns

All rights reserved.
No part of this book may be reproduced or transmitted in any form by any
means, electronic or mechanical, including photocopying, recording, or by any
information storage and retrieval system, without permission in writing from
the publisher, excepting brief quotations in connection with reviews written
specifically for inclusion in magazines and newspapers.

TABLE OF CONTENTS

ACKNOWLEDGEMENTS

Very seldom is the writing of a book the result of one person's effort. This is especially true of the work that you are about to read. It is the collaboration of hundreds of stories pertaining to kids and their travels through youth baseball.

I would like to express my sincere gratitude to my baseball family for providing me with the memories and responses to my incessant questions that kept me going.

I would like to thank John Zingaro for the book, *Spellman, One Man's Influence*, which helped inspire me to take on the challenge of writing.

I would like to thank my wife, Sheryl. Her years of living through the transition of being a mother of a youth baseball player, and being the wife of a baseball coach, was an inspiration to write this book.

I would like to thank the thousands of parents who "get it," who understand that building character and teaching life lessons are much more important than throwing a fastball.

And of course last, but certainly not least ....

Thanks Eric

PREFACE

Truth be known, I've wanted to write a book for as long as I can remember. It just never happened and as time went on the once vivid goal of being an author slowly burnt out. The blame of not seeing my project through was a combination of lack of time, money, and subject matter.

That's what I thought...........

Then it happened.

I don't know what a ton of bricks would actually feel like if it hit me, but that analogy is the best way that I can describe the tremendous emotion that took over my body the moment that I *knew* that this book would be written. I have never felt anything like it. There was no huge life changing experience that prompted this action, only a very subtle comment made by a very dear friend and father of a youth who played baseball for me.

The remark was stated over a very casual dinner after one of our kid's baseball games. It was one simple sentence, "We're not looking forward to leaving something that has been so good to us." That "something" was a baseball program, that "us" was his wife, son and himself. The reason for their leaving is one of the core issues of the book and their departure is only a small window into what has really happened to baseball.

Before I left the table that night, I knew what I was destined to do. The road blocks that I continually put in front of me for not carrying out my dream of writing all of a sudden made no sense. Matter of fact, they had disappeared immediately.

I was going to write a book! I found my subject matter, but more importantly I found my inspiration. Now two years later, I have completed the first part of the journey. The easy part, the words on paper, has been finished. What is left now is for the readers to find something in the following pages that can be related to, its significance understood, and those particular messages communicated to another person for his or her benefit.

I hope in reading this book it brings back memories of your childhood when things seemed peaceful, fair, honorable and innocent.... like "back in the day." All good memories are wonderful, but baseball memories are, well, you know—very special. I hope a light bulb goes on at some point in reading this book, perhaps when you learn something about the game, or more importantly, learn something about yourself.

Whether you are a coach or parent or just a plain baseball fan, I hope you teach children the right lessons about life as you go through the baseball process. I hope I've done a good job with my son. The truth is, I probably won't really know for years.

I do know that my son has as much passion and drive for the game of baseball as he did ten years ago. I know that he loves and respects the game of baseball. I know that I'm very proud of his baseball accomplishments, but even prouder of the young man he has become. I do believe that a lot of his positive attributes were captured on a baseball field. He has learned teamwork and discipline. He has understood the significance of a good work ethic and hard work. He has learned, through some coach's character flaws, how necessary it is to be persistent and have a good attitude. He has learned the power of confidence and that by the proper outlook you can truly control your own destiny. He has learned so much! I'm very confident that as long as he lives he will look back at baseball, and his life lessons, with good memories.

That's the purpose of this book, for each of us to learn something about ourselves, to improve upon one thing, to acknowledge a bad habit or character flaw, to better understand the importance of life's lessons over winning, to perhaps just for a moment take us back to a better time.

I hope you find your own answers to what happened to baseball.

CHAPTER I
DO YOU REMEMBER ME?

"Baseball, it has been said, is a game of inches. But even more, it's a game of innocence. It is a child holding tightly to his father's hand as he is taken to his first big-league ball game. Some twenty years later the scene is repeated-the child, now a man, has his own hand clasped just as tightly by his son as they approach the ballpark together for the first time.

The father, as his father before him, knows full well that baseball is as much business as sport. He also knows that the world is not just and that life is not fair. But, given the slightest encouragement, mind and heart keep to their separate orbits. As father and son pass through the turnstiles, walk side by side through the damp passageways under the stadium and then suddenly emerge into the dazzling brightness – the vast green playing field laid out like a magic carpet before them - they share that excitement that today is something very special for both of them. The parent passes on the wonder and awe of his own youth to his children, and in so doing renews it within himself."

—Lawrence S. Ritter

One day about five years ago I went to my mailbox and inside was a hand-written letter addressed to me. It was from the town of Cottage Grove, Wisconsin. The name on the envelope was one that I hadn't seen for over 30 years and the title that accompanied it was one that shocked me even more. The piece of mail was from John Zingaro—the *Reverend* John Zingaro.

When I think of John, I think of a journalist or a math teacher, maybe even a scientist, but not a *Reverend*. It's not that he didn't possess the redeeming qualities of that vocation, he certainly did. It's just that it took me by surprise that he had chosen this profession. I went to high school with John and remembered him only as the sports writer for our daily local newspaper. I hadn't talked to him since graduation and here I was, standing in front of my house staring at this thick piece of mail from my former classmate.

**John Zingaro as a senior from
the 1972 school yearbook**

I immediately assumed two things. One was that the information inside the envelope was an invitation for our upcoming 30th high school reunion for the class of 1972. That would be nice, a chance to go home and see some of my old schoolmates, reunite with John and talk about the "good old days." The second assumption was that this was fate, getting a letter from the high school sports writer at this particular time. Baseball, after many dormant years, was beginning to influence my life again, just as it did when I was a teenager. Here I was holding a package from an individual who I would remember quite vividly from playing baseball as a youth.

During my last two years of high school, John probably had more nice things to say about me than I deserved. We weren't close friends, but we had a common interest; baseball. He was the writer for my high school baseball team and I was the star player. I was not only the star player, but also the star pitcher. All diehard baseball fans know that the pitcher always gets more credit than he deserves and I was no different. John's interpretation of what he saw on the baseball diamond was printed in our daily town newspaper, *The Ledger*. He had an uncanny way of not only reporting the facts, but also telling a story. It wouldn't have surprised me a bit if he had become a writer rather than a man of the cloth.

Seeing John's name on that letter triggered a lot of memories, mostly of my high school teammates: Rich Herman, Eddie Prence, Mark Crofton, and Donnie Mancini. More than winning or losing, I remembered the fun that we had playing baseball. Who could forget the long practices in cold weather, the "running of the poles," the reputation that we as teens were trustees of the top area baseball program, the excitement that went through the town when baseball season finally arrived! I had a lot of great memories of these players, and others, and the pure love of the game of baseball. Most of my thoughts, however, were of one person.

Coach Spellman.

My thoughts always went back to "Coach."

In hindsight I wish I had taken the time to properly thank John for all the nice things he wrote about me. No one at the age of 17, however, thinks about thanking the local sports writer for doing his job. Perhaps this piece of mail, this apparent invitation to our 30th high school reunion, would give me an opportunity to see John again and finally show him my gratitude.

I walked toward my house tearing open the envelope. Inside was a one page letter along with a questionnaire. It was not the reunion invitation I expected.

It was much better!

April 16, 2002

Hi Jeff!

> Remember me? I'm writing a book about Coach Bill Spellman. I'm sending this survey to as many of his former players as I can find. I plan on using the surveys to conduct as many follow-up interviews as I can. I hope to tell the story of a very interesting man who lived life to the fullest and who influenced many young men. His family is fully supportive of this project.

> I'm now the pastor of a Presbyterian church near Madison, Wisconsin. This is the 3rd book that I hope to publish. I've been thinking of doing a book on

Coach Spellman for several years now, and I'm finally moving on the idea.

Wow—how cool was this! There was going to be a reunion, not of our high school classmates, but rather a reunion of all former baseball players who played for Coach Spellman. I couldn't believe it! Although I hadn't talked to anyone about Coach for many years, I was thinking about him constantly for the last few months! Instantly, a warm feeling came over me. I knew this was more than a coincidence. Now more than ever I knew this letter was fate. The timing was incredible, the fact that it arrived at about the same time that I started getting interested in coaching baseball. That's why I'd been thinking about Coach Spellman so much. My son Eric was 12 years old and he was now totally entrenched in his baseball experience. We had recently moved from the only baseball organization that we had known to one that was new and exciting and full of hope. I hadn't been real involved in baseball for over 20 years, but now I was starting to get that feeling again, the same feeling I had when *I* was 12 years old. And now this letter! It was just what the doctor ordered, a shot of adrenaline!

Only at this time did I realize that John had not only become a minister, but he in fact was a writer, and a published one at that. I knew how well John wrote back in high school, as I had my scrapbook clippings to prove it. This would be his third book and I somehow knew at this moment that he would produce something really special. It would be a book with great interviews and wonderful stories. He would bring together all of Coach Spellman's former ball players and do right by him. I imagined others just like me scattered all over the country, opening this letter and learning about the book project. This wouldn't just be John's project – it belonged to all of us! We were going to recreate our youth. It wouldn't simply be high school memories – it would be baseball memories!

Baseball the way we knew it.

That was the project that John would try to create and we the players would help him. As much as we all selfishly believed how great each of us was as a ball player, we all knew that the central figure back in the day was Coach Spellman. Soon to be a book!

Over the next few months John collected surveys from more than 200 former players and coaches. He tracked players down in Florida, Tennessee, and California. Just about everywhere in the United States! Lots of players, some of them former teammates of mine, were interviewed. I spoke to John three or four times myself during the information collecting process. He finally assembled all of the surveys, all the notes from the phone interviews, all the stories from the former players, coaches, friends, co-workers and family members. The end result was a brilliant book that brought back a lot of terrific memories to a bunch of guys who thought they could play some pretty good baseball.

The process of John writing this book gave me a chance to relive a lot of stories and by doing so, unlock a lot of baseball memories that had been put away for more than 30 years. There's nothing quite like them. I could still hear the crack of the bat, the feel of hitting a ball squarely, the smell of leather, and the taste of dirt while diving into second base.

It was all so real again. Talking to John about my high school coach and the book in general was bringing out memories and emotions that had been lost for a very long time. During this time I learned a lot about former players and teammates that I had never known and more importantly, I came to realize what they thought about me.

The title of the book was perfect—*Spellman, One Man's Influence*. His life was all about influence, and the book was supported by stories told by former players, rival coaches and managers, and many friends, family members and acquaintances. The day that my copy of the book arrived in the mail is a day I'll always remember. Opening the package and seeing the book was pure excitement. I began to read it and any real work that I should have been doing was temporarily put on hold. It was 262 pages of pure joy!

The book was written in chronological order, with each chapter representing a calendar year. Chapter XXIII, 1970 – 1971, didn't take me long to find. That's where I would discover my best high school exploits. Although I graduated in 1972, and also played for Coach Spellman in 1970, my best year was 1971, which was Coach's last year at the school. I opened the book to page 185 and began to read quicker than I thought possible. Once I finished reading the next 20 pages or so about my time in the limelight, I did what any former player would do; I reread them again, and again, and again—no shortness of ego here! I enjoyed it more every time I read it. You need to realize that I was reading about myself from 30 years ago! I was reading about what *other* people thought of me. Taking in the compliments and accolades made me feel great. It took me back to that time, back to the day, when life was simple, innocent and pure—where I didn't have a lot of responsibility or cares in my young life. I could remember myself standing on the mound, ball in hand, staring at the batter who had absolutely no chance of hitting the fastball that I was about to whiz by him. What a wonderful memory—even after all this time. It had been *years* since I thought about being out on the mound… larger than life… invincible.

Thanks to the book I was back!

I finally pulled myself away from focusing on me. Reading this book was a reminder of when I would read the local newspaper the day after I pitched a game. It was usually a win and most of the time there were a lot of complimentary things said about me by the local sports writer – the same John Zingaro. I would read his article the first time quickly. Then I would sit back and enjoy reading the article again, and enjoy it even more the third time! John was a great writer, even as a high school student. As I read more of his Coach Spellman book, I realized John, like a good wine, only improved with age.

I glanced over the other pages of the book quickly. I then turned to the collection of photos which were located in the middle of the book. Maybe I would be in one—there goes that ego again! I wasn't but that was okay. There were plenty of other good pictures. One of the photos was of Coach Spellman's first varsity baseball team from *1954,* the year I was born. Two of his players on that team, Don Schaly and Bill Frasier, went on to become two of the most successful college baseball coaches of all time. Both played for Coach Bill Spellman on the very same team, on the very same field as I played. Both learned from Coach Spellman. Both became extremely successful.

That kind of says it all.

I then went to the very beginning of the book and started reading from page one. By the end of the day I had read more than half the book. I'm sure that I could have finished the whole book the first day, but it was more than just reading. It was going through a few pages, then playing it back in my mind... all of those great memories. Sometime in the early evening of that same day, I sent an e-mail to John asking him to please send me 20 more copies and include the cost. He gave me a price for the additional books that did nothing more than cover his expenses. His main motivation for writing this book was not to make money. Rather, it was a labor of love. Within the next few weeks, the copies of *Spellman, One Man's Influence,* arrived at my home. I couldn't wait to give them out! I handed a book to each of the players on my son's baseball team at the time and the rest of the books were put in my office waiting to be given to someone who I believed could appreciate it. Those books, along with 25 other copies that were later ordered, have long since been received by deserving individuals. I still couldn't believe that I was actually reading about my life 30 years ago!

I was floored by the information that I didn't know about Coach Spellman, my coach and more importantly, my hero. Knowing that I was under the tutelage of a great coach was always a good feeling. I knew he was a good man, but for the first time I truly understood just *how* good he was. He was selfless and fair and completely full of integrity. The game was never about him. He always shied away from the adulation that he certainly earned and deserved. Instead, he spent his time and energy helping, encouraging, and empowering others.

He was a class act.

In the three years that I was under the influence of Coach Spellman, he managed to instill in me something that is hard to explain.

But when I was on a ball field, I felt it. It was a feeling that far surpassed joy and excitement. At the same time, it was a calming of the soul and an exhilarating passion.

And it came from him—I know it did.

From the time I stepped on the field as a high school player until my final game with Coach, I felt it. When I read John's book all of those emotions that had been stored away for so many years came rushing back. Those feelings have never been duplicated in anything else that I've done in my life. When I finished reading a page from the book, I would stop, reflect, and realize how much emotion was contained in the words. No one spoke of Coach Spellman's wins and titles, rather they spoke of the man and his far-reaching influence and character.

The calming of the soul and exhilarating passion are two gifts Coach Spellman gave to me. He gave them to many people, but I believe I was fortunate enough to fully understand their significance. I can only hope that others did as well. They are priceless and I will treasure them forever.

I only came to understand these feelings by playing for Coach. Soon after high school baseball ended, my dreams of playing professional baseball were also shattered. Without the baseball diamond as part of my life these emotions slowly faded away until I no longer felt them. They were dormant, locked away somewhere in the back of my mind with all of those other wonderful childhood memories. Like most people, life takes a good grip on you and jobs, spouses, children, and bills take over. If you're lucky you find time to occasionally "smell the roses" and appreciate things in life that are important. If you're really fortunate, as I have been, you get a chance to rekindle your childhood memories, to replay them all over again…..and again….and again.

The catalyst to unlocking these memories was my son Eric. He could have decided to play football, basketball, or a multitude of other sports. He could have decided to be in the band, chess club, or some other organization. He chose to play baseball which I believe is the best sport in the world. My wife and I signed him up for T-ball that first year and the rest is history.

Once the juices got rolling and the lid came off of all those old baseball memories, it has been nothing short of an insatiable appetite for not only the game of baseball, but as it has turned out, a passion to share Coach Spellman's gifts. What better way to share these gifts than with your son!

One of my goals in my life is to share these treasures with as many other people as possible, to other ball players, coaches, and parents—and anyone else who is open and passionate enough to receive them. Some people have been recipients of them already. They're lucky and blessed, and they can thank Coach Spellman.

As I said, John's book was published about the same time that I started coaching youth baseball on a full time basis. There was no doubt in my mind that fate was playing a huge part in all of this. As I read through the chapters the one thing that was most telling was how things were back then as a child and how things are today. The more I delved into the book, the more apparent is was of just how different things have become—both on the baseball field, and in life.

Sadly, they are different mostly in a bad way.

With all the "improvements" in baseball—better equipment, improved training, higher level of competition, more parent involvement, and more money through fundraising efforts, you would think that baseball would be a lot better off now than in the past.

Unfortunately it's not.

You would think with all the improvements in our lives— improved health care, modern conveniences, higher education, career opportunities, and high technology—that life would also be much better off now than it was years ago. Again, that's not the case.

The more I read and thought about the characters in the book the more I came to understand the beauty and innocence of being young, a child growing up in the 60's. The values that were learned on a baseball field stuck with us forever in our everyday lives.

I go to baseball games now and want so badly to just be able to magically take these kids back to a better time, where playing baseball was fun, where parents and coaches had their priorities straight, and the experiences stayed with you longer than the game itself. It was wonderful back in the day, but like everything else, baseball and life have changed.

Somewhere along the line we lost our way. Not the players, but the parents and the coaches. We really don't have much of a clue anymore. We have managed to drift way off course and when we try to figure out why, everyone seems to point the finger somewhere else.

Maybe by trying to give our kids everything we didn't have, we took away from them what we did have. The truth is, we had everything growing up.

When the coach told us something, you could take it to the bank.

We had consistency.

When the coach saw that you were working harder than the other kid, you got in the game.

We had fairness.

When the coach saw you not hustling, no matter who you were, he did something about it.

We had discipline.

When you played really hard and did a good job, you were praised. The coach set the example. The coach gave proper attention and credit to the players. Back in the day, the star players didn't get treated differently. Matter of fact, because they were so good, the coach expected more from them. The stars were expected to hustle more, get to practice earlier, set the best example. The stars never embarrassed the coach by giving less than 100% and the stars were humble. Coach Spellman made sure of that. The stars didn't get special privileges, easier classes, or their own set of rules.

Consistency, fairness, discipline …where did all of this go?

You may think that we still have those things, but you are just fooling yourself. They are long gone. Sure, there are still coaches out there with all these great qualities, but they are becoming downright scarce. Parents will tell you that, players will tell you that, even other coaches will tell you that.

Every year tens of thousands of teenagers enter the ninth grade, full of excitement and expectations about high school baseball. These same kids have parents who are hoping that the high school coaches will be role models for their children, teaching them not only the game of baseball, but also the game of life. The hope is that the coaches will set a good example, be consistent and fair, motivate, educate, teach, and encourage the kids.

Like Coach Spellman.

I've been lucky enough to work with some baseball players who started with me as 13 year olds and are now very entrenched in the world of high school baseball, or have moved on to college. They go to different schools and play for different coaches. I talk to their parents and I also talk to lots of other parents who have sons who play baseball throughout the area. I've heard a multitude of stories about lots of coaches, many more than I care to remember. There are not many Coach Spellmans out there.

One of Coach Spellman's former players, Mike Esoldo, probably said it best when he was quoted in John's book – hitting the highs and lows of coaches in one paragraph—"Credit is often delayed for a coach. Teenagers sometimes don't see until years later what they have gained. When you're a young kid, you didn't know that he (Spellman) was teaching about life. If you can only teach a kid how to play baseball, you aren't winning."

Unfortunately, too many coaches, and parents, aren't winning. The life lessons are lacking, and all that is left is a number of wins and losses. Ten years down the road, the numbers of victories will only be important to that particular coach. In some distorted way, he feels that the total wins he garnered on the scoreboard are the indication of his success as a coach.

I believe that is truly sad.

Baseball today has taken a life of its own, not necessarily a good one. Kids are kids. They aren't the ones steering the boat, they're just passengers trying to get a smooth ride while the coaches and parents fight over who's navigating the ship. Egos have taken over along with power struggles and politics. Parents too often are trying to take a short cut that's not there.

You shouldn't teach your kid to hit the ball 15 feet further, but not teach him to be a good teammate. You shouldn't spend thousands of dollars on "showcases," but not a cent on a tutor for a class he's failing. Coaches are trying to win at any cost, at any age. What 16-year-old star pitcher hasn't already had some sort of arm problem? It's not just on the field; it's off the field too. It's embarrassing to what extent certain parents will play up to the coach, anything to get their son more playing time. Everybody sees it other than the parent. How did it get like this? Is it too much to ask to have players, parents, and coaches on the same page, the right page?

Maybe things haven't changed as much as I think. Perhaps it has always been like this and maybe it just *seemed* different before. Maybe I was looking at the game as a kid through "rose-colored glasses." I'm really not completely sure what has changed to what degree.

What I do know, however, is that it's difficult to watch a baseball game now, to see the disrespect this great game now seems to get. When players walk on and off the field, when they throw the bat, when they swear at the umpires, when they're more concerned about their personal stats than the team, I believe there's a problem. It may seem like a player problem, but these players have coaches who have set the example, or should I say, have failed to set the example. This type of behavior by the youth is nothing more than a reflection of you and me.

When parents are completely out of control about "showcases," holding their kid back in high school to get another year of baseball eligibility, flying all over the country to pitch one game for a team in a tournament, there's a problem. Are we really doing all of this for our kid? That's a nice thought, but we all should know that there are larger motivations at work here. Maybe some of this, or a lot of this, is actually for us. In a lot of ways, we perhaps are trying to re-live our youth through our son. We are trying to feel good about ourselves.

Other than my former high school teammates, I have never heard the word admired used when players were describing a coach or an ex-coach. Not one time. I heard it used several times in the making of Coach Spellman's book as I spoke to my former teammates and listened to John talk about the interviews he did with former players. Not once did any former player ever mention to me how many wins Coach had or how many championships were attained. They all talked about how Coach influenced their lives.

How many of you have had a coach that truly influenced your life? How many former coaches did you admire? How many coaches does your child admire? How many heroes are out there on a baseball field?

We need more Coach Spellmans out there leading baseball teams in high school, summer leagues, youth baseball, and T-ball.

So many coaches today don't have the knowledge; so many others lack the passion.

As I continued coaching youth baseball, something interesting happened. Baseball became not only part of my life once again, but it actually took over my life. Not in a way you might think. It wasn't the thrill of winning or the need to protect my son that was my strongest motivations, although they were present. The driving force was the incredible opportunity to influence young people beyond the baseball diamond. I was blessed with the privilege of having parents put their children in my care, to teach them not just how to hit, field and pitch, but also those life lessons that were necessary in their development. I'm sure most parents didn't see it at first as that profound, but the fact is a coach truly has that kind of power and influence, and if done correctly, that coach can work wonders. When that certain, special coach works wonders, not only does a light bulb go on in the kid's head, but perhaps the parent also realizes the tremendous value of a good coach and what has been accomplished that has nothing to do with baseball. Life lessons are what's happening out on those fields, baseball is simply the vehicle to carry it out. Coaches, players, and parents all need to understand and embrace this fact.

Baseball is the most beautiful sport in the world by far. It was crowned "America's Pastime" for a reason. Despite all the things wrong with today's game, coaches, players, and parents, baseball will not only survive, but will prosper. The excitement and passion generated during the course of competing in this sport will always outweigh any arrogance and ignorance toward the game.

I miss baseball the way it was. Most of all, I feel bad for what we have taken away from all of these kids. A lot of them will never have the opportunity to appreciate the game the way I did. So many people have lost sight of what the real purpose is out on that baseball diamond.

But *I* remember.

Yes, John .... I remember you.

CHAPTER 2
THE PICK-UP GAME

"This field, this game, is a part of our past. It reminds us of all that was good and could be good again."
   —James Earl Jones as Terrence Mann in *Field of Dreams*

Baseball was special in my hometown of Ellwood City, Pennsylvania, which is located about 30 miles northwest of Pittsburgh. This small community has no real claim to fame other than being the birthplace of Hack Wilson. Most people still would not consider that much to hang your hat on since most people have never heard of the man. Only real baseball fans would recognize this name. Playing professional baseball in the same era as Babe Ruth, Hack Wilson set a major league record in 1930 that will probably never be broken. He drove in an astounding 190 runs. Nobody in the last 77 years has come close to this record, even with the diluted pitching and the inflated stats of hormone enhanced power hitters.

Hack Wilson actually played his youth baseball on the same ball fields as I did when I was growing up as a kid. While our rival schools in western Pennsylvania were hotbeds for future football stars such as Beaver Falls (Joe Namath) and Aliquippa (Mike Ditka), we were all about the baseball diamond. The annual drubbings that our football teams took on the gridiron were on most occasions avenged on the baseball field. My initiation to baseball didn't start in high school, though. Long before I came to know Coach Spellman, I was honing my skills on a ball field in a community situated between Ellwood City and another small town, Portersville; hence the name Ellport.

Baseball used to be all about community. That no longer exists. Our fathers worked together in the steel mills, our mothers saw each other in the grocery store, or the laundry mat, or the Cub Scout meeting that all boys seemed to belong to. If I hit a home run or pitched a shutout in one of my high school games, I went to the Dairy Isle and Mr. DeLoia would give me a free hamburger, and say, "Nice game Jeff. Tell your dad that I said hello." The school used to supply the bats. If you wanted your own bat, you went over to Carmen Beatrice's Sports store on Wampum Avenue, put down your $4.99 and picked up your 34" Jackie Robinson. If the bat broke, you screwed and taped it back together. Dad didn't buy you a second bat.

Nowadays, you don't know who half the parents are on the team, what they do for a living, or where they live.

Now community is an empty feeling. Players move into apartments with their dads to get into a desired school district. Families sell their house and buy another one a mile away so they can attend a certain school. Kids are home schooled and held back a grade so they can have one more year of high school baseball eligibility. Back in the day, there weren't instructors or camps or lessons or radar guns. Showcases and travel teams didn't exist. But somehow we managed to play some pretty good ball.

Amazing, isn't it!

I can't remember what age I was when I started playing baseball but I know that I was very young. Matter of fact, I can't remember not playing ball. With three older brothers you had very little choice other than to join in.

It wasn't like it is today. Back in the day we had teams and leagues but most of our ball playing was what we organized ourselves. League games were a couple of hours. Pick-up games lasted all day.

This particular July morning in the year 1963 started out like any other morning.

I suppose the teams were pretty even. Our team had me, my brother Rich, Kenny Gebhardt, and Jerry Mesko. Our opponents were Pete Sheeler, Bob Maine, and Frank and Nick Tukalo. If the teams weren't fair, the only person that could be blamed would be your captain. We took picking teams very seriously as it was as important as actually playing the game. You never just picked teams, you had to go through the ritual of winning the opportunity to have first pick—the infamous "throwing of the bat."

The throwing of the bat, like so many other parts of the game of baseball, is a lost art. This doesn't happen anymore. Youths today seldom have the type of pick-up baseball games we had when we were kids. If they do put a game together, the sacred throwing of the bat wouldn't be part of the ritual. Back in the day, however, selecting teams in this manner was not only important, it was paramount.

The two best players were always captains. Pete picked up the bat and threw it to my older brother Rich, who caught it – now it began in earnest. With my brother holding the bat upright like some kind of sacred candle, Pete wrapped his whole hand around the bat, with his hand snug against my brothers. Rich followed likewise.

It was on!

Congressional pages choose up sides on the mall in Washington, D.C. in 1922. Back in the day, all baseball games started with this ritual.

Although their hands were still pretty far down on the bat barrel, Pete countered with the three middle fingers. Rich responded with the straight one finger, which was done by making a Churchillian "V" with your middle and index finger—only not vertical, but horizontal. Actually, at our age, we would not have thought of the "V" from the indomitable British lion of World War II that our parents would have connected with. We would have thought of Moe from The Three Stooges giving a forked poke in the eyes to Curly. At any rate, you formed a "V" with your fingers, and slid the bat in between them. The only three grips allowed, the whole hand, three fingers, and one finger, had all been used.

Now Pete had a dilemma. You could see him frowning. He was trying to figure out the next move, knowing full well his options were limited and basically non-existent. Pete finally countered with the "V." Rich came back immediately by grasping the bat with his whole hand, grinning smugly like a wiser, older man (though he was only 11). Pete knew at this moment that he was done. If he went with the one finger, Rich could go with the whole hand and there would be not enough of the bat left to grab. If Pete went with the whole hand, Rich could get enough of a grip to throw the bat the necessary 20 feet for the victory. Pete acknowledged the loss without even attempting the last few grips of the bat. Like a beaten chess master, he conceded.

It was 1-0, Rich. Pete, being the oldest, and the best player, was not too happy to have lost that throw. But it was always best of three; there was an opportunity to come back.

The exercise reversed itself. Rich now threw the bat to Pete and the game was on once again. Their palms and fingers worked with spidery efficiency up the bat toward the knob. It ended up with Rich barely having hold of the handle. With that tenuous grip, he had to throw the bat the necessary distance to secure the win. He swung the bat back and forth and finally heaved it with a grunt. It fell way short of the necessary distance, and the score was now tied up at 1 - 1.

Up until now, we the future draftees stood around watching with the kind of intense silence that our teachers wish they could have instilled in us in the class room. But now with the fate of the next few hours awaiting the outcome of this unbreakable covenant, we broke into shouts. Advice, strategy, body language…it took only moments for the two of them to work their magic on the bat once again. Pete had the final grip on the bat and now the only question was whether he had enough of the handle to throw it the necessary distance. Everyone moved back. The shepherds in Bethlehem could not have given way with more reverence.

A line was drawn in the dirt. After rocking the bat back and forth a few times, Pete seemed satisfied that he had the necessary momentum. A grunt—the heave—the upturned eyes…the bat went high. We watched it arc through the air end-over-end, not only watching the bat but mentally computing where the projectile was in relation to the line on the ground. Even before the piece of lumber landed, we knew the outcome. Pete won. Now, and only now, we could pick teams and play ball.

This meant more ritual, worked out over time with considerations of history and tradition and the unanimous consensus about lop-sided games. In other words, we would have fair teams. Whoever took the first pick, the other captain got the next two picks; and then the selections were rotated until all players were members of a team. Pete immediately gave up the first pick to Rich, who without hesitation picked me. My brother and I could fight like hissing polecats at home. Sometimes we couldn't even look at each other across the table at dinner.

But this was business.

This was baseball.

He knew I could hit, throw and field. Therefore, he made the only logical choice and picked me first. Pete, suspecting I would be Rich's first pick, was well prepared. He responded immediately with Bob and Frank, saying the names so quickly it sounded like a species of grouse: "bobnfrank!"

Pete had this all figured out. Although I was the next best player after the two captains, Pete knew I was also Rich's brother. Being his sibling, Pete knew from experience it was just a matter of time before we "got into it" on the field of play. Therefore, he forced Rich to pick me and he ended up with the next two best players. George Steinbrenner never negotiated better. Rich then followed by picking Jerry, and then the final two players were selected.

It was four on four, which meant hauling out the accepted conventions agreed upon over the ages:

- The pitchers mound was considered first base in terms of throwing someone out.
- It would be a nine inning game.
- Anything hit to the right side of second base past second base was an out.
- The player pitched from the third base line for a left hander.
- Anything a lefthander hit foul of third base past third base was an out.
- No bunting.
- The team hitting supplied the catcher.

Of course the most important rule, the one rule that created the most fights, was that the fielding team was the umpire. What they said was final… sort of. In a lot of cases on close plays where both teams were adamant they were "getting hosed" if the call went against them, the argument usually led to a negotiation, the batter would hit again. Since Pete won the bat toss, he also got the choice of dugouts. Naturally, he took the third base side. Nobody liked the first base side because it got all the sun.

We all went in to our dugouts and got the lineup from our captain. Although each team had a total of only four players, we acted as though this was an immense decision to make that would take incredible managerial experience. It was no more than Rich blurting out the names, but our minds created so much importance to this ritual. Of course, Rich, as was the custom of the captain, batted himself fourth. Back in the day, whether you had four, six, or nine guys on the team, batting fourth was the sign of respect. Everyone wanted to be the "clean-up hitter." In our neck of the woods it represented Willie Stargell, the star slugger of our hometown Pirates.

The bats were placed against the outside of the dugout wall in a straight line. No crisscrossing of the bats. Who knew that six years later that I would come to realize that this would be one of Coach Spellman's biggest superstitions; absolutely no crossing of the bats!

By now, it was around 10:30 a.m. This was the normal time that all the conventions and rituals were completed, and the game could begin. It was important to have a clear head and be focused on the game knowing that no parents with arms crossed would be waiting for us at home. All of us were smart enough to make sure there were no house chores left unfinished before we left for the field.

Our parents understood our passion for playing baseball. That was the one way they got through to us. When chores weren't done, the dreaded sentence would be dropped upon us: "No ball tomorrow for you." And they meant it. When our moms and dads said something, that was it. Today, it's the start of negotiations. In our day, it was over - end of discussion!

We learned quickly. Once we got up in the morning we would say, "Mom, I'm going to go play ball at the field, is there anything you want me to do first?"

We were surprised how often the answer was no. I think the moms were just happy we asked—what a great son, offering to do housework! By the time all of us went through this daily routine, it was usually 10:00 a.m. or so before we arrived at the field. An upset parent showing up at the field was one of the three things that could ruin the whole day. The other two possible problems were both out of our control. One was the weather and the other one was the older kids showing up and throwing us off the field. We at least made sure we properly prepared for what we could control.

We loved baseball, and we played all summer long. Sometimes the game was four on four, sometimes three on three, or some other variation depending on how many players showed up that day. We improvised a lot. If there was an odd number, we may have an "automatic pitcher" or an "automatic hitter." We used designated hitters way before the American League instituted that policy. We used "ghost runners." We played three on three without ghost runners, where if you had men on first and second base, the runner on second had to score when the ball was hit.

On this particular day, the game was four on four and it started out like any of a hundred other games played on that field over those last few years.

It became a day that I'll never forget!

I remember that we batted first and we had the first base dugout. There were only eight guys playing ball on this day, but we used different dugouts. Why? Major League teams don't use the same dugout!

I'm not sure which Major League team we represented, but if I was a betting man, I would guess that it was the Cubs. Pete won the first pick, and therefore the right to select his team. I knew he would take the Pirates. We lived an hour away from old Forbes Field in Pittsburgh. Everybody wanted to be the Pirates and everybody wanted to be the team's best ballplayer, Roberto Clemente, #21. What a great ball player! Little did anyone know at the time that his life would be cut short by his humanitarian efforts! Little did anyone know at the time how great of a person he was! But the Cubs weren't a bad team. They had Ernie Banks and Billy Williams and Ron Santo. We never picked an American League team. For some reason, if your home team was a National League team, you were considered a traitor if you rooted for an American League team.

It's just the way it was.

We played the first game and our team lost. I hated losing—at anything! But it was twice as hard when it was baseball and you were on the short end of a game to Pete. He really knew how to give it to you—before, during and after the game. I can't say he was a bully. He was just bigger and better than the rest of us. He was 12 and I was 9 and at that age, the difference in physical stature is tremendous. I can't remember the score of the game, but does it really matter when you lose? Not to me, I was all about winning.

Winning was everything.

We asked for a rematch; I remember that. The first contest must have been close. Usually, you picked different teams after every game. The only reason you requested a rematch is because you were really pissed off that you lost. You wanted revenge, especially if it was a game you could have, or should have won. You just wanted a chance to get even. The winning team didn't have to give you a rematch, it was their choice. That was another rule back in the day. This time they decided to be nice and they granted us an opportunity to avenge the first game loss. I'm not sure why, but it was probably because they felt that they could beat our butts again.

Before the start of game two, we took a break as we always did between contests. There was only one thing on our minds. We all ran over to Pete's house which was directly across the street, and headed for the side of the house. There it was; what a beautiful sight!

Water!!!

One by one, we picked up the long green hose, put the end in our mouth and chugged water out of it. Back then, you didn't grab a soda from the refrigerator. That was a luxury. Most families didn't have "pop" in their house and Gatorade was not yet invented. That rubber hose was a welcome sight. It had that awful, funky, funny taste, but we didn't care. The water was cold and we were thirsty. Back to the field we went.

Once again, it was game time.

We started the second game and it didn't take long for our team to be looking up at a pretty good deficit. We once again were getting our butts kicked. I was really pissed! Yes, I can still remember to this day how mad I was. Nothing was going right. There was no way these guys should have been beating us.

It was about the fifth inning of this game and from my position in the outfield I could see out of the corner of my eye a very familiar sight. It was Pete's dad walking toward the field. Because the Sheelers lived so close to the field it wasn't uncommon to see Pete's dad Joe come over to watch us play ball. By this time, it must have been 3:00 p.m. or so because that's when he usually got home from the mill. He, like most of our dads, worked at U.S. Steel. The steel mill was by far the biggest employer of the town of Ellwood City.

Joe loved kids, and he loved baseball. Anytime he had the time he would come and watch us play. Even from a distance, you always knew when Joe was approaching. He had this certain odd manner in which he walked. I never knew the origin of the "limp," just one of those things you don't ask as a kid. We enjoyed any parent watching us play ball, but especially Joe Sheeler. Along with being a supportive father, he happened to also be our Little League coach.

On this particular day Joe walked toward the third base side and stopped on the far end of that dugout with a good enough view to see the action. Unfortunately for Pete, he was out of the sight of the team hitting, Pete's team.

Well, those dreaded Pirates had been batting for a while and were really pouring it on. The score was something like 18-7. They just kept hitting it where we weren't and when they did hit it to us, something bad happened. To make matters worse my brother Rich was giving me a hard time.

Pete was right again.

Every time Rich and I were on the same team there were problems, especially when we were losing. We were yelling at each other and Pete, along with the rest of those knuckleheads on his team, was having a great time laughing at our expense. I tried not to say too much back to Rich for the simple reason he'd beat me up. He was 11 and I was 9 and I could never get the best of him. Although I was pretty strong for my age, I was no match for my brother who was built rather powerfully, even as a young boy. It was just so hard to keep my mouth shut, I had such a temper. Pete knew this and he was playing us like a fiddle.

We finally got them out, and we were coming off the field. I should say we were running off the field. Yeah, even back then we ran off the field, even though we were getting trounced. Why? We did this because we were a Major League team and that's what they did. So that's what we did! Pete, being Pete, was really letting us have it now. He then uttered a line that, although sounded quite harmless, will never be forgotten by me.

"Are you sure you girls want to finish the game?"

"Pete! Come here!"

The booming, deep voice of Joe Sheeler!

Joe, without anyone noticing, had made his way from the third base dugout area to behind the backstop.

The problem was Pete hadn't seen his dad walking over from his house—the way we did—didn't see him standing behind the third base dugout, the same dugout he happened to be occupying, and obviously didn't see his dad make his way to the area behind home plate. Pete was too busy enjoying the spats between my brother and me. He certainly didn't notice his dad when he hit a hard grounder to Jerry Mesko at shortstop that took a bad hop. Bad hops were commonplace on our baseball diamond. There was no such thing as dragging the field. Hundreds of small stones covered the infield. Well, the sharp two-hopper that Pete hit took a very nasty bounce as Jerry was about to field the ball. It was a direct hit to the face. Bright red blood immediately covered his lips as he crumbled to the ground. He quickly got to his feet, but we could see Jerry was a little stunned. He was just standing there, head bowed, working his tongue and jaw—a sure sign that a tooth was loose.

Jerry began to cry, but even at nine years old, he was tough as nails and wasn't about to quit. The game had to be held up for a moment while he took off his jersey and used it as a towel to wipe the blood from his face. That didn't matter much to Pete, who like the rest of us, didn't possess a whole bunch of compassion on a baseball field.

Pete yelled—"Maybe you should wear the glove on your mouth!"

Of course, we weren't going to let Pete know that his dad was standing in the background taking all of this in. Those words certainly would not have rolled off of Pete's tongue if he knew his father was present. We were all full of barbs and smart ass comments, but never were these comments uttered in the presence of our parents or any other parents. We all knew better.

Mr. Sheeler was probably ready to intervene right after Pete's remark while Jerry was bent over spitting out blood. But maybe the old man was giving his Prodigal Son a grace period.

But another remark by Pete, "Are you sure you girls want to finish the game," was more than Mr. Sheeler could tolerate.

Revenge is so sweet.

There is a few times in life that seeing something in person is priceless. Forty years later—I can still see Pete's face.

When 12-year-old Pete heard his dad's voice, he was about 20 feet from me, heading in my direction. I was running off the field; he was running on the field. As soon as the words came out of his dad's mouth, Pete literally turned white; adrenalin shooting through his body—his mind racing—the fox surrounded by the hounds. The tone of the voice made me feel that this was just the *start* of Pete's ordeal. When Pete turned around to walk toward his father, I actually began feeling sorry for him. We never, ever felt bad for each other, especially on a baseball field. Usually, we were delighted when somebody got in trouble with their parents. But with that tone of voice, we all winced knowing what was in store for him.

We all knew "the voice." Each parent had it—male or female. Joe Sheeler's version of the voice was encountered by Pete on this day.

He meekly went before his father. No convict has stood before a judge with more desire for mercy and less hope for it. We couldn't hear what was going on but we saw Mr. Sheeler speaking to his shaking son. We were all frozen in place.

Silently, Pete went directly to the side of the dugout where his bat was leaning, straight up and down. He picked up his bat and started across the street to his house. All of sudden, "the voice" boomed louder than ever: "No, no, no! You stay and *watch!*"

I never heard Mr. Sheeler use that tone of voice before. I had seen him plenty angry, like the time we all got caught standing by the back window of our neighbor's house, scaring a young girl while she took a bath. Or the time Barney Hempfill talked all of us into walking the streets of Ellport at 4:00 in the morning when we were "sleeping out." Or the time Mrs. Zekeli phoned Mr. Sheeler when we soaped her car windows at Halloween. All of those times, he was just real mad. But this —"No, no, no; you stay and watch!" We hadn't heard this tone before—we weren't sure what to do.

At this time, we all must have looked like we were playing "freeze tag" and were all captured. All bodies were motionless, just stuck in time waiting for the next move to unravel.

Mr. Sheeler just stared out at the field with an odd glare on his face. He obviously was expecting to see the game proceed. Pete now stood beside him, looking straight ahead. Not a word passed between them. The two were just staring. We figured that Mr. Sheeler expected us to continue since he ordered Pete back to *watch*, so we continued the contest. We better put a game on for them!

Another rule of four on four games came into effect. If you lose a player, tough! Pete was by far the best hitter on their team, plus they now had only three people in the field. That didn't seem to bother Joe Sheeler much, the fact that he had pretty much messed up our ballgame. I remember we actually felt uneasy playing the rest of the game. Mr. Sheeler and Pete kept watching. With the two of them just standing there, we obliged them and kept playing. In the next few innings we went from losing 18-7 to winning by a score of something like 39-18. Our opponent never scored again.

The game finally ended. Any other day, there would have been hot exchanges of words and a call for another rematch or we would have picked new teams and played the rest of the afternoon.

However, on this late afternoon the field was strangely silent.

Mr. Sheeler and Pete still hadn't moved. The Great Sphinx could have been replaced by either of these two. We gathered at home plate, no more than ten feet from Pete and his dad. We just looked at each other. We found ourselves in uncharted waters because this had never happened before. One player broke the ice of this uncomfortable situation by deciding that he had to be somewhere. One by one we all agreed and found reasons to leave. No one said much of anything, we all just kind of quietly scattered in different directions. We left Pete and his dad just standing there stone like.

At this time, there was only one thing on my mind – Robosky's. This was the local store. It was our summer hangout, what we affectionately referred to as our "pop shop." Everybody went to Robosky's after playing ball. It was the only place in Ellport unless you wanted to walk half a mile to Herberts grocery store. You needed at least 17 cents to make the trip worthwhile. That got you a 16 oz. bottle of pop (12 cents counting the two cents deposit for the bottle) and a bag of chips (five cents). Back then, there was only Snyders or Wise—no other brands. Wise were the salty chips, the ones I liked. Pepsi and Coca-Cola were natural choices, but RC cola was also another favorite. And of course, there was Hires root beer.

On this day I probably would have gone to the store with *no* money. I just wanted an excuse to walk past the ball field again on my way home and see if Pete and his dad were *still* standing there.

My brother Rich was in agreement. An hour ago, we couldn't stand looking at each other, now we were best buddies, discussing Pete's dilemma. That's how brothers were. It was amazing how everyone had something to do after the game, riding off on their bikes or walking in different directions, yet we all ended up at Robusky's 15 minutes later. Pete and his dad were the only topic of conversation.

Rich and I finally finished our business at the store and walked home, which took us right past the ball field. As we started past Hemphill's house, which was located behind center field, we got a glimpse of the area where Pete and his dad had been standing over 30 minutes ago.

The view that Pete and his dad had of me and Rich walking past the field. The Hemphill house is on the right. Years ago, there was no nice fence and it was just a field. Now, it is deservedly called Sheeler Field

They were still standing there! Pete and his dad were still in the same spot! When we walked a little further past the field, we felt justified in staring; and we just couldn't believe that they hadn't moved.

If this situation wasn't sticky enough, there was another little twist of fate that needed to be dealt with. Our little league team, the Ellport Pirates, had a game that night and we would be back together in a few hours. Pete, my brother Rich and I were all on the team. Mr. Sheeler would become *Coach* Sheeler. I thought this day was about as bad as a day could get at the ball field.

I was wrong.

Other than our team, the Pirates, there were only three other teams in the Little League program. None of them were any good. They all stunk. The best of the bad teams was the Juniors, our opponent that night. We enjoyed playing them the most because they at least gave us a little competition. We usually beat them by six or eight runs, while the other two teams frequently gave up over 30 runs against us. Back then, there was no "mercy rule" about being ahead by ten runs. The only thing that stopped a brutal whipping of another team was darkness. Looking back, I'm not sure how these little league teams were picked but I think Coach Sheeler may have had a lot more knowledge of the kid's potential than the other coaches or perhaps just a lot more say in the selection process. They certainly weren't fair teams.

The other two teams were the Cubs and Wayne Township. The Cubs always beat Wayne Township. The Juniors always beat the Cubs and Wayne Township, and we always beat everybody. We thought that we were so good! Not exactly parity in this league, but even at that age, I knew that I was obviously on the right team. I always pitched against Wayne Township, my brother Rich always pitched against the Cubs, and Pete always pitched against the Juniors, our opponent that night.

The season was almost over and the games went fairly routinely... until that night!

I was always one of the first players to get to the field and this evening was no different. In fact, with all of the happenings of that day, there was a special buzz in the air and a good reason to arrive earlier than usual. I wanted to hear all the gory details of what happened between Coach Sheeler and his son, the best player on our team. I wanted to be the first to know how long they stayed at the field, whether his dad was talking to him, and what punishment was doled out.

Nowadays when something like that happens a bunch of cell phones immediately start ringing. If someone isn't calling their buddy, they're sending a text message. Back in the day, we seldom even talked on the phone. If we were talking for more than five minutes, our mom would tell us to get off the phone because an important call might come in.

No one on our team other than my brother and I knew what happened that day and I was more than willing to spread the word when I saw the other players.

As I arrived at the field, Coach Sheeler was there. The helmets, bats, and catching equipment were already out of the bag and a few players were tossing the ball back and forth. Everything was normal except one thing.

There was no Pete.

I started warming up, craning my neck to look around for Pete.

He wasn't anywhere to be seen.

I looked at the warm-up mound, which was down the left field line.

Again, no sign of Pete.

This was very odd.

I continued to throw the ball, and players continued to arrive: Billy Boy, Pat Boyle, Steve McDevitt, and Miles Heinzenrator. All of the players, except one. Our best player was inexplicably missing in action.

Yes, Coach Sheeler was there and at times was standing within three feet of me. No, I didn't ask him where Pete was. Something inside my 9-year-old brain knew not to ask any questions. As badly as I wanted to know where our star player was, my mouth would not let the words come out. So, I just wondered like all the rest of my teammates. Coach Sheeler wasn't forthcoming with any information and it was obvious that all the other players had the same built-in protection mechanism as I did. They all seemed to know not to ask the one question that was on everyone's mind.

Although no one on our team other than my brother and I knew what happened that day, everyone sensed something. I couldn't figure it out until my eyes wandered over to the visitor's dugout. Frank Tukalo was sitting there smiling like a Cheshire cat, as were the other players.

Why were they all smiling?

Then it suddenly dawned on me that there were other kids present that day at the game, not just my brother Rich and me. Only later did I find out that a few of the players in our game earlier that day spent the late afternoon riding around Ellport on their bikes, talking about what transpired that day to anyone in the community who would listen. Sort of a Paul Revere situation, but instead of "the British are coming" it was "Coach Sheeler came and punished Pete." The whole Junior team knew what happened that day.

Our players started to realize one by one the absence of our team leader. They all wanted to know where he was. This was my time to "spill the beans" and tell all, how Pete had really made his dad mad, how Pete and his dad stood at the field for over an hour saying nothing, how his dad used a voice that was beyond anger. But once again, the words did not come out. I think in some strange way I was fearful for Pete that perhaps something terrible had happened to him. So what occurred earlier that day remained a secret.

By now, it was getting close to game time and all of us seemed to be watching every movement Coach Sheeler was making. I guess we were waiting for some official announcement regarding his absent son. He must have known that we were all wondering, but he was just sat at the end of the dugout involved in his usual ritual, scorebook in hand, making out the line up.

All of a sudden he put the score book down, went over to the team equipment bag and retrieved a new ball, as he had done a hundred times before the start of a game. This was another little ritual he had, presenting the new ball to the starting pitcher and sending him and the catcher down the left field line to warm up.

The only difference tonight was that we had no idea who the ball was going to be handed to. Pete was nowhere in sight and he always pitched against the Juniors. Both Rich and I wanted the same thing. We wanted that new ball to be placed in *our* hand. Neither one of us had been given a chance to pitch against the Juniors all summer and tonight was obviously going to be an opportunity for one of us. Coach had no other choice. No one else had pitched all year.

I wanted that ball so bad!

Coach Sheeler grabbed a new box that held a shiny white ball. He methodically started opening the box which took way too long to do. He then walked the length of the dugout, ball still in hand. He walked right past both Rich and myself. That brand new white baseball was put in the hands of another player. None of us could believe our eyes.

He gave the ball to Chip LeViere.

Chip LeViere!!!

Chip was an outfielder, and he would convert to the catcher's position when my brother Rich pitched. He had never pitched. We were playing the second best team in the league and the coach handed the ball to an outfielder who had never in his life pitched an inning! Coach Sheeler and his new pitching ace then headed down the third base line toward the pitchers mound to warm up. We all thought this had to be a mistake.

As we stared down toward left field at this unusual set of circumstances unfolding in front of us, Coach Sheeler patiently warmed up Chip. Usually my brother Rich, our starting catcher, would warm up the pitcher, which was always Pete in these games against the Juniors. Tonight he wasn't asked to warm up the pitcher and Rich didn't bother to volunteer. As Chip loosened up, more often than not he threw the ball into the dirt and more often than not the ball scooted past Coach Sheeler. Every time this occurred Coach Sheeler got up, went and retrieved the ball and threw it back to Chip with the patience of a saint. Although it was hard to even watch how often the ball bounced past Coach Sheeler, none of us for a moment took our eyes off of them. The other team, the Juniors, had now wandered over from the first base dugout to join us in watching the spectacle. They were all asking, "Where's Pete?"

We all wished we had the answer.

Suddenly Coach Sheeler stood up and started walking in the direction of our dugout. Chip followed closely behind. We all quit staring and tried to act cool but we were all kind of nervously walking around. The other team hustled back to their side of the field.

As Coach Sheeler arrived back at the dugout he simply said, "Guys, have a seat." We had never heard him say that before, at least not in the tone it was presented. It normally took a while for the players to assemble and get settled and stop fidgeting. Not this time. Whoosh! We were seated.

For the first time that I could remember, the whole team was quiet at the same time. Not only was it silent but the parents were closer than normal to the dugout. They kind of sensed something was going on, but not knowing what. I'm sure they had all realized by now that Pete, the coach's son and the team's best player, was missing. Perhaps we were ready to get our answer.

After a long, uncomfortable silence, Coach Sheeler started talking. It was apparent from his first words that the tone of his voice was much different. I'm not quite sure of everything he said. My mind was busy enough at the age of nine trying to piece together the events of the day. I assumed that what Coach Sheeler was saying to us at this time had something to do with what happened earlier in the afternoon. He seemed really upset. He never gave speeches before a game but this was different, and it felt different. He rambled for a while and it was hard listening to him, trying to sit still for what felt like a very long time. In addition to this, I knew all of our minds were somewhere else. We were all thinking the same thing.

Where was Pete?

Coach never mentioned where Pete was or why he was absent. He never mentioned him by name during his pre-game speech but we all knew he was speaking of his son. He spoke for much longer than he ever did previously before a game. Of all that Coach Sheeler said in his tirade, one line stood out. I don't know why I caught this one sentence, but I did. Maybe that's a sign of truth, it catches us in spite of ourselves. This one line is one of those locked up memories that now have come back to life. I hadn't thought of it for all these years, but it somehow stuck with me.

"Always compare yourself to someone better."

I'm sure he didn't just say this out of the blue. I'm sure he led up to this in some way, but I wasn't listening too well. Yet this one line stuck for all of these years. What was odd was the fact that it didn't even make sense to me at the time. I had absolutely no idea what he meant by always comparing yourself to someone better.

Why?

Wouldn't that make you feel bad, always seeing yourself as less than adequate? Why would you want to admit someone was better than you? What did this have to do with Pete? Besides that, where in the hell was Pete?

We still didn't have our answer.

But at this time, at this moment, all I knew was that he said it, and Pete was missing, and Chip LeViere had warmed up, and everybody was totally confused.

The game started and as usual, I ran out into the field to my position in centerfield. Yes, I ran out and yes, I do remember running out to my position that particular day, that particular game. I had a warm up ball in my glove and I stepped on second base on my way out to my position. I always ran out to my position in centerfield and I always stepped on second base. It was always with my left foot. I can't explain why, I just did it. Centerfield is where I usually played if I didn't pitch. Centerfield, like batting fourth, was a status thing. The centerfielder was always better than the leftfielder. The leftfielder was always better than the right fielder. Right field is where you put your very worst player on the team. That's where we put Randy Blinn. The best outfielder was always in centerfield. Occasionally, I played first base. Because I was left-handed, I was deprived of playing any other infield position or catcher. It took me years to realize that being left-handed was not a curse but a blessing. As a boy growing up there weren't too many left-handed players and less left-handed pitchers. I became known in baseball circles, even at the age of nine, as "Lefty." This name stayed with me throughout high school. Most kids called me Jeff, most parents called me Lefty.

So I played centerfield that evening—had the perfect view for watching Chip walk four guys in a row to start the very first inning.

The first four guys walked! I don't think any of them ever took the bat off their shoulders. As the first runner for the Juniors jogged across home plate, being forced in from third base on the walk, Coach Sheeler slowly started toward the mound. The bases were still loaded and there was nobody out.

Boy did Coach Sheeler screw up this game, I thought.

As he approached the mound, my only thought was whether he was going to call me in to pitch or would it be my brother Rich, who was the catcher that day. I mean Pete wasn't there! That was really his only two options. I knew he would have to put in one of us. Why did he even start this other guy? Why did he walk past both Rich and me in the dugout before the game with that brand new baseball? Why didn't he just hand it to one of us? Why was he punishing our team like this? Well, it didn't matter. We'll come back and beat them. I mean we are 14-0 and we are the best team in the league by far. We don't need Pete to beat these guys. Let's just get out of the inning.

Coach Sheeler arrived at the mound and started talking to Chip. I felt bad for him considering the fact that he had never pitched before, and he didn't even get anyone out. His head was hung, his shoulders were sagging, and he was staring at his feet. I'm not sure, but I think tears were running down his cheeks. Even at that age, I knew these were the signs of a beaten pitcher, someone who just wanted the coach to take mercy on him and get him off the mound. Coach Sheeler took the ball out of Chip's glove and put his hand on Chip's shoulder, as if this was going to comfort a kid who basically couldn't throw a ball over the plate. The hand on the shoulder is the universal sign that the pitcher is being replaced and comforted at the same time. Coach Sheeler just stood there for a few moments and then he signaled Rich from behind the plate out to the mound. I guess he was going to have Rich pitch and not me. I didn't like that but I could live with that. Anybody but Chip!

Rich arrived at the mound and now there was a three-way conversation. A few moments later, Rich started back toward home plate, not to the dugout to change his equipment! Coach Sheeler was still on the mound, ball in hand. Chip was still there and had managed to pick up his head. I was getting pretty pumped as I knew that he was going to call on me to pitch!

Come on Joe, give me the sign, I thought to myself.

Call me in to pitch! I'll get us out of this jam.

At the time, I didn't realize how bad of a teammate I really was. I did not support Chip before the game. It would have been so easy to go over to him as he was waiting for the game to start and give him a couple of words of encouragement. It would have been so easy to let him know that the team was behind him. I mean he did look really scared as he waited for the game to start. But I failed to do this, and I guess deep down, I really didn't want him to do well. I wanted to win the game and I guess I wanted to be the hero. As I stood out in centerfield all I could think about was me going in to pitch and how in a way, I wanted Chip to fail.

A few seconds later, however, my elation turned to shock when instead of signaling me to come in to pitch, he took the ball and placed it back in Chip's glove and walked back into the dugout. After all of this, the only thing he did was talk to Chip and return to the dugout!

What was he thinking? What positive signs did he see with a guy who just threw 16 straight pitches with not one of them crossing the strike zone? Sixteen balls in a row! After that performance, he patted him on the shoulder and gave him the ball again! What kind of coaching was this?

The game started again and here we were, still in a "pickle", and no light at the end of the tunnel. We finally got out of the inning, somehow, someway, but we were down four or five runs. Chip did a little better after the talk with the coach. He at least threw some strikes but he wasn't pitching as well as Rich or I could have pitched. Why couldn't Coach Sheeler see this?

I remember that we scored several runs but we never made up the deficit from that first inning. We ended up losing the game and our perfect record went down the tubes. Every time we scored a few runs and our hopes lifted, Chip would be sent back out on the mound and he would without fail give those runs back. During the game, Coach Sheeler must have gone out to the mound five or six times, but he never took Chip out of the game.

I couldn't figure out how he had become such a bad coach so quickly. Before that night, I always thought he was a good coach. We always won. What exactly were his motivations in what he was doing? Perhaps he wasn't as good of a coach as I thought.

The other team, the Juniors, was having a ball… Greg Hampton, Buddy Harper, Ed Wojtkiewicz, Joe Tomon, all of them. They were having a great time at our expense. The Juniors had beaten the mighty Pirates. Some other teams may have seen this as a hollow victory, beating a team who used a player who never pitched before and missing their best, most dominant player. Trust me, they weren't thinking hollow victory. They didn't care who played and who pitched. This game, this win, made their summer. This game ruined our summer.

Sometime after the game started, about the third inning, Pete walked over from his house to the field. He was not in uniform, rather in street clothes. He sat at the end of the bench—said nothing to any of us the whole game. We returned the favor by leaving him alone. We could tell he had been crying. Once again, all of us somehow knew that this was not the time to take advantage of his weakness. Perhaps this was the day we all learned about compassion on the baseball field.

This was all like a very bad dream. Okay, punish your kid …big deal…but why punish all of us? Why ruin our whole summer in one game? None of it made any sense.

I don't know if what Coach Sheeler said or did that evening affected anyone else, but it affected me. No one ever talked about that day after that day. I guess we were still trying to figure it all out from our own childhood logic and vantage point. But from that day on I looked at Pete, and Coach Sheeler, quite differently. I felt bad for Pete but I wasn't sure why. I had plenty of conversations with him *after* that day, but never *about* that day.

Joe Sheeler continued to coach baseball for a few more years, never working with kids older than Little League. He coached me until I was 11 and in my mind, never made another coaching mistake that came close to the fiasco of that loss that night that made us less than perfect. After that evening I thought he recovered and became a good coach again. I don't remember many of the details of any other games that he coached me. I do remember, however, that I never again made fun of another kid that wasn't as good as me.

Well, at least not in front of Coach Sheeler.

From the time I was 11 until I graduated from high school, I would occasionally run into Joe Sheeler. He would always ask how my parents were doing and he would always say something nice about a write-up in the local paper that he had read about me. Baseball was so popular where we lived; our local daily newspaper covered every level—Farm League, Little League, Pony League, Colt League, American Legion...let alone High School. I was making headlines every summer.

I would always think of that one summer day when I was nine—and what Coach Sheeler said to the team. I could just envision him, standing with Pete, stone like, watching us finish the game on that rocky, dirt field. I have often wondered about what the two of them went through that day. The anger that I felt toward Coach Sheeler finally went away. I still didn't understand everything about that day, but I had this feeling that there was a logical answer ... I just didn't know it.

Now, over 40 years later, I realize how often my thoughts go back to a memory on a ball field and what life lesson was being taught that day; a lesson that I would not understand for maybe 30 or 40 years. How many of those other kids that day learned something or kept some memory from another childhood game? Coaches were teaching all kinds of lessons and I know that now. Unfortunately, it's too late to thank our childhood coaches, but it's certainly not too late to learn from them.

Coach Sheeler is an old memory to me now. I haven't spoken to him, or Pete, in over 30 years. But that summer day in 1963 was locked away somewhere in my head for all this time. I didn't realize until very recently that when I'm coaching and I'm not too happy with the players, I will say to them, "Have a seat," exactly the way I remember Coach Sheeler saying it that night.

When a player now gets a little too big for himself I think of Pete and his dad. I often wonder what was said that day between them, sitting at that field or in their house that afternoon or perhaps after the game that cost us a perfect record.

I now realize why he said that one sentence, why you *should* compare yourself to someone better. After all these years, it hit me. We ended up 14-1 and beat the hell out of every team really bad. I remember at that time how great it was to have dominated those teams so easily.

I thought that we were so good!

But now I have a different perspective.

We weren't that good; we were just playing kids who didn't have as much talent. That's what Coach Sheeler was trying to tell us. That's what he was trying to tell Pete that day. I came to realize that he wasn't a bad coach the day he put Chip in to pitch. Rather he was displaying some great coaching skills.

Teaching a life lesson was more important than winning a game, even if it cost us a perfect record. I really had no reason to be angry at him. Now I understand the lesson that was being taught. I hope as a coach that I would have no problem doing that myself. It has become obvious to me that under that particular circumstance, there really was no other good choice. What is sad is that a lot of coaches would never dare to do that because winning is just way too important.

What's so good about beating up on lesser teams? What's so good about making fun of a kid smaller and younger than you? You see coaches today puff out their chest and act condescending when they beat up on a team with much less talent. They act like they're the reason the team won, that they're such a good coach.

The most important game that year was the game we lost. I didn't know it at the time, but now it is crystal clear and a life lesson well received. The one game I remember that summer was that loss, and the one game that affected me in the most positive way was that loss. I just didn't know at the time how much it would impact me.

Perhaps when I bench our clean-up hitter for throwing the bat or our star pitcher for mouthing off or our starting second baseman for not looking at the signals, it is really Coach Sheeler doing that. Or maybe it's Coach Spellman, Dave Dobi, Fred Takas or another coach who taught me that particular lesson. It's a little voice saying that winning is a temporary high, life lessons last forever.

Maybe that's why it's just not that important to win at all costs. Maybe I learned from Coach Sheeler that you only get better by playing better teams. You get better by comparing yourself to someone better.

I hadn't thought of Coach Sheeler for all of these years. Then the writing started, and soon after that the flood of memories followed. Perhaps there was no reason to think of him then, but now there is.

I regret the fact that I never thanked Coach Sheeler for coaching me, even when I was older. I never truly appreciated what he taught me, all the life lessons. But now, it is all so clear to me.

Pete went on to eventually be a star outfielder in high school and American Legion baseball. He threw right-handed but batted left-handed. He could hit a ball further than anyone I've ever known, routinely hitting balls well over 400 feet. This was done with a wooden bat. He had amazing power, along with one of the strongest outfield arms that I have ever witnessed. But Pete had no foot speed and tryouts with a few major league teams did not lead to anything promising. He played ball in the area for years and years after graduation and ended up being the head baseball coach for four years at the high school where we both graduated.

I'm sure he was a good coach. I'm sure he taught the kids the proper way to play baseball and the proper way to conduct themselves on the field. Also, I'm sure as he was coaching, memories went back to his childhood playing days; perhaps back to that day at the ball field with his dad.

Looking back, I'm glad we lost that game. I'm glad that 12 kids across the field had a memory of knocking off the mighty Pirates. Perhaps somebody else at that game that night learned the right lesson, and in the 40 years since, has taught it to someone else.

He can thank Coach Sheeler.

C H A P T E R   3
THE BROKEN BAT

"Life will always throw you curves, just keep fouling them off... the right pitch will come, but when it does, be prepared to run the bases."

—Rick Maksian

Back in the day, whether it was on a baseball field or life in general, we had everything we needed. By today's standards, one would look at us back in the 1960's and say we were "broke," we really had no money. We probably were broke, but the key was that we didn't know we were broke. Therefore, in our minds we had everything because we just didn't know any better. There was no such thing as CD players, big screen TV's, and cell phones to even wish for. We didn't waste our time thinking about the things that we couldn't afford. We were too busy playing baseball.

Baseball was king. Nothing else really came close to it. Yes, there were pick-up football games in our yard, and yes we went down and played basketball at Bill Soltes's house for hours and hours at a time. And yes, we spent some days down at the creek swimming, building dams, and swinging off the vine. They were all fun times and great memories.

They just weren't baseball.

I can remember every one of my 12 coaches, from Frank Clark at seven years old through Coach Spellman in high school. I never had the impression that any of them had any other agenda other than being a good coach and helping the players. They all seemed to have a real excitement about teaching and the game of baseball never seemed to be about them. When you acted up, which was seldom, they put you in your place. Then you had the privilege of going home and facing the wrath of your dad who didn't want to hear your side of the story. All he knew was the coach had to talk to you. You must have been wrong or showed some sort of disrespect.

How things have changed!

We played so much baseball as a kid that you couldn't help but improve as a player. Today's terminology would be "muscle memory" but back then we just knew it as playing ball until it got dark. We played games and then home run derby. After that, we raced around the bases, had bunting contests, throwing contests, and hit fly balls. We learned to be creative and make our own fun.

When the big guys came up to the field; Dickie Rogers, Art Butler, Ed Chantos, my brother Jim (six years older than me), Tony Bucci, we prayed that they wouldn't have enough players so we could play with them. If they had enough bodies, they would do the unspeakable. They would throw us off the field, and do it without an ounce of remorse. They cut us no slack.

We played ball morning, noon, and night. We played in the rain. We played with old bats, old balls, and old gloves. It was not uncommon for our game ball to be kept together with electrical tape. We played before our weekend league games, then turned around and played after the league game. We played baseball until we had no more energy, but the setting of the sun usually came first.

Then we had no choice. We had to go home. If there was a game, I wanted to be there. Not much stopped me from playing baseball.

Except the day my bat broke.

That day began as a lucky day for me. Really lucky! It had been a routine day. Then some of the older guys showed up and it was just a matter of time before they threw us off the field. They wouldn't be nice about it. As soon as enough of them showed up, they would literally take over the field. It wouldn't matter to them the inning or situation. They simply would announce, "You guys are done." This particular day turned out to be no different. It was like an oncoming storm … the sky got darker and darker, the air got cooler, the rain was inevitable, but you weren't sure of the exact time. The older guys were like the dark clouds, and when there were enough of them, the announcement came. I think this particular day it was Art Butler who delivered the bad news to us—get off the field!

Anyone who has ever turned on a light in a room filled with cockroaches can appreciate what we looked like in the next

60 seconds. We scurried around with no plan, only to get away from the oncoming attack. Grabbing our shirt, bat, and glove, we scurried off the field. There was never any talking back, until of course we were far enough away on our bikes to throw out some four-letter words. Yeah, you wouldn't have believed the language we used outside the ears of an adult.

I say the day was lucky for me because as the rest of my buddies retreated as fast as their bikes could peddle them away, I stayed to see if there was a chance, any chance that they would ask me to play. I knew that I had a small advantage over most of my friends, the fact that I had two older brothers, Jim and Dave. They were part of the older gang who would perhaps give me that opportunity to play. Rich was older than me but by only by two years and that wasn't enough for him to be considered part of that older group. Even with the inside track on my buddies, there were two chances of playing with the big boys. One was slim and the second was none.

Today, this particular day, the baseball Gods were on my side.

"Jeff, you're on my team," hollered Tony Bucci.

Oh, my God! Tony Bucci actually called me over to play on his team! Wait until Rich hears this! I can't believe it! I knew they would bat me last and send me somewhere out in the outfield to an area as insignificant as possible. It didn't matter. I was in the game! I was playing with the big boys! You have to understand how it felt to be ten years old and playing with kids 15, 16, and even 17 years old. There was nothing better! Nothing!

The game started, and as expected, I was batting last and was told to go out in the field and stay out of everyone's way. That was okay with me. Every inning I ran out to the outfield and took my position with a smile plastered on my face. When an inning ended, I ran off the field into the dug out, with the same happy look. When it was my turn to bat, I hustled up to the plate and took my swings. Although I don't think I ever reached base, I'm sure that I hustled on every play. I must have batted three or four times and although I was hitless, I couldn't have been having a better day. Life was perfect.

Then it happened.

I broke my bat.

Years later, I used a Jackie Robinson, 34". But back as a ten year old, it was a Nellie Fox, probably 28". I swung at a pitch and the ball rolled weakly to the shortstop as the bat cracked. You knew the feel and sound of a cracked bat, something you never wanted to experience as a baseball player. Perhaps you need to be a little older to appreciate the despair of having wood splinter in your hand as you swing the piece of lumber, causing that tight firmness of the bat handle to give way to a weak insecure piece of wood. Anyone today under the age of 30, in the metal bat era, would never relate to this awful feeling.

Freddie Mohrbacker, the opposing pitcher, started laughing at my anguish. Once I hustled down the line trying to beat out the throw, I started crying. I don't know why, I just did. Mohrbacher was a jerk, I never liked him. Tony Bucci, seeing the combination of abuse given to me by Mohrbacher and the tears rolling down my face, found it in himself to surprisingly show some compassion. He walked up to me and said quietly "Go home and fix your bat." This was unusual. You never left a game to go fix a bat. Instead, you borrowed another player's bat and fixed yours later after you got home. You just never left a game and quit playing but I guess he had his reasons for saying that and I certainly wasn't going to argue with the one person who let me play in the game.

So off to the house I went, running the whole way. We lived about 200 yards from the field so it wasn't much of a trek. Bat in hand, I ran to the side door that went to the cellar (back then they were cellars, not basements). I needed to make sure I snuck in the side door so my mom didn't see me. Not that I was in trouble or anything, but she might have found something for me to do. If she was downstairs doing laundry, I might have had a problem. Luckily, she wasn't. I ran over to an old dresser and opened up the top drawer where I kept my "supplies." They consisted of a small tack hammer, screws, nails, an old screwdriver and electrical tape. We always had that type of tape in the house because my dad was an electrician.

Now, like a skilled surgeon, I went to work fixing the bat. The first thing I did was to survey the extent of the injury. In other words, how bad did I crack the bat? Different types of cracks needed different types of nails and screws. Unfortunately, this was a severe break and therefore needed major work. It would need a screw, but I first had to put a small nail in the bat to stabilize it. If you couldn't find nails small enough, you needed to use one that went completely through the handle and actually stuck out the other side. In that case, like what happened on this day, you needed to pound the nail back into the bat handle. Once the nail was pounded in, I inserted the screw, and then tapped in a second nail. Once this was completed, electrical tape was run around the handle of the bat covering the nails and screws.

Back then, ten year olds didn't have the technology to countersink the screws and nails into the bat. Therefore the electrical tape served the purpose of allowing us to comfortably hold the bat without hurting our hand from the sharp metal heads of the nails and screws. This was done many, many times before without a hitch, it was an easy repair. On this particular day, however, I was in a real hurry and didn't do a real good job with the tape.

Back to the field I went with my repaired bat. The whole process probably hadn't taken more than ten minutes; but they were ten precious minutes. Remember, when you lost a player … for any reason … you played without him. Although I was nothing more than window dressing for my older teammates, it was big time being selected to participate and I didn't want to miss any part of the experience.

I got back to the field at a perfect time. My team was just coming off the field and it was time to hit. Little did I know at that moment that my day was about to take a very bad turn for the worse.

The next hour or so of my life is a hazy memory. All I can recall is that in this time frame I managed to completely bloody a shirt and cut open my hand so severely that I still have the scar today. It's a little v-shaped scar that is directly under my middle finger on my right hand. Since I hit left-handed, my right hand was my dominant hand when I swung.

The problem was my bat.

I noticed immediately upon hitting that I didn't put enough electrical tape on the bat and the screw head was tearing into my hand every time I swung. I managed to get through my first "at bat" and now my hand was throbbing.

It hurt an awful lot, I remember that. But after a while, the pain subsided. I probably knew at the time that not hurting anymore wasn't a good sign, but I kept on playing. I mean, how often do you get to play with the big guys? If I quit now, they may never give me another chance.

So now we were back out in the field and my hand was not only throbbing but there was evidence of blood on my glove. I was a bit woozy and my stomach was upset. For the first time that I can ever remember on a ball field, I was praying that the ball was not hit to me. I couldn't even imagine the pain that I would have experienced if a fly ball landed in my glove, directly against my bleeding and sliced up hand. Luckily, my wish came true and no ball fly balls came my way. The next thing I remembered was that we were back in the dugout and it was once again my turn for the next plate appearance.

The condition of my hand had now changed to extreme pain as blood was now oozing through my fingers. Off came the shirt that I then wrapped around my bat as I walked up to the plate to hit. The skin was sliced open, blood dripping everywhere and I wasn't feeling good at all.

Matter of fact, I was getting down right dizzy.

For one of the few times in my life I quit playing baseball in the middle of a game. I remember dropping the bloody bat while still up at the plate and mumbling to no one in particular, "I've got to go home." I ran down the alley, past the Sheeler's house, past the Migut's house, and through my back yard, blood now running down my arm.

I was in so much pain.

I remember opening up the back door which led into our kitchen. With the shirt wrapped around my hand and blood dripping everywhere, I headed toward the living room. I quickly went around the corner and ran directly into my mom.

This was not good.

She took one look at the shirt which was now the color red. I guess through her experiences with six kids, she simply said, "Show me." I removed the shirt from around my hand and she made this horrible face. I knew it was bad because my mom was used to seeing cuts, bruises, blood, and it didn't usually affect her. This time she was squirming.

"What happened?"

"I hurt my hand playing baseball."

"How did it happen?"

"I don't know." (real intelligent answer)

"You need stitches."

I told her that I would go wash my hand off. I went upstairs and put my hand under cold water. It burned so much and it kept bleeding. It seemed like an hour that I sat on my knees running water in the bathtub. It was gross, and extremely painful.

She was right, I did need stitches.

But I never got them.

Looking back, I'm glad I didn't.

I'm sure I caught hell from my dad when he got home. I'm sure he came home, saw my hand and made sure I wasn't dying before he started yelling. I'm sure I missed a few days, perhaps a week, of baseball and I'm sure that it was really a dumb thing to do.

But I have the scar, I have the memory.

I'm not exactly sure why the memory of this particular August day in 1964 was the one that wouldn't leave my head on another day almost ten years later. I hadn't thought back on that painful day very often, but of all the thoughts that could be with me now on this particular day, why the memory of that game and the broken bat? Here I was, going through probably the toughest day of my life, and the best comfort I could find was once again feeling the intense pain of that broken bat. All I could seem to do on this dreadful day was continually look at my scar on my hand.

I just stared at my hand and remembered the intense pain!

It was an early March morning in 1974. I don't recall the exact date as it wasn't something that I wanted to remember. I was sitting outside the office of Hoot Evers, who was in charge of minor league baseball players for the Detroit Tigers organization. I don't remember his exact title, but again, that wasn't important. What was significant was the fact that I was summoned to his office and my baseball future was at stake. I wasn't feeling real good because I knew how the meeting would probably end.

Since my arrival in Lakeland, Florida the previous month I had pitched poorly. When you are a 19-year-old pitcher who is trying to make a minor league baseball team, pitching poorly is a recipe for disaster. You just can't pitch poorly. When that happened, you were usually summoned to Mr. Evers office where he handed you an envelope. When the envelope was opened, there was an airplane ticket – a one-way ticket home. I was sitting there, nervously awaiting my turn to enter his office, much like the many times I waited my turn outside the assistant principal's office in high school. On all of those occasions it never ended well. I had the same feeling on this day, but it was even worse. The stakes were much, much higher.

I was once again staring at my hand, at my scar.

I was once again feeling that awful pain.

The door suddenly opened and out walked another player. It was obvious that his conversation had not gone well. As he walked by me with a stunned look on his face my stomach tightened even more. I then heard a voice say, "Jeff, come on in."

I walked into the office and immediately noticed how dark it was. There was a huge desk in the middle of the room with what appeared to be an extremely comfortable chair that was occupied by Mr. Evers. Across from his desk was a very plain looking chair, the only other one in the office. It was directly in front of his desk.

Mr. Evers, without looking up from the note he was writing, instructed me to have a seat. Trying to act as comfortable as possible, I sat down. I had been in his office only once before, and that occurred the previous year during spring training. I believe that's about the time Mr. Evers began to not like me very much, the day I told him just what I thought of a decision he had made. More about that later, and to be honest, that really wasn't important at this point in time and it really had no bearing on what was happening now. I realized that how he personally felt about me had nothing to do with how poorly I had performed that last month or so.

He wasn't to blame.

With his head still looking down at the note he was writing, he asked how I felt that I had pitched since arriving in spring training.

My response was honest, "Not well."

How does your arm feel?

Again, I felt honesty was probably the best policy and responded accordingly, "Not well."

He then raised his head, pen still in hand, and looking directly at me said, "Mr. Potter, you've had a tough time getting started in this profession."

He was right.

I had a very tough time as a Detroit Tiger minor league ball player. When I arrived at spring training the previous year, hopes and expectations were high. The organization had just invested $8,000.00 in me and I knew that they were expecting big things. Compared to today's standards that amount of money is nothing, but back in 1973 it was substantial and a very real investment on their part.

I had planned to produce to their satisfaction.

About two weeks into spring training, I pulled a muscle in my arm and was out for a few weeks of practice. Because of the missed time, Mr. Evers assigned me to Lakeland of the Gulf Coast League as a "batting practice" pitcher. The coach of that team took me to the side one day and explained this to me, saying that I would travel to the games and be on the roster, but they wanted to take it easy with me. I could throw batting practice for two months. Then in June, I could go back to the second spring training and go on from there.

I don't remember exactly what time of day that this was communicated to me, but I do know that I was knocking on Mr. Evers door within seven or eight minutes of this notification. That's how long it took me to briskly walk across the confines of Tigertown, the complex of the Tigers, to his office.

Once he gave his blessing to enter his office, I walked in and simply said,

"Mr. Evers, I understand you have assigned me to Lakeland to throw batting practice."

He said, "Yes, we want to take it easy with you. So instead of sending you home for two months without getting paid, you can throw batting practice for the team and we can keep you on the payroll."

I guess he thought he was doing me a favor, and he probably was. I thought differently however. The next words out of my mouth probably weren't well thought out and thinking back probably weren't said in the best of tones.

"If you don't think I can pitch, then send me home, but I don't want to go to Lakeland. I'm not a batting practice pitcher."

Based on the sudden change of color of his face, I assumed that he was taken back by my comments. He immediately opened the drawer on the left side of his desk, pulled out a piece of paper and declared, "You don't want to go to Lakeland, okay. I'll tell you what... I'm sending you to Clinton, and I'm going to put your paperwork right on the top."

He then took my chart and firmly set it on the top of the stack lying on his desk. I said thank you and left his office. I wasn't sure at that moment whether he was insulted with the candor I displayed or that he appreciated my self-confidence in my abilities. If I knew what was in store for me, I would have never thanked him. I found out rather quickly what he thought of our discussion. He did send me to Clinton, which is in the state of Iowa. It wasn't to pitch however. He gave me my wish, but in the end, he got his way. I sat on the bench and pitched very little.

He was still doing what he wanted to do but he was teaching me a lesson.

It was a long, cold, lonely spring. A five day road trip to Wisconsin Rapids and Appleton via a school bus to sit and watch four games being played in 30 degree weather was not my idea of fun; especially when you don't play. The meal money at that time was always paid in full before you left on your trip. So as you got on the bus to start your five days of bliss, you were handed your full allotment of money for the entire trip, which totaled 25 dollars...five dollars a day! For some, that money was gone in the card game on the bus ride to our first city.

Once June came around, Mr. Evers then transferred me back to Lakeland, Florida for a second spring training, just like he had planned all along. I drove from Iowa to Pennsylvania, stopped at home for a day, and then drove to Lakeland, Florida. Well, at least I would now get a fresh start.

Two days into the workouts, I was through.

I shattered my wrist running into a wall. Although I was drafted as a pitcher, I also was a decent hitter and I guess they wanted to see me in the outfield.

The very first batter of the intramural game hit a ball over my head that I ran down. Unfortunately the cement wall in left field was stronger than my wrist. I thought that the important thing was that I caught the ball. I went home for the rest of the season to recuperate. The wrist never healed correctly and I spent the following spring training trying to pitch with a throbbing wrist. My arm was in constant pain and I pitched dreadful.

So yes, it was difficult getting starting in this profession.

A little more small talk by Mr. Evers did not mask the fact that I was there for only one reason – to be handed my envelope. He spoke briefly about my bad breaks and misfortune and his regret that things didn't work out.

He then stood up as he picked up the dreaded envelope.

Handing it to me, he simply said, "I'm sorry, but we need to let you go."

I'm sure most of what he said to me in that 10-minute period was a "canned" speech that he had memorized over the years. There were hundreds of young baseball hopefuls that had been delivered that same message in that same office, probably the same words. Perhaps he did feel bad for me, the fact that I had shattered my wrist the summer before and the arm never healed correctly. Perhaps he knew of my disappointment and anguish.

I'll never know.

I never told him that my arm was killing me every time I pitched that spring and that it obviously didn't heal correctly. I never told him a lot of other things. I just got up and left the room.

All I knew was that it was over.

All I knew was that I couldn't stop staring at my hand.

The rest of that day was extremely long. I somehow managed to get a taxi to Tampa Airport and fly back to Pittsburgh. I was no longer a part of the Tiger organization and I was no longer playing baseball. My career was over and for the first time in about 13 years, I had nothing to look forward to the next day—nothing.

The only thing I can remember once I left the confines of "Tigertown" that day was of the experience ten years earlier when I broke my bat. I just kept looking at that scar on my hand all day. Perhaps it was the symbolism of something broken. This time it wasn't a bat, it was my career, my dreams, my future.

I think back to that moment a lot, right when Mr. Evers handed me the envelope. There was a dull, aching pain in my stomach; the combination of anger, bitterness, embarrassment, and fear. That feeling stayed with me for a long time before finally fading away. Now, once again, I still occasionally dream about that day, and yes, suddenly I become conscious in a cold sweat.

Not every day do you wake up and find your world has completely changed. I just knew that I was good enough to make it to the Major Leagues.

Baseball was everything to me.

I wanted to be a Major League baseball player ever since I was seven years old. Every kid who picked up a baseball glove did. I wanted to be the next Sandy Koufax, who happened to be the best pitcher around when I was growing up. It was just a dream when you're a small kid but every time we went up to the field to play ball we lived out that dream.

I played baseball nonstop all those summers. We played hundreds and hundreds of games at the field in Ellport. Then all those Little League games, and Pony League, and Colt League, and High School, and American Legion. I became a high school star who was scouted. I was drafted and given a bonus by the Tiger organization. It was all meant to be, and now it was being taken away.

Dreams turn into nightmares very quickly.

I really didn't know life without baseball. If I wasn't playing baseball, I was looking forward to playing it. Now I'm not even 20 years old and I'm left with no baseball, a throbbing wrist, and the thought that I had turned down major scholarships to several colleges. I said no to all of them so I could go play the game that I loved.

Now it was gone.

The bonus money that they had paid me less than two years before this had disappeared.

Life can really suck.

This was the worst thing that ever happened to me.

What was I going to do?

I never thought about an actual occupation in life other than "professional ball player." I had no skill, I had no real opportunities that I could envision, and I had no money. My girlfriend was away at college so she wasn't around to feel sorry for me. So, along with having nothing, I didn't even have any sympathy.

Could life get any worse?

Little did I know at the time that it was just the start of my life and yes, life can get worse. Matter of fact, it can get a lot worse. But looking through life with the eyes of a 19 year old, I had lost one love in life and I was at the bottom of a very deep hole with no idea how to climb out of it. I didn't even know where to start.

We all eventually find our way, and it was no different for me. I went years and years without baseball and eventually learned to live without it. As the trials and tribulations of life took hold more and more, the memories of the game of baseball became fainter and fainter. Eventually, it was no longer difficult to walk into a stadium, as it was right after my playing days were over. Softball games became nothing more than entertainment, not the burning desire to win at all costs. The discussions with new friends and co-workers about playing professional baseball were more of an anecdote rather than striking a raw nerve. It was over; it was a lifetime ago.

The real life started; the one with bills and pressures and mortgages and kids; the life with sick parents and jobs that were never just right or paid quite enough money. I, like most people, can look back at a lot of lost years. Not that we didn't have good experiences and accomplish noble things, and improve our standard of living.

We just stopped allowing ourselves to be kids.

We stopped being passionate.

There was no time for childhood dreams anymore.

There was no time for broken bats.

Other than that one terrible day that I was released from my employment with the Detroit Tigers, I went 30 years and seldom looked at the scar on my hand, which is hardly visible now. There was no reason to look at it except, I guess, for that one day. For the last six months, a day hasn't gone by that I haven't stared at it and been taken back to a better time and enjoyed being a kid again.

Nothing has changed except my perception.

I now believe there is every reason in the world to take my five minutes every day to do nothing but stare at my hand. There are chores to do, bills to pay, errands to run: things that will never get done. The world is still revolving at a breakneck speed. Expectations are high and the day to day pressure can get to you.

Don't let it!

Take those five minutes every day because believe it or not, the world will wait for you.

I have come to realize that.

If you allow life to take such a stronghold on you, there will never be time for any of the things that should be precious, like living your childhood all over again, teaching a little boy to play ball, or learning something new about yourself.

Find your broken bat …find your memory.

It will make all the difference.

CHAPTER 4
BILL SPELLMAN

Coach Spellman eyed the Waynesburg game carefully.

"He (Spellman) was such a wonderful man. I remember Christmas caroling with the concert choir and making a special stop in front of his home. He and his wife came outside, gave Mr. Gehm a monetary donation, and then his children came out with hot chocolate for the entire choir. I wondered what it must have been like to grow up in a family with such deep commitments to family values. I learned a lot from Mr. Spellman on that cold winter night."

—Nancee Condell Huggins, former student

As a little leaguer, I remember two things that could happen after a game that brought excitement that now, 40 years later, I can still feel. The first one was going to the frozen custard stand. For those of you who have never heard of, or tasted, this ice cream-like treat, you have missed one of life's treasures. There were three of these establishments in the Ellwood City area; J&T Custard on Route 65 going south toward New Brighton (home town of current Boston Red Sox manager Terry Francona), Four Bushes, the opposite way on Route 65 going north toward New Castle (hometown of Chuck Tanner, former Pittsburgh Pirates and Chicago White Sox manager), and the third one was right there in Ellport. There was nothing like frozen custard and black cherry was without a doubt the best tasting and certainly my favorite.

Although I can still to this day close my eyes and remember that black cherry flavor, there was a bigger event that was offered to us on occasion, one that we never turned down. Unlike the first treat that was provided to the whole team, whether we won or lost, the second one was a gift to a few chosen players. Coach Sheeler would occasionally take me and my brother Rich to the side once our little league game had ended, far enough away where no one else could hear. He would simply say, "How would you like to go over to the park?"

Back in the day most of the baseball games for kids in Pony League (13-14) or older were played in a corner of Ellwood City that was named Ewing Park. It was an area of streets and houses lined with shade trees. It was home to the city's only real picnic area, the city's public swimming pool, and to the school's football field. We all knew it just as "the park." It was the hub of summer activity for the entire town.

That's where everyone went and spent their summer nights. That's where one would meet his girl friend or just hook up with friends. That's where small kids would watch in absolute awe the high school guys take the field for a game "under the lights," and dream of being one of those players some day.

There was only one baseball field in the "Park" and that's where all the games were played. It was a great place. There was always a 6:00 p.m. game and then a night game under the lights.

When the lights went on, it became magical!

The bleachers down the third base side went well past the infield, probably 60 feet or so into left field. At the end of the bleachers, in an area that was somewhat dark, the dads would congregate on a nightly basis. No kids or teenagers or mothers were present here. It was the area that six or eight fathers would stand, smoke their cigarettes and cigars and talk about who knows what. Perhaps they spoke about work that day at the mill, perhaps about national news. I don't know about that but I do know one topic of conversation that was always present; baseball. They were well-respected adults who had a reputation as real baseball people.

That's where they would stand.

That's where you would see Coach Spellman.

Bill Spellman lived in Ewing Park, not more than two blocks away from the field. For him, it was a leisurely five minute jaunt to take in a game. He would join in with the fathers at the end of the bleachers and talk baseball. Very seldom did he walk any closer than that to the area behind the third base dug out where the real social action took place, where hundreds of kids ranging in age from 7 to 17 would be standing and talking for hours. He would just keep his distance. Little did I know at that time that he was displaying one of his greatest assets; selflessness. It was never about him and he never wanted the spotlight. To a stranger who didn't know better, it would appear that his attention during these games was more focused toward his conversations with the dads.

But we knew better.

He was all baseball.

Although he talked non stop the whole night with the men of the community, he missed nothing on the ball field.

When he was at a game, you knew it. Everybody knew it. He was bigger than life and word would spread quickly of his presence. When you were fortunate enough to be playing when this occurred, adrenaline immediately shot through your body.

He had that influence.

One would run a little faster, throw a little harder, and "talk it up" a little more. You would not dare give less than a complete effort in his presence.

When I now say to my players, or any young ball players, "always hustle and give 100%, you never know who's watching,"

I guess I'm thinking of Coach Spellman standing over at the end of the bleachers.

I believe he is still watching.........

As a young little leaguer I had never met the man, but I was in awe of him. While a lot of the kids my age would find something else to do during their visits to the park, I would stand beside the home dugout and listen to the players talk. They would be joking and kidding and having a good time. Then one of them would say, "Hey, Coach Spellman is here." The dugout would instantly get a little quieter and a little more serious.

As time went on, I heard more and more stories and came to respect his stature. My brother Jim was the first of three Potter brothers to play for Coach Spellman. He was followed by my brother Rich.

Then it was my turn.

Bill Spellman never coached in the summer. I never really wondered why, it was just one of those things. When school ball was over the first of June, American Legion baseball started for the high school players. Two brothers, Harry and Al Miller, coached the team. It just was always that way. When the summer baseball ended in the middle of August, the baseball spikes were packed away and football took over the school and the community. There was no fall baseball, off-season workouts, or showcases.

From Labor Day until the beginning of spring our only communication with Coach Spellman was an occasional conversation in the hallway at Lincoln High School, or perhaps a hello at a basketball or football game.

That all changed, however, on the first day of March. That's the day that all Lincoln High School baseball players waited for, the day that baseball came back to life for all of us.

That was the day that Mr. Spellman once again became *Coach* Spellman.

When you showed up for baseball practice that first day he was ready. He knew who his ball players were. He didn't need to time you with a stopwatch, he knew who was quick. He didn't make you bench press as much weight as you could, he knew who could make contact and hit. He didn't make you throw a ball as hard as you could the first day of practice because he knew who could pitch, not throw.

Nowadays, coaches may spend the first week of practice compiling all the information that Coach Spellman had already stored in his head. He would laugh at today's coaches with stopwatches and jugs guns. He had done his homework the summer before.

He was a real coach. He didn't measure a player just by numbers. He measured by heart and head and instinct. He had smart players. He had intense players. He had heady players. The radar gun doesn't give you that information.

He learned to be a great baseball coach by being on the field, watching, learning, teaching, and even asking questions of his players. He threw batting practice before each game. The ball was pitched to certain spots for a reason and he expected the ball to be hit to certain spots for a reason. You just learned to do it.

He knew the game of baseball at a level that I have not since seen. He was incredibly perceptive.

He knew who was quick but not fast, who could lay down a bunt, who could make the throw from deep short to first, who could hit the ball a mile but couldn't hit the down and out curve ball. He knew who got into proper cut off position, which players could draw a walk, and what pitchers performed better pitching from the stretch than others.

Today, coaches huddle around with their little notebooks, stopwatches, and jugs gun. They write down all the information that they feel is pertinent, grading each kid on arm speed, strength, and foot speed. If there are 30 kids trying out for the team, they are given a grade 1 through 30, with 1 being the best and 30 the worst. Once they grade the kids in all three areas and mark them down, they then add the scores. For instance, if a player was #1 in arm speed, #7 in strength, and #12 in foot speed, the total score would be 20. All 30 players then would be graded on their total score.... and Voila! You would have your list of players from the best to the worst in those three areas.

The coaches run around with this list, proud as peacocks, like they have discovered the cure for cancer. This list has absolutely no bearing on anything other than a certain kid may have physical prowess over another one. It has very little to do with the game of baseball.

Coach Spellman never went through this ridiculous exercise. He didn't have to. It was, and still is, a complete waste of time.

Instead, Coach spent this precious time fine-tuning the players, getting them to work on the little things that made a difference: pick off plays, first and third situations, bunting, cut-off plays, suicide squeeze, rotation plays, positioning your body correctly for turning a double play, catching a fly ball on the run with a man tagging up. This was all done in the first week. Nowadays, you have coaches still writing down numbers.

Why don't coaches today know who their players are? Why do they waste so much precious time doing such ridiculous things?

Along with being keenly aware of the physical and mental skills of his players, he was very cognizant of the emotional shortcomings, and needs of these same players. Looking back now, with much more mature eyes, I realize that I was a project for Coach Spellman. I was temperamental, immature, and did not possess the best of team building skills. It was all about me as a young freshman coming into high school. I came to him with lots of talent as a ball player, but very few life lessons learned. That scenario changed, sometimes painfully, over the next few years. He became my mentor, my teacher, my motivator, and my disciplinarian, all in one.

Most of all, he became my hero.

William Spellman

Most of all, he became my hero

He was a man of great character. John Zingaro said it best in his book.

Chapter One of the Spellman book is titled *Builders vs. Destroyers*. The chapter speaks of the morning of Tuesday, September 11, 2001, the day now remembered simply as 911.

He writes:

"It is a sad truth about life what takes years to build takes only minutes to destroy. The 110-story towers, from the point of ground-breaking to completion, took eight years to build: from the point of the first jet crash at 8:45 a.m. to the fall of both towers-one hour and 44 minutes to destroy. This had been a hard fact of life since ancient times. One of the wonders of the Ancient World stood for 200 years-The Temple of the Greek goddess Artemis at Ephesus in present-day Turkey – a structure so overwhelming that two Lincoln Memorials could have fit within its space-was burned down in one night by a malcontent.

Any nut can destroy. Dearer to a society are those who build. And dearer still are those who build not structures but that element of a nation which shows its true strength.

Character.

Bill Spellman occupied roles that would be crucial in any society: family man, educator, coach. He lived each aspect of his life with all the fullness he could. But, above all, the role he is most remembered for is: building – and building that which is most needed in a nation.

Character."

There were a lot of other players who went through the Spellman process that could have been characterized as projects other than me. I was only one of many of those young, immature, unfocused youth. No baseball player enters the ninth grade without flaws, some athletic, some academic, and some just plain old personal flaws. You're 14 years old and in the realm of the big picture of life, you're a small child who has not experienced even a fragment of life's experiences.

He molded everyone, like a fine sculptor with a raw piece of clay. Never did I feel that a player disrupted the team by his actions, or act like a primadonna; not for long, anyways. Coach would reel those players in very quickly, and find the effective way to teach the right lessons. Never did he choose winning over teaching when a lesson needed to be taught. He was a builder. I should know. Some life lessons taught to me were extremely painful.

There was always some sort of life lesson to be learned. As I started my high school baseball career the lessons came fast and furious. The problem was I missed most of them. As a kid, you can only grasp something through your eyes, you usually don't "get it" until years later. Looking back today, with much more wisdom, I realize that there were so many lessons I missed.

When I heard all of the horror stories about Coach Spellman as a freshman and what he did to these poor ball players, I assumed that he was just this guy who wielded power and was much like a dictator. Most of these stories were related to me through my brother Rich, two years my elder. He was 16, right in the middle of everything. He would come home and relate to me all of these tales that kind of scared me; like the one about Chuckie Nardone.

Rich came home one day and said, "Nardone got kicked off the team"

"Why"

"He missed practice"

This was Chuck Nardone's sophomore year in high school. He wasn't a starter on the varsity, but he was good and everyone knew he would become a star. When John Zingaro wrote his Spellman book a few years ago, his story took life once again. It was nice to hear the story directly from Chuckie.

As he tells it, he made a bad calculation as a sophomore by missing a practice one day. It had been raining and he assumed that there was no practice. He made an error in judgment. When a teammate of his got home that night, he looked him up.

"Chuckie, Coach wants to see you in the morning."

Chuck went in to see the coach in the morning and Mr. Spellman said nine words to him, "Never come back, you're done, turn in your uniform."

But before he left the office, Chuck said "I *begged* him to keep me on the team."

He remembered Coach Spellman's response – you could come to the practices, and you could run around the poles the entire time while we practice for as long as I think you need to, and it will probably be weeks, and after that I *might* consider letting you back on the team.

Nardone did just that.

It was never fun running for Coach Spellman, especially the poles. But Chuck did it for weeks. He would come to practice and just run, not sure if there would be any payoff for all of this hard work and humiliation. Finally, Coach Spellman gave him back his uniform.

I guess the risk was worth the reward.

Years later, Chuck would say he didn't resent the discipline. "He (Spellman) was in control, which is how you have to be with kids." The next two years, Nardone started in centerfield. Spellman would later say that Chuck had the purest swing that he had ever seen.

Chuck Nardone, Pete Sheeler and about 20 other former players became coaches at either the high school level or higher. Twenty! Something happened to them as young kids that made them move toward coaching. It was more than the competition or the power it possibly wielded. I believe it was the way Coach Spellman affected you. He could be tough and fair at the same time. You hated what he did to you on occasion but you somehow knew he was right and you were wrong. He didn't care who you were when a situation arose but he cared about everyone. He felt a tremendous passion to win, but a bigger passion to do the right thing; to teach the right lesson. He would mentally and emotionally beat the other team down, anything to gain an advantage in order to win. But he would give up that win in a split second to do the right thing. It wasn't all about winning. Lots of coaches now soak up their lofty titles and wins, telling the world of their accomplishments. What you really need to do, however, is talk to the players who have been out of school 10 or 20 years, see what principles they live by and whether that coach they had way back in high school was the inspiration for some of their convictions today.

Rick Coughlin was one of Coach Spellman's players in 1969 and 1970. He graduated in 1970 with my brother Rich and Chuck Nardone. The preceding year he played with Pete Sheeler. Rick was one of those "three sport stars," starting in basketball and football as well as baseball. He was also an excellent student and decided upon the Air Force Academy. He later became an orthopedic surgeon. After six years in his own practice, he became associate clinical professor of orthopedic surgery at the University of California, San Francisco.

Teaching, he says, is one of the greatest things you could do.

"(Spellman) was truly a consummate teacher in that way: motivator, mentor. How many years later, I certainly have to doff my surgical cap to his instilling deeply in me those qualities. I learned that my great passion in life is teaching. I am probably more like Bill Spellman as I reflect because I'm a pain in the ass, especially to the younger residents. They tend to fear me – but it's a great relationship. I have a chance to spend five years making somebody from a medical student to a surgeon. I spend tons of time watching people grow up- much like Spellman did as a coach watching kids from junior high finally be smart seniors. I watch them the first time they put a knife on skin until they finally graduate. When you have a chance to watch people mature over a period of time, it's a pretty amazing opportunity. It's a job that every day I'm happy that I have."

As I eventually moved into *my* high school years, I found that the coach was not a dictator, only a leader. All you needed to do was "get with the program" and you would be okay. He treated people with respect and he only wanted the same in return. Almost any problem between a player and Coach could have been avoided if the player had shown the proper respect.

Some of us were slow learners, however. I lost the second part of my sophomore year because I kicked some dirt and mumbled a few choice words under my breath. You never get that time back.

It's lost forever.

Bill Spellman played minor league baseball. I didn't know that. Nor did I know that he was a professional scout; or that he was a certified umpire, nor did I know the hundreds of stories of his childhood, college life and the Navy that he so proudly served in. It was part of his personality to avoid the attention that he so much deserved.

Today, you see coaches walking around at these showcases and tournaments and baseball camps acting as though they have "never been there before." They throw around names and walk around with their briefcases, holding in their hand their mighty jugs gun. It's hilarious. Most of them together wouldn't have had the influence that Coach Spellman had by himself. But Coach never acted as if he had influence. He never tried to impress anyone. He never threw names around that he certainly could have.

I played for him, I was drafted out of high school, and I didn't even know he was a scout! I didn't even know he was influencing other scouts to come and watch me pitch. Bringing attention to himself was not his nature. He was so confident and secure in himself that he didn't need to create some importance for himself. Tell me what Coach today is like that!

I've come to realize that coaching is a privilege. Knowing a man like Bill Spellman was an honor. To this day, he projects such a large shadow on me that it makes me feel totally inadequate when I'm on a baseball field. However, you do the best you can. You teach, motivate and inspire others the best you know how. And along the way, by teaching these things, winning ball games will find a way into the equation. Coach Spellman taught me that lesson.

How many coaches do you know now that would bench their starting high school shortstop during a playoff game because he was caught drinking?

Coach Spellman did.

How many coaches do you know now that would bench their starting pitcher because he showed up late for the team bus?

Coach Spellman did.

How many coaches do you know now that would cut a promising underclassman because he skipped a practice?

Coach Spellman did

For Coach Spellman a life lesson learned always won over his desire to win games. Yet Coach Spellman won games too—he did both! Ask any player at the time, and they would have told you the most important thing was winning. However, ask any of those players now, 30 years later, and they'll tell you the important thing Coach Spellman taught them was lessons about life. Winning isn't everything. It's a temporary high until the next problem or issue arises. Life lessons, however, are forever.

These young boys and young men, who go out and play youth and high school baseball, are not professional athletes. They are just kids. They themselves don't think so, but they are. They have yet to find out who they are, or what they want to do in life. In most cases, they are searching for someone to guide and influence them in a positive way. They desperately want someone to look up to, craving a really good coach they can admire. More often than not, these individuals are disappointed. Coach Spellman influenced these young men in a positive manner. He built confidence and character and taught them that you really have no winning without these qualities.

In 18 years of coaching baseball at Lincoln High School in Ellwood City, Pa. Coach Spellman's teams were first or second place 15 times. His worst year was a record of 14-8. This was done in the toughest section played in the WPIAL, which is the second largest high school baseball association in the country! And when people speak about Spellman, his illustrious winning record and titles are nothing more than an after thought. It's not that his former players aren't proud of the wins and successes. It's just the fact that those accomplishments are dwarfed by the personal traits possessed by Coach.

Bill Spellman was born on October 25, 1926 and died on November 20, 1983 at an age much too young... 57. But as a former Lincoln high School principal, Rich Santillo said, "Years need not be many to be full, if they were only 57 years, they were 57 *good* years."

Spellman filled those years as well as anyone could. He was a builder, not a destroyer.

Coach Spellman retired from coaching baseball at Lincoln High School at the end of the 1971 baseball season with a record of 304-79. The last game he coached was bittersweet. It was pleasant as it was the championship game of the Pennsylvania WPIAL (Western Pennsylvania Interscholastic Athletic League) baseball season and was played in a major league stadium. The game was unpleasant because it was a stinging loss, the type you never forget or want to forget. I was lucky enough to have played in that game. I was his starting pitcher that day.

I still remember the line-up that Coach Spellman presented to the umpires at Three Rivers Stadium on that sunny afternoon. The date will never escape me. It was June 14, 1971, my 17th birthday. It was Bill Spellman's last high school game as coach.

Line-Up	Position
Lagana	3b
Foley	2b
Ferruchie	rf
Pertile	lf
Potter	P
Prence	ss
Kish	cf
Herman	C
Huffman	1b

Thirty-six years later, I still think we had a better team than our opponent that day. But after all these years, the score hasn't changed: Highlands 5, Ellwood City 4.

It was a tough game to lose as four of their runs were unearned. We played a very sloppy ball game, not a real good example of the discipline that "Coach" taught us. I pitched all seven innings and the result just wasn't good enough. I wanted to win that game so badly. It was Spellman's last game and we all would have given anything for a victory.

We were down 5-2 going into the last inning and rallied valiantly, but with two outs and two men on base, Ed Prence went down swinging, and the game was history. A photographer took a picture immediately after the game showing two teammates consoling Ed as he walked off the field with his head hung. In the background, you could see Coach Spellman heading over to congratulate the other team. It was typical of him. Back then, there was no "lining up" to shake hands after games. Yet Coach always made a point of seeking out the other coach, in victory or defeat. It is one of my favorite pictures and I re-visit it often.

One of my favorite pictures. I hadn't talked to Ed for over 30 years until recently. The book made it possible, and necessary.

Coach Spellman was 43 years old at the time, a young man when you consider coaches who regularly are still at the helm well into their 60's. There are currently only three major league baseball managers out of 31 younger now than what Bill Spellman was when he left the high school team. He still loved coaching and was in excellent health. His passion for the game was unsurpassed.

But he was leaving.

So why would a relatively young man who loved coaching, who was loved and respected by everyone, leave the game?

The truth is he didn't leave.

He was thrown out.

Even back in the day you had politics. It was something that has never quite left me, a bad taste that you can't quite ever get rid of.

On March 5, 1970, the Ellwood City Area School District met as they usually do for their monthly meeting. On this particular day, however, the school board had an agenda. They wanted to get rid of the basketball coach, L. Butler Hennon. Mr. Hennon was well known in the area and was asked to come to Ellwood City five years before this to resurrect the basketball program. Although he came with very high credentials, he was a bust and they wanted him removed from his position. They could have just approached him and been straight and forthcoming, but they elected to take another route. Through some back door maneuvering, realizing that Mr. Hennon was also an assistant to the school superintendent, they concocted a devious plan. The school board, instead of just giving Coach Hennon the bad news, attempted an end run by making a new policy that anyone who was considered an administrator could not also coach. That took care of that, now they could all pretend that it wasn't their idea, they weren't the bad guy. It was this new policy. They washed their hands of their little problem; except for one small detail.

Coach Spellman was a guidance counselor at the school. Although this policy had no intent to do anything but rid them of the basketball coach, Mr. Spellman was technically considered an administrator. The powers to be, in their infinite wisdom to eliminate the basketball coach by being "cutesy," managed to remove the most successful coach they had ever had at that school in any sport. Mr. Spellman was forced out, only allowed to finish his contract, which went through the 1971 season, which would become his 18th and final season.

The team was devastated, especially those of us who would be back in 1972. We went through the 1971 season like we were on a mission, and we were. It was Coach Spellman's last year and we knew it. We played good and we played hard, compiling a record of 30-7 before losing that championship game. He was a classy man. Too classy to be treated that way.

Coach never talked about the injustice that was done to him. Many times he was interviewed and asked questions about his impending ouster, every time he simply said "No comment." He never made it public and never made an issue about it. He deserved to be able to say goodbye on his terms. He deserved a better fate.

So Coach Spellman was officially retired. The following spring we were back on the field, but without "Coach." It just didn't feel right. The whole season became a bad dream. Nothing went right. It rained most of the spring and many games were cancelled. We ended up the season with a 12-6 record. Not bad for a lot of teams, but Ellwood City came to expect more. We felt we left the whole town down. Worse than that, Coach Spellman never came to watch a game.

Not one.

I'm sure it would have been painful for him to come and watch, but that's not the real reason he stayed away. He just didn't want to put any undue pressure on the new coach. Again, that's how he was, classy. His absence certainly didn't help me. He wasn't there to coach me ... or support me or talk to the scouts for me. Not only was he not in the dugout, he wasn't even sitting down in the left field bleachers ... like he did all of those summer nights for years and years.

The new coach did as well as he could, but he was not Coach Spellman. I didn't pitch as much as the year before. I still got drafted fairly high (sixth round), but at the end of the previous year I was told that I would be drafted much higher. It was a very tough spring.

Coach was gone, but unbeknownst to many people, including me, Mr. Spellman wasn't sitting still. He was putting together another baseball team, Ellwood City's entry in the North County League. He, along with another long time resident, Carmen Beatrice, was going to coach the team. This was same Carmen Beatrice who sold you the 34" Jackie Robinson for $4.99 in his sports store off of Wampum Avenue.

Coach just couldn't stay away.

This would be different though, because he had never previously coached in the summer.

This new team started playing ball in the league in the middle of May. For the third game of the county league season, they found themselves with a depleted roster. It was prom night at Lincoln High School. The date was Friday, May 19th and that's where the seniors who played on Spellman's summer team were spending that evening. In addition to this, the game was to start early at 5:00 p.m. and some of the other players were still working.

All of us have been through the "fire drill" of trying to put a team together at the last moment. It's not fun. Spellman tried to round up additional players, but to no avail. Game time came and there were eight players, and Spellman. Coach was 44 years old now, but he was ready to play. The fire was still burning. Several of the players present that day were left-handed and there wasn't a catcher. Without hesitation, Spellman said, "I'll go back there."

Even though it was only mid May, it was a hot and humid evening. To make matters worse, the starting pitcher was Wayne Alexander, who during his high school days of only two years prior, occasionally got the ball up into the mid 90's. I know that, because I batted against him during my school days. He threw harder than anyone that I have ever faced. I still have the clipping of the only time we faced each other on the mound. I was lucky enough to beat him in nine innings 1-0. I had 16 strikeouts, he had 15.

He could bring it!

Spellman loaded up the catcher's gear, went out there and caught Alexander's screaming fastballs. The game went on – nobody else showed up for the team – and Spellman kept catching.

The first baseman was Pete Sheeler, the same guy who stood with his dad that July day eight years prior watching us finish that four on four ball game. He was now three years removed from high school, but still playing ball. In the second inning, the pitcher attempted a pickoff. The ball skimmed off of Pete's glove, striking him in the eye. It swelled shut and he not only had to come out of the game, but was sent to the emergency room of the local hospital. Now they had eight players. They kept playing, Spellman kept catching, and nobody else showed up.

About the third inning, while crouched behind home plate, Spellman suddenly called time.

He walked out to the mound.

"What's up", said Alexander.

"I don't feel good."

Alexander figured he was throwing in the 90's.

"Mr. Spellman, do you want me to take it easy?"

"No, you throw the way you usually do."

Spellman then returned behind the plate.

In the fourth inning, another player showed up, so Ellwood could now play once again with three outfielders. There still, however, was no relief at the catcher's position for Coach. Ellwood came to bat in the top of the fourth and Spellman came out for his second time to hit. He smacked a grounder to the shortstop. Half way down to first base, he uncharacteristically peeled off and jogged toward the dugout, directly to the bench. As he sat there, Spellman broke into a heavy perspiration. "He was very pale and perspiring", said Chuck Nardone. "We were very concerned about him. We knew something was wrong." Yes, the same Chuck Nardone who four years earlier had begged Coach Spellman to let him stay on the high school team, who had missed a practice and was thrown off the team. Two years removed from high school, he had come back from college to play summer ball for Coach Spellman.

Spellman lay on the bench, still insisting he was okay. He then started talking incoherently and the players became alarmed. It was obvious that help was necessary so a spectator who lived near the field ran home and called for an ambulance. At the local hospital, Pete Sheeler was sitting in the emergency room having his eye worked on. He saw Coach Spellman being wheeled in. "I had no idea what was going on, so I went back and played the last two innings." Ellwood ended up losing the game 2-1, but no one's attention was on the game. Coach Spellman was now in intensive care.

He had a heart attack.

His condition remained so delicate that the hospital personnel didn't remove his baseball uniform for four days.

I was at our high school prom when I heard the news regarding Coach Spellman. He had twin daughters, Rhonda and Saundra, who were in my class. One of them was at the prom with Rich Hermann, my catcher for the last two years of high school baseball. I believe I got the news from him. I was sick to my stomach. My very first thought was of that damn school board who threw him out of his job. That's why he was back on the field coaching summer ball and worse than that, playing and catching. In his 18 years of coaching high school ball, he never coached in the summer. They are the reason he had a heart attack. At least that's how I felt.

Coach Spellman eventually recovered enough to function, but never truly regained his full health. He looked weak and sickly, only a shell of the man I remembered out on the field. If he would have only said goodbye to the game when he left the school.

But he had to come back.

There were so many things left to do, so many more life lessons to teach, so much more passion left for the game. It was just an unfortunate twist of fate that brought down a great coach. Had Bill Spellman not been forced out of his position, life over in Ewing Park in Ellwood City would have been more robust for years.

But he was forced to leave.

Between 1972 and 1993, The Ellwood City Wolverines baseball team managed to win a section championship exactly one time. Former player after former player came in and tried their luck with the team; Bill Smeltz, Ray Foley, Pete Sheeler, Vic Sharek, Dave Blazin, Jeff Meehan, Donnie Wick... one section title in 23 years. They all had knowledge and wisdom and a good work ethic. They were all taught by the master. They just **weren't** the master. They didn't possess that thing you just can't put your finger on. We've all played for that one particular coach who just could bring out more in you than we knew we had, the passion he possessed, the calming spirit he displayed, the intensity that he exuded; those Spellman qualities.

We all come to that time in life where we need to say goodbye ... to something. Perhaps it's time to move on from what our life is to what it should be. It may be a change of jobs, a change of residence, or just a farewell to baseball. It's never easy, but something inside of us knows it's time to move on. We just feel it.

Coach wasn't ready to leave. It wasn't time.

After several years of poor health, William Shelby Spellman died on November 20, 1983. After his death, the tributes kept coming. A monument was erected at Sanders Memorial Field and dedicated on September 21, 1984. A likeness of Spellman's face is carved on the monument:

William Spellman
In recognition of one of the State's finest
baseball coaches and a true
community leader. During the nineteen years
from 1954–1971 and 1979 he amassed 320 wins
against 87 losses winning eleven section Championships
and two W.P.I.A.L. crowns ... Coach Spellman has
served as a model for dedication, discipline and
effort to those who knew him.

Later the same year, the high school began a "William S. Spellman Scholar/Athlete Award." Along with that, a "Bill Spellman MVP Award" began at the school. Nearly ten years after Spellman's death, on April 26, 1992, he was inducted into the Lawrence County Hall of Fame, the county where Ellwood City is located.

I found out about all these wonderful accolades as I read through John Zingaro's book on Bill Spellman. I was happy for his family and all the deserving recognition that had been showered upon him. They are without a doubt memories that symbolize his life and his accomplishments. More important than these tributes, however, is the fact that he lives in all of us. We all had been taught, motivated, and inspired by him, and in our own way have tried to continue his work. It's taken me most of my life to realize the impact he has had on me.

Baseball made that possible.

Coach Spellman is probably looking down at all of us now with a smile on his face, just shaking his head. His smile probably turns to a laugh on March 1 of every year. That's the first day of baseball tryouts at a lot of high schools throughout the country. He's looking down and watching all the coaches with their stopwatches timing every kid on the 60-yard dash. He then looks over at each kid struggling to put the bar bell over his head, while another coach is marking down the weight each prospect struggles to put over his head. Then his laugh probably turns to a look of concern when each player is sent over to an area and instructed to "throw the ball as hard as you can" in the 42 degree weather ... with very little warm up.

He asks himself the obvious question, "Is this really progress?"

Why would you need to do such foolish things when you should already know everything you needed to know? Coach understood that these were just numbers and they didn't make a ball player. He took the time in the summer to watch his future ball players play real ball. We all came to understand that when we went out for the high school baseball team, Coach had already scouted us. He knew what his intentions were for every player. He had watched all of us, making mental notes each summer on perhaps a hundred kids. Not just the high school kids, but younger players who would someday be part of his program.

He was so much more advanced than today's coaches. Instead of coaches today whipping out a stopwatch or jugs gun, perhaps they should take in a few summer baseball games of the upcoming freshman and sophomores, or perhaps head over to a little league field.

Only years later, did all of his former players come to find out just how much they were being watched. During an interview at one of the dinners honoring Coach Spellman, we learned that he had a "draft board" in his basement. He actually had every single ball player rated on a board at his house and for all those years of coaching, and that fact never became evident. He would walk down from his house, take in a game or two, and go home and chart each player's progress.

If he really is looking down on me, he sees a man who to this day is overpowered by his huge shadow, a man who feels humbled every time he steps on a ball field, a man who can only hope of some day approaching his character, a man who thinks about him on a regular basis.

There isn't a week that goes by that I'm not using the Spellman book as a reference – searching for inspiration or some nugget of information. Anything I can use to be a better coach.

Anything I can use to be a better person.

CHAPTER 5
WINNING ISN'T EVERYTHING

"Credit is often delayed for a coach. Teenagers sometimes don't see until years later what they have gained. When you're a young kid, you didn't know that he (Spellman) was teaching about life. If you can only teach a kid how to play baseball, you aren't winning."

—Mike Esoldo, former player

On a hot, sunny afternoon, a small boy stepped up to the plate. The crowd watched like hawks for his move, waiting for the sought-after home run that most likely wasn't going to be. After all, these kids were five and six years old, much too little to stroke a ball past the pitcher, if at all.

The little guy's determination showed in his stance: gritted teeth, slightly bulging eyes, hat-clad head bobbing slightly, feet apart, hands with a death grip on the bat. In front of him was a small soft-ball, perched like a parrot on a lone tee, awaiting the six swings the batter was allowed.

Strike one.

"Come on, you can do it," came a solitary voice from the bleachers.

Strike two.

"Go for it, son," the proud father yelled encouragingly.

Strike three.

"Go, Go, Go," the crowd joined in.

Strike four.

"You can do it! Just the father and a couple of viewers crooned, others losing interest and turning to bleacher conversation.

"You can do it!," and suddenly the ball hit the bat, amazing the crowd and the little boy, who stood rock still, watching it travel slowly past the pitcher on its way to second base.

"Run"

The stands rumbled with stomping feet.

"Run, run" the little boy's head jerked ever so slightly and he took off toward 3rd base.

"No," the crowd yelled, "The other way!"

With a slight cast of his head toward the bleachers, the boy turned back toward home.

"No, son," the umpire waved him toward first base.

The kids on both teams pointed the way. The crowd continued to cheer him on. Confused, he ran back to third base. Then following the third baseman's frantic direction, he finally ran toward first base but stopped triumphantly on the pitchers mound. The pitcher moved back, not sure what to do next. The crowd stood, shaking the bleachers with the momentum. All arms waved toward first base. And with no thought for his position, the first baseman dropped his glove and ran toward the pitcher.

"Come on," he yelled, grabbing the hand of the errant batter, and tugged him toward first base while the crowd screamed its approval. The ball lay forgotten as a triumphant twosome hugged each other on the piece of square plastic which marked the spot where lives are forever shaped.

Two little boys, running hand in hand, toward a goal that only one should have reached and both boys came out winners. In fact, there wasn't a loser on the field or in the stands that day, and that's a lesson none of us should ever forget.

Winning is more than being number one. Winning is helping another when the chips are down. It's remembering to love one another, as biblically directed, despite the flaws that sometimes appear in the fabric of everyday life.

No one will ever remember the score of that summer day encounter. Competition, usually fettered by jeering remands, lost to sportsmanship, an innate formula for winning.

When you get to first base with opposing teammates, families, friends, and grandstanders behind you, a home run is never far down the road.

Great competitors are bred, and great sportsmen are born. I came to that conclusion at a Little League t-ball game in Davis, California, for which my son, Matt, was umpiring. This conclusion was cemented solidly just last week when a friend of mine related a horror story from her son's little league game.

"One of the coaches just ripped off a kid's head for making a mistake," she noted "What does that teach him?"

In both of our books, nothing

We have become a nation addicted to winning. "We're number one puts smiles on sport fan's faces. Running a good race doesn't always."

This premise relates to every facet of life, whether at home, at church, at school, at work or at play. Numbers are crunched, awards are pursued, and emotions are stifled in favor of one upsmanship. Even the Jones' have a hard time keeping up.

Life too often becomes a tough game with more losers than winners. When claiming the prize eliminates the good in playing, no one wins. Real awards come from teamwork, and playing the game unselfishly for the good of the whole.

Yes, when I read the preceding short story and the following comments from one of the many inspirational books (Mary Owens from *Chicken Soup for the baseball Fan's Soul*) that I have amassed over the years, my thoughts immediately drifted back to my son Eric as a T-ball player, his first year of structured baseball. No, he didn't hit the ball off of a tee and run to third base as this youngster did, but I do remember the time that he ran all over the field directing traffic when he was supposed to be playing centerfield. On another occasion, he was on second base and his teammate hit a ball that went into the outfield. Rather than run to the next base as urged to do by the third base coach, he chased down the batted ball and threw it into the infield. Like most teammates that year, much of his time playing the outfield consisted of picking the pretty dandelions. He was only seven and this was his first experience with a sport. He picked the one that I wanted him to select; baseball, and I was thrilled.

This was the sport that I grew up with and learned to love; the sport that as kids we played non-stop, the sport that gave me so many great memories and taught me so many life lessons. I had privately hoped that Eric, like his father, would also play baseball and perhaps eventually feel the magic of the game. At first glance, it appeared that my wish may come true. He looked happy out on the field and I'm sure I looked happy off the field. He was only seven, though, and as we all know, things change. Maybe I would get lucky and he would stick with baseball for a while.

There were two very nice men who served as coaches for Eric's first team and they both did a very good job in that capacity. It's all about expectations. Place them too high and you'll be disappointed. I had no expectations, and therefore shielded myself from disappointment. The two dads who coached were patient and mentoring with the kids and despite making the decision of forcing my son to hit right-handed; they did a great overall job. There wasn't an over abundance of favoritism toward their children and they didn't go too overboard showing everyone how good they could coach. That happens a lot more than it should, coaches trying to impress everyone with their expertise and knowledge.

Fortunately for our team it was not the case.

It was all good.

Only a few times did they attempt to teach 7-year-old boys 12-year-old lessons. The advice of "squashing the bug" only means one thing to a very young boy, and it isn't the method in which you turn your back foot when you are in the process of rotating your hips into your swing. To a youngster, this term has a completely different meaning, one in which young girls scream when they see you literally squashing a bug. We got past that little advanced lesson with no damage done to anyone.

My only hope for that first season was that the coaches did not sour my son toward baseball in any way. That's all I asked for and because that was accomplished, I gave the coaches a big fat A on their report card.

I couldn't have been happier.

Eric did well and actually, with some practice, learned to hit right-handed. It was very uncomfortable for him to do this as he was a natural lefty, like his father, but he listened to the coach's direction and did his best. When he asked me why he had to hit right-handed, I told him that the coaches already knew how well he hit left-handed, and they wanted to see if you were one of those special kids that could do it with either hand. He smiled and gave me the impression that my answer would suffice. We moved on and never talked about it again. Over the years, however, I have thought of this little minute conversation that I had with Eric many, many times. Not so much the substance of the talk, but the presentation. It's all in the presentation.

During the course of this ball season I never felt that it was necessary to question either coach on how they conducted themselves, ran practices and games, or generally motivated and supported the kids. It seemed to be all about fun and all the kids having a good experience, like it should have been.

On days that Eric didn't play, we would occasionally go outside in the yard and catch. As I was ready to throw the ball to him, he would put his glove up in the air, and I would try to hit the glove with the ball. Sometimes it worked, and when it did, he would smile at his accomplishment.

Those were special moments for both of us.

When it got close to starting the next season, Eric, pardon the pun, "threw us a curveball." He decided to play soccer instead of "America's Pastime." I believe that I may have been a bit disappointed in his decision, but that fact was never made apparent to Eric. It wasn't that he didn't have a good time playing baseball. I just think he wanted to try something different. Soccer probably looked like more fun than baseball. The sport of soccer gave you a chance to stay active and run and kick, not stand out in the outfield totally bored. From the perspective of a small child, it made sense. In addition to this reality was the fact that a few of his friends had registered for soccer in the same organization. So off to soccer Eric went without a single concern from my wife and me. We wanted him to do what he wanted to do and there was no sense trying to sway him to play this sport or that sport. Go out and have a good time, and he did.

Sure enough, a season of soccer was completed and he returned to the baseball diamond. Now he was playing both. With sports being played spring, summer, and fall, it gave kids an opportunity to try different things. Who knows what I would have done as a kid if all of these different sports were there at my disposal!

The return of baseball introduced Eric to "coach pitch." Two different dads were now in charge and they, like the former coaches, also did a very nice job handling the young baseball players. The parents were all encouraging and very grateful for these two fine men who took the time and effort to work with all of our children. Everybody hit, fielded, played, and the support and playing time was meted out evenly to all the kids. Again, the coach's kids did not appear to be treated extra special. That was a concern of mine, something that I had heard happened quite a bit. So far so good for us, though! Life was once again, for the second baseball season, going very smoothly. The kids were having fun.

Baseball started out far different for Eric those first two years than it was for me as a child. We played non-stop and had much less "pampering." When we were kids, if our mom came to a practice, we were laughed at and called a "momma's boy." That's just the way it was. As seven and eight year olds we spent most of the day in the summer at the ball field. Our bikes got us there, not our parent's cars. Our neighborhoods were safe and therefore, we could do that. Life was innocent and pure and baseball was king. I can remember my mom on many occasions just saying, "Be home before it's dark."

Now, parents can't leave their children out of their sight for a minute. Dads no longer work ten minutes away at the steel mill and get off their jobs every day at 3:00. Nowadays, they are busting their butt just to make the last three innings of a game; or they miss it completely because they are at their daughter's soccer game. Remember, back in the '60's girls didn't play sports. It was all boys...and it was all baseball. Baseball now must compete with soccer, lacrosse, field hockey, computer games, paint ball, and a multitude of other activities. Back then, baseball competed with nothing.

During this second season, Eric somehow transformed back to left-handed, his natural way of hitting. I was elated that it happened without me having to intervene. I believe the few times that I took Eric to practice early so he could get some extra hitting really helped with this change. I made sure that the coaches saw that he was hitting left-handed, not right-handed. The coaches obviously took the cue and that was that. Somehow it just happened without a word being uttered. The coaches once again, as in the first year of Eric's baseball, did all the necessary things in a satisfactory manner. There was no issue too large that a few extra deep breaths couldn't neutralize. Like I said, both coaches had boys who played on the team, but if another parent just showed up in the middle of a practice and didn't know the kids, picking out the coach's sons would have been difficult. That's a great sign of good coaches, when a fellow parent has no idea which young boys happen to belong to the men in charge.

As time went on, I realized that this situation was the exception.

A friend of mine has told me more than once that the greatest compliment ever given to him in all the years that he coached was an eight-word question that a parent once asked of him. After three or four practices of a newly formed team, the man walked up to him and said, "Do you have a son on the team?

He did, but you wouldn't have known.

I didn't realize at this time how uncommon it was for men to coach young kids without having a son of their own on the team. Growing up, a lot of my coaches did not have sons on the team (Frank Clark, Dave Dobi, Al Miller, Fred Takas, Harry Miller, and Frank Sanders) and only later did I understand how deeply this relationship affected all other players and parents on a team's roster. I believe this fact alone, having all parents of players as coaches of teams, is one of the biggest problems in youth baseball today.

I still wasn't sure at this time that baseball would be king with Eric. There was basketball in the winter and soccer in the fall that also seemed to have his attention. Sheryl and I tried to not sway him toward any particular sport, but I was personally rooting real hard for my son to continue on the baseball diamond. I don't think at this age Eric even knew that his father played, and loved, baseball when he was younger. There was no real reason to ever bring it up in conversation. He never asked and I never volunteered the information. I guess my thought was that if I brought it up, then I may be swaying him unfairly to stay with baseball. I wanted him to remain with whatever sport he liked, but it needed to be on his own terms. If it was baseball, it needed to be his decision.

I would have loved to have told him about the hundreds of pick-up baseball games that we played as kids, the throwing of the bats, the wooden bats, to pick teams. I would have loved to have told him that we played real baseball. I would have loved to have explained to him the feel and look of a real bat, the one that had those nails in it, the balls that were taped together, the fact that kids had to share gloves, how bases were sometimes nothing more than a piece of cardboard, how a field was never "dragged" before a game. When a ball was hit squarely, it was the crack of the bat, not a ping that metal bats manufacture.

Real baseball with real memories.

This conversation, however, would surely have met with deaf ears and a glazed stare. He was only eight, way too young to understand my memories. So I hoped that he would learn the beauty of baseball on his own. There would be time for these stories later....

The following year was when baseball started in earnest. It was the first time that kids actually pitched to each other and played baseball the way it was meant to be played. Real baseball was upon us. Preparing myself for that third year, I assumed that the style of baseball may change a bit. The fact that it was real pitching and keeping real score may make winning a little more of a priority. I was bracing myself for a bit more conflict and confrontation. I saw what was happening with the "older boys" in the program and therefore assumed that life as I knew it up to now would become a little different on the baseball diamond. I was braced for the upcoming changes for my son and me. I felt he had played adequate up to this point, but he was still small in stature and did not appear to be nearly as aggressive as I had been as a child.

Although I knew things would be different for this third baseball season, I must admit that I was not prepared for what was about to happen. It was like someone turned on a switch and changed life, and specifically this youth baseball program, from night to day. We went from kids picking flowers in the outfield to coaches arguing with umpires and arguing with each other, actually screaming across the field while they were coaching first and third base. It was almost like the coaches understood that while the kids were playing "coach pitch," one was not supposed to focus on winning. Once the coach pitch was done and the floodgates opened, there was very little semblance of order.

It became chaos over night. Not that there wasn't some sort of organization and structure. There certainly was. Matter of fact, the organization did an excellent job of setting dates for tryouts and having coaches in place to work with these kids. The problem was that in most cases the people assigned to be coaches were the wrong people, and were put in place for the wrong reasons. It no longer was a problem of finding coaches. It was amazing how difficult it was to find fathers who had the time to coach when their kids were playing T-ball and coach pitch when it was more fun and exercise. However, once it was all about winning and the competitive juices start flowing, the coaches came out of the woodwork. They now found the time. This organization was no different, and dads now were lined up to take over the reins of teams.

The emphasis came off of fun and became competitive real quick. It's hard to say which part of the equation (players, parents, coaches) had the most influence on creating "the winning at all costs" mentality, but from what I remember, I would say it was the coaches. Things got serious and coaches now felt that they needed to display their attributes relating to knowledge of the game. A lot of them really didn't know the game very well.

Even though this was only nine year old baseball, lots of coaches were just not properly prepared to be in charge of these kids. This included the two gentlemen who were in charge of Eric's team. Very quickly, it became painful to watch. Although the kids in general still seemed to be having some fun, which should have been the priority, they were getting very poor instruction in the game of baseball and certainly weren't learning the proper "life lessons." Fun is good, though, and it seemed that there was still enough of it, so all the parents appeared to go along with the program. I wasn't in a position to coach at the time, so I had no right to criticize someone who did have the time and was willing to do the job. Of course, even if I did have the time, it wouldn't have mattered. There were already too many coaches lined up for too few jobs.

Just because I wasn't coaching and just because the kids still seemed to be having some fun didn't mean that I wouldn't sit there as a parent and occasionally get upset. I got agitated and aggravated more than once. At times, I would tighten up and get pretty "zoned out." More often than not, I would not go a full practice or game without biting my lip or grabbing the chair a little tighter than necessary. When I was real upset, I would close my eyes and take deep breaths, like I was trying to get myself under control. I would always do this from a distance, however, never making it apparent to another parent, or to the coach, that I was upset. It was my way of dealing with the situation. If I was sitting in near proximity to other parents or the coaches, I would always try to watch a practice or game with a newspaper firmly in front of my face. That way, the only one that knew that I was upset was my wife.

She always knew....

At these tenuous points in time, she felt it was her cue to kind of get to the bottom of what was bothering me.

"Jeff, what's the matter?"

"Nothing"

"You have that look!"

"What look?"

"The look that you're not happy with what's going on"

"I'm fine"

"Is the coach doing something wrong?"

"He's doing fine."

"Then what's the problem?"

"There is no problem."

Well, we both knew there was a problem, or at least something that created all of my animation. Something that the coach was doing was making me very uncomfortable and she knew it. This was the time that she would "cut to the chase", ask that one question that I would need to answer.

"Would you want him coaching you?"

I would always laugh and say, "He's putting his time in, I'm not."

And that's the truth.

These tens of thousands of coaches out there every year, in almost all cases, are not paid.

Not a dime.

The time and energy that they put in to these teams are donated free of charge, and in fact, many of these coaches take a few bucks out of their pockets to cover some expenses. No one pays for their gas. The Gatorades and waters that were brought to some practices might have been reimbursed, but not always. The coaches should all be commended. It's so easy to run the team from the stands. We're all great "Monday morning quarterbacks." Most of us can more readily see a coach's miscues rather than his attributes, and I am as guilty as the next person.

I take my hats off to all of these coaches... that is if they are truly doing it for the right reasons. There's the rub, if they are doing it for the right reasons. Protecting and showcasing your son isn't the right reason. Trying to relive your childhood isn't the right reason. Showing everyone how much baseball knowledge and expertise isn't the right reason, nor is being on a power trip the right answer.

The only thing that we can hope for at this age is that the coaches are out there to show these kids the proper fundamentals of the game, have fun, and be fair. Too many times, however, this is not the case. Winning becomes the emphasis at an age much too young. Eric was only nine... way too young for what was happening.

This third year of baseball demonstrated the true significance of good coaching... and of bad coaching. Although the first four coaches of Eric's young baseball life exceeded my expectations, I'm not really sure that they knew baseball. The truth is that they didn't really need to know the game as much as they needed to be good babysitters who made sure everyone had the same amount of attempts at the plate and rotated around in the field. There were no scores or averages, strikeouts, or winners and losers. There were no star players, strategies, or planned line-ups. There were no politics, pressure, or agendas. It was nothing more than being introduced to the game of baseball...and having fun. Little did I know at the time that baseball knowledge really wasn't as important as people thought in terms of the effectiveness of a coach. Matter of fact, it's pretty far down the line.

The two coaches who were selected to lead this 9-U baseball team must have been selected in one of three ways; either they were the first two men who volunteered, their names were picked out of a hat, or they were related to the baseball commissioner. None of these selection processes was the right one, and therefore the chance of having the most deserving or qualified coaches were slim. Twenty minutes into the first practice of the year this fact was painfully apparent.

It appeared this was going to be a long spring!

You just get a feel for people real quickly, whether it is new neighbors, a fellow employee, or perhaps a salesman who you are doing business with. The same rings out for parents who want to coach a baseball team. They were without a doubt the wrong people for the job. They did compliment each other, but only in a bad way. When I felt that the situation could not get any worse, I would just need to wait until the next practice or game to prove myself wrong. Neither man seemed to have much baseball knowledge and both of them seemed to have even less positive personal attributes. I am not saying that they weren't good people. They just shouldn't have been put in charge of molding young kids.

I stayed on the sidelines for most of Eric's third year of baseball, which was his first year of *real* baseball. I watched as the coaches began teaching the wrong lesson that winning at any cost is not only okay, but it's necessary. I watched some of the parents buy into this thought process. It was apparent that favoritism was rampant, and in most cases it was the coach's sons who benefited the most. As one of my colleagues so often says to me about his experience with youth coaches, "They promoted theirs at the expense of mine and yours." It happens all the time.

By the middle of this year, the fun part was wearing off, even with the kids. The players who needed the most help weren't getting it because the coaches were trying to win at all costs. These kids started to play less innings and the parents started noticing. Because of lack of playing time, the boys were a bit more nervous and up tight when they did get into the game. That caused them to struggle even a bit more. This did nothing but get them a seat back on the end of the bench. The coach couldn't possibly get them more playing time, more at bats, more fielding, and perhaps build their confidence. Doing all that would necessitate a lot of time and energy, and perhaps cost the team a game or two in the standings. Winning just one more game was too important.

1999 CROFTON CARDINALS
MVP'S

Eric, on the right, and Jesse Leszczynski, left took a minute to pose for the cameras before a game at Crofton. Two years later, they were still teammates, but they were then wearing a different color for a new organization.

One memory of that 9-U team still lingers in my mind...

About half way through the season, I found myself entwined in a conversation with one of the fathers made me very uncomfortable. I was at a practice and going through my usual ritual of placing the daily newspaper in front of my face. On occasion I would actually be reading the paper, but most of the time it was a wall between some of my many expressions that I would make and what was happening on the field. My displeasure regarding the particular coaching techniques was *my* problem and there was no reason to share my personal issues with anyone else. So on this particular day, like most, I was shielding myself from the world, minding my own business. I'm sure I had a fresh cup of coffee within arms length. I was friendly enough to the other parents as I arrived at practices, always smiling and going through the usually greetings. I would then attempt to move far enough away from the group of parents to not get involved in further conversation, but not far enough away that I appeared to be anti-social. It was a balancing act. On this day, I didn't move far enough.

This certain dad was a very nice fellow and on this beautiful April morning decided to sit his chair right beside me. I was about 40 or 50 feet away from everyone, strategically placing my chair down the third base line as I always did. Usually this father was sitting with the majority of the parents in their group. Today he planted himself directly to my right side. In my mind there was one of two reasons that he did this. The first consideration was that he really liked me a lot and thought I was a great guy and wanted to get to know me better. After about three seconds of evaluating that theory, I decided that I thought the second option was more sensible. He wanted to talk.

Within a minute or so, my thoughts were validated. To this day, I do not know why he sought *me* out. Perhaps he had tried with other parents in the past and it was my turn.

And it began ......

"Hey, how's it going today?" he asked.

Considering the fact that the newspaper was still in front of my face and I had not until this time even acknowledged his presence, I reasoned that he really wanted to talk.

I took the paper away from my face, and as nicely and politely as I could, smiled and said, "Great, and how about you?"

I guess the response that I gave, including the words, and how about you, gave him the opening to now break into a lively conversation.

I have had more fun at the dentist's office than what occurred in the next 30 minutes. It wasn't him, it was me. *It was all me.* He was fine, just trying to talk. I was the one who had the attitude and to be honest, it wasn't a great attitude. He never knew of my displeasure, but that did not change the fact that I was not real comfortable in this monologue.

Almost anytime that someone seeks another person out to talk, there is an agenda. We all have an agenda. Sometimes it makes us seem almost mysterious by nature. The person may start out with small talk or act like it is just him or her being social. Before long, though, the true purpose of the conversation is unveiled and this discussion was no different. The father wanted to relay his displeasure with the coaching staff, the unfairness shown to his son, and most importantly, his personal credentials as a baseball coach. I listened as though I was his best friend in the world and I, too, was feeling his pain.

This was not a good strategy.

I should have stopped him real early in the conversation and told him the obvious; you need to go to the coaches with your concerns, and if you want to help coach, tell the proper people. I knew better than to patronize him and make him feel that I was his number one supporter. I had been down this road before and I was handling this in about the worst possible manner that I could. I should have known better.

But there was just something about him that made me feel that he was going through some real pain. It took me only a few minutes to realize why I was attempting to be so compassionate with him. It was the way in which his son was treated in a game a few weeks previously.

His son had asked the coaches to let him pitch all year. He really wanted to pitch more than anything in the world. The coaches kept finding reasons to not give him the opportunity to throw in a game. Finally, either out of need of a pitcher or sheer frustration in the boys continuing persistence in asking, they decided to give him his chance.

The boy started this particular game on the mound for the first time in his young career. He was a small kid with very little confidence and to make matters worse, he had a very uncomfortable behavior of crying when he did not do well. This is not a good combination for a pitcher as I knew through personal experience.

These kids are nine years old, however, and this is when you work with them and see what skill level each possesses at different positions. This is where you work with ball players mentally and emotionally and this is where you build confidence.

This is real coaching.

As the game started, it was apparent that the young boy was extremely nervous. He walked the first batter with none of the pitches coming close to the strike zone. As he trotted down to first base with the free pass our one coach looked at the other one and said, "I told you it wouldn't work."

That was a real uplifting thing for a coach to say! And it wasn't said in a low tone, rather barked out for all people within 50 feet or so to hear.

The four straight balls obviously did nothing to improve the pitcher's confidence. He was now shaking and it was apparent that tears were not far away. The next two pitches were also off the mark. The coach who had not so subtly let everyone know that it wouldn't work, called time and marched to the mound. No, he didn't walk to the mound; he had to march to the mound. He had to let everyone know that he was not happy and was very frustrated with the boy's performance. He had to put on a show for every one. As he arrived at the mound it was apparent that the pitcher was being chastised, not calmed down. The coach's face was beet red, and he returned to the bench with an angry look plastered over his face. Those tears now started flowing and as we all had already realized, the next two pitches were also not strikes.

This was more than our beloved coach could take. Back out to the mound he marched, and it took him no time to replace the shaken young man with another pitcher. It was terribly uncomfortable for everyone at this point, about as bad as it could get. But the coach somehow found a way to make it worse. Upon leaving the mound area, even before he got to the bench, he screamed out at the starting pitcher, "That's why you don't pitch."

Suffice to say, this was the start of the unraveling of the team. Most of the inconsistencies and shortcomings of the coaching staff were overlooked until this time. This was too much to look the other way. This was not poor coaching, this was poor conduct. This was a coach displaying a terrible character flaw.

So back to the present time, and the dad who I felt for, and I knew was hurting inside. I thought perhaps our conversation would let him blow off some steam and he would feel better. I thought he wanted to in some way have me nominate him for a coaching position on the team. That agenda started to make itself evident as the conversation continued. Everything was going along fine. He was somewhat bragging in regards to his baseball background, and I continued looking at him with awe of his previous baseball exploits. Perhaps this would be the impetus for him to have the courage to approach the coaches.

But as he was relaying his baseball resume to me, and I was showing great admiration for his accomplishments, he asked me that question that I always hated. Right after he listed his selection to the all county team, the junior college he played for, the two home runs he once hit in the same game, he asked me, "Did you play any baseball when you were younger?"

I didn't want to go down this path… for many reasons. Yes, I did play ball and yes, I was actually pretty good, but that was a long time ago…a lifetime ago. Lots of disappointment in the way it ended.

My answer to him was pretty much to the point.

"Yeah, I played some ball."

Perhaps this would get me off the hook and he would move on to some more of his baseball highlights.

I wasn't that lucky.

Like a very good criminal lawyer, he felt the need to dissect my answer to his question and to learn not only more about my baseball experiences, but my life in general. It was miserable and uncomfortable. The more he asked, the more I said. The more that I said, the more it was apparent to him that his resume wasn't that great. Worse yet, it may have appeared that I was patronizing him and that certainly was not my plan. The conversation ended abruptly once he had sucked out the last of my baseball highlights. I think he was embarrassed though he had no reason to be.

Although the conversation came to an end, he quietly sat there for about 15 more minutes before politely excusing himself. He walked directly up to the coaches and began to have what appeared to be a very cordial conversation with the coaches. Perhaps by me sitting there and listening, I had helped the father come up with the courage to communicate his concerns or perhaps offer his assistance to the team. That's what I should have told him to do in the first place. Several more minutes of discussion took place between the father and the coaches. Although the exchange still seemed to be friendly and constructive, both parties looked over at me every few minutes.

I didn't like this.

As I was trying to figure out in my mind why the glances toward me were occurring, the three gentlemen suddenly started walking directly at me. I really didn't like this. As they approached me one of the coaches spoke, "Mr. Potter, we would like you to help with the team."

Before I had a chance to respond the other coach added, "Why didn't you tell us that you played professional ball?"

Because of my schedule and a few other personal things, I was not in a position to make a commitment to coach. I told them that I would help out as best that I could. I would like to stay out of everyone's way and just work with the pitchers a little. They agreed.

The extent of their excitement in the fact that I had played professional ball was way out of whack. They shouldn't have been so enamored with that fact. They were connecting my playing ability years ago directly with the winning result that surely meant for their players. That was a big mistake on a couple fronts. First, and foremost, winning should have been far down the list of goals for the coaches on this team. Secondly, even if winning was the top priority, equating someone who played well to someone who could coach well wasn't a great idea. As time went on, I realized how big of a misnomer that truly has been in youth baseball.

I finished up the year working with a few pitchers on the team, one of them being the boy who threw eight straight balls and was taken out of the game crying. I told the coach to give him another chance, let him pitch and let me talk to him during the game that he pitched. He agreed to give him another chance but told me, "You know he can't throw a strike." More words of encouragement!

I worked with the boy a little for the next few weeks. I informed him that he would pitch again and that he would throw strikes. His problem wasn't that he couldn't throw strikes. The problem was that he wasn't shown how to throw strikes. It was actually a very small adjustment that made a very big difference.

He never looked at his target. Yes, he looked at the target before he went into his motion and he was looking at the target after he threw the ball. During his wind up, however, his head was flying all over, just not at the target. It took him about three sessions to work that out, to where his control was pretty good. I then asked him if he would like to throw even more strikes.

He said yes.

I asked him what he thought about when he looked at the target. He said, "Nothing." I asked him why he looked at the catcher's glove if he had no purpose in looking at it. I told him that you need a purpose in everything you do on a ball field. I told him to pretend that the target was the coach's head and that his goal was to hit it every time: that same coach that ridiculed him and told him that he couldn't do it and didn't really give him a chance. I told him to hit the target every time and really give the coach a headache. We both laughed. I told him that it was our secret and he couldn't tell anyone. He smiled and said okay. I guess that wasn't the most respectful thing I could have said to him, but I said it and it sounded fair at the time.

He went out and pitched again. No, he didn't remind me of Roger Clemons or Randy Johnson, but he did throw strikes. He pitched about four innings and I can't remember whether our team actually won the game. I can remember the smile on his face, though, and the satisfaction and pride that his dad showed on the sidelines. For some reason, winning the game wasn't important that day, and remembering whether we won or lost was even less significant. Bigger things were happening.

About a year ago, I ran into his dad at the high school that both of our sons attended. He asked how my son was doing and I said fine. He said that his son was doing really well also. After a little small talk, and completely out of the blue the dad said, "Thank you." No reason was given ... and no reason asked. I'm not sure what he meant, but I have a pretty good idea. When I look back at that year of baseball, I have no idea what the team's record was. I tend to remember the other winning that took place.

My son was fortunate enough to have at least average ability and therefore that fact allowed him to get a decent amount of playing time. Not as much as a coach's son, but enough that I could deal with it. He played the outfield and first base and pitched a little.

What was hard to deal with was the fact that these coaches had very little idea what they were doing yet didn't realize it. Very few players had the opportunity to pitch. The few that threw the hardest pitched over and over. Basic fundamentals of the game were not taught and there was very little discipline. It was painfully apparent that progress would not occur on this team this year for any of the players.

It was more and more difficult to watch the games as the season went on. The newspaper that I always brought to the field was now held tighter in my hands and closer to my face. Most of the time I couldn't bear to watch, not because of the kid's performances, but because of the anguish that most assuredly was apparent on my face. Although I felt the coaches were ill equipped to lead a team of nine year olds, the fact was that they were out there giving their time. They didn't deserve to be embarrassed, ridiculed, or talked about. They thought that they were doing a great job and I didn't think it was my place to burst their bubble. I mean if it was truly that bad, I could always have volunteered to help if I could have added something of substance. I elected to not volunteer full time so I really had no right to complain.

The biggest problem was that parents were selected to coach not by their experience or ability, but how well they knew the baseball commissioner. There were not coach's clinics, seminars, or any type of coaching lessons. There was no oversight of the coaches by anyone and they were never evaluated at the end of the year. The coaches just followed their kids up to the next age group and once a coach had a team it was hard to replace him.

So far in Eric's short baseball career, he had been introduced to six men who served as a coach to him. Some were better than others. There was no Coach Spellman yet. Nor was there a Joe Sheeler, Dave Dobi, Frank Clark or any of my other youth coaches. Maybe the next year there would be a coach who measured up to my childhood hero, my high school coach; or maybe I was just asking for too much. As time went on, I came to realize that this was an unfair comparison for me to make. No one would ever measure up to Coach.

Was my high school coach, Bill Spellman, really that good? I thought so, and still do, but I have run into some skeptics. Those non-believers, not surprisingly, are coaches that now must run a high school team under a lot of different circumstances. Society has changed, and many coaches now believe that parents, administrators, players, and the public have made the job so much more difficult in the present than in the past. Pressures come from all directions and situations are much more scrutinized. Some coaches, when reading my thoughts about how Coach Spellman disciplined us, reminded me that they could never get away with some of that stuff today. Parents just wouldn't put up with it, and would certainly march down to the administrators of the school bemoaning how terrible their young son was being treated. Perhaps this is true.

March of 2000 was now upon us and like every other spring of every other year, baseball had a new beginning with new hopes and dreams for everyone. That's the beauty of the game; just ask any Chicago Cub fan. As they say in spring training, hope runs eternal. If it wasn't for hope, what would we have? We lived in the little town of Crofton, Md., which is nestled neatly between Annapolis, Baltimore, and Washington, D.C, Although on a much smaller scale than the major leagues, some adults were hoping for a successful CAC (Crofton Athletic Council) baseball season. My wife and I were two of these people. There was no doubt that Eric wanted to play baseball and the sport was now in his blood. We had all put last year, and some of those embarrassing situations, behind us. The important thing was that nothing from the past seemed to impact my son in a negative manner. If he did have a problem, we didn't notice.

One of the coaches was back for this year and the other one was gone. The returning father was fairly harmless. He would show favoritism toward his son and always play him. He really didn't know baseball and I doubt that he ever played baseball as I only remembered him speaking of playing high school basketball. He was involved with other sports in the association, and coached those sports. I believe that is how he got the job as the baseball coach. He was an ineffective coach but he could be dealt with.

The other coach was a different story. He had to go. He was the one coach who had absolutely no social skills, the one who embarrassed the little pitcher, who constantly screamed across the field at the other coach during the games. He was the one that had no clue. He was replaced with a man who did not have a son on the team and therefore didn't seem to have an agenda. He had more baseball experience and knowledge and seemed to be good with the kids. They all liked him and his presence seemed to have a calming affect on the other coach. It was a very good mix.

It was also a good season for Eric. His talent level started to improve versus some of the other kids on his team. I believe the reason for this was that he now played baseball consistently and this was his fourth year. Some of the other kids were in and out of baseball and it seemed that they had not made a full time commitment to this game. Eric seemed to now have a love affair with the game. I once again stayed on the sidelines. Occasionally I was asked if I would help out and I would always oblige, hitting some fly balls or grounders or every so often throw batting practice for the team. Because of the improvement in coaching, the newspaper disappeared a lot more from in front of my face and it was a bit more relaxing to watch the games. The kids were now having fun again. Yes, there was still way too much emphasis on the wins and losses and yes, there was still too little development of the fundamental baseball skills, but it was a big improvement over the year before.

**Eric as a young pitcher. Good form was never
the problem.**

Despite the more positive experience of that year, it was becoming more and more evident that the organization that Eric
played ball in was not a well run operation. Not only were there a
lot of incompetent coaches running teams, but more importantly,
there was no indication that things were going to improve. We had
no idea who would be coaching the next year and that concerned
me. I knew that the new coach who had come on this year, the one
who brought some stability to the team, would not return.

Well, the next year came and the spring season was over before we knew it. Eric's team played a total of only 11 games, which I realized was not nearly enough baseball to remain competitive with other serious ball players. Actually the season should have been 12 games, but the baseball commissioner made sure that final game was not played. He was very upset because a game was rescheduled without his knowledge and approval. So to prove a point he did not allow his boy to play that game for us. Yes, his boy was on our team, and yes, his boy happened to be ninth player that day, and yes, he forced us to forfeit. That pretty much said everything about the organization, the commissioner, and baseball in this program. That was the last straw. We decided that we were leaving for another opportunity, that greener grass that everyone seems to seek.

We had given five years to this organization and no improvement had been made in the manner in which the program was run. Not once did they ask for input, not once did I remember them putting into effect a suggestion from a parent. The commissioner's motives and motivations did not seem to parallel the kid's having a positive experience on the ball field. Coaches seemed to have more job security than was merited.

The coach of Eric's team that year was someone who I would consider an improvement over the other coaches who he had been associated with up to this point. I thought the man was fair and knowledgeable. I thought he knew the game of baseball well and I thought he tried to the right things out on the ball field; for all the kids, not just his kid. I felt it was unfortunate that he had an opportunity to only coach 11 games and to work with the kids a few limited months.

The good news was that this coach had to also leave the organization the same time Eric did, and he also had to go to the new organization that Eric was headed. He went there and stayed with Eric from that time until the present day. He did everything he could do to not only make Eric a better ball player, but a better person. He really cared about Eric a lot. He coached him and mentored him and pushed him and supported him. He tried to praise him enough, but not too much and do likewise with the reprimands. He tried to teach him not only baseball, but also all those life lessons that were necessary.

That's what dads do…

Yes, I became my son's coach when he played in the 11U age group. He actually had tried out and made the 12U team, but looking at that situation, and coaches, I thought it would be best for Eric to stay back and play with his age group with me as his coach. Perhaps I was being over protective by wanting to coach my son and perhaps I just wanted to coach and it was more about me than him.

Maybe I was being selfish. I hope that wasn't the case.

Along with my decision to coach, some good fortune came our way. The head coach's son also made the 12U team that spring and he opted for the route to join those players. So I now had become the head coach which made me feel much better. I'm not a real good assistant; I like to be in charge.

To this day, I am not sure of my true motivations. All I know is that I feel it worked out for everyone. I just knew that it was time to get involved. I took my own advice; don't complain if you're not willing to do something about it. I became a coach. It only lasted two months and 11 games, but it was enough to get the juices going once again. It was enough to start unlocking some of those memories, some of Coach Spellman's wisdom and knowledge. It was enough to start hearing those voices again.

Eric had now established himself as a pitcher and first baseman. His talent level was a little above average in regards to kids on his team and it became clear to me that he had some real natural ability for the sport. Most importantly, he still loved the game.

At the end of this spring season Eric and a teammate, Jesse Leszczynski, joined the 12U team for a weeklong tournament in Cooperstown, home of the baseball Hall of Fame. It was a fun experience and Eric's first exposure to teams who years later would be called "showcase teams." Little did either of us know at the time that these showcase teams and showcase weekends would be a big part of our lives in years to come. In regards to baseball, it would become the way of the world. This tournament would be the last time either of these players would ever wear a uniform for this current organization.

We left and never looked back.

When I was a kid, the option of leaving an organization, good or bad, was almost non-existent. We played with the same teammates for years and years. We may have changed teams, which meant that one summer a player was a teammate, the next year we were playing against each other.

But it still was all within the same association.

I think today it is too easy to move on when something doesn't go your way. The solution always seems to be to find another place to go. Perhaps my wife and I had become those parents that took the easy way out. I don't know, but I do know the option was there and it became an easy decision. I thought that we had made a fair effort to this organization.

Five years of baseball and my son still loved the game and I loved to watch him play. He was a natural. He didn't run real fast, hit real far, or throw real hard, but he was a natural out on the field. I had watched him progress to the point that staying in this organization would have deterred his progress which probably would have ultimately sapped the excitement for the game out of his body.

I couldn't let that happen.

I remembered what baseball meant to me as a kid and I knew if the game was half as much fun to Eric as it was to me, I needed to give him every opportunity to keep the passion. I knew there was a good chance that if he could be put in the right environment, baseball would take a hold of him, and never let go. There is no sport like it; no other feeling goes through your body as when playing this great game. I also knew that you can have all the passion in the world for something, but in most cases you need to have an environment which allows you to feed and nourish what you care so much about. The baseball surroundings that Eric had participated in for the last five years were lacking in this area. There really was no other choice but to find the right home.

Baseball was still a great sport, but we all seemed to have lost what baseball was supposed to be about. I could tell. I could see it slipping away. You went to the games and the feel just wasn't right. The passion was not in the air, the excitement that we had as kids playing this game was not present, and the reverence for the coaches had vanished. We, not only as a team but as a society, had lost our way.

We have always had winners and losers in baseball, but at one time winning wasn't at the expense of sportsmanship or development or fun.

Now it seemed to be.

When I was Eric's age, I was all about winning. Winning was everything, nothing else mattered, and I never thought about anything else. The difference back then, though, was that the coaches and parents did care about the other things. They kept things in perspective and gave us the proper balance. We could think about winning because the adults found the way to teach the right lessons while we could eat, drink, and sleep about winning. The coaches and parents kept everything in check.

That doesn't happen anymore. Today, the coaches who we expect to keep the balance are far more winning at all cost than is healthy. In five years of youth baseball for my son, I couldn't remember a coach teaching a life lesson. Not once. When there was a choice of winning a game or acting in a way that would perhaps teach a child a valuable lesson about teamwork or hustle or attitude or responsibility, the chance of victory was always taken.

Baseball has come a long way from its earliest days, when the sport was considered recreation, not competition. It used to be an honorable sport. It no longer is. It is still beautiful and still the best sport played, but we have lost that honor and respect. Until we get that back, we will have too many coaches and parents who don't understand the true beauty of the game.

Golf is a game of honor.

Sure, we all have hit a drive behind a tree, and upon inspecting the location, looked around and when no one was gazing our way, gently kicked the ball far enough to have a playable lie. It's done thousands of times every day on golf courses scattered throughout the country. We all laugh about it as we have a beer in the clubhouse after the round or perhaps keep it to ourselves out of shame of cheating.

In reality, the real golfers don't do that.

Most of us are individuals who occasionally find our way on to a golf course with no real intention of following golf's policies to a tee (pardon the pun). We are weekend warriors, certainly nothing that resembles the professional golfer.

The real golfer still considers the sport honorable and treats it that way. When he approaches a ball to strike it, and by accident nudges the ball ever so slightly, he will call a foul on the play, and be penalized, even when no one is watching. Or if it is realized that a rule has been broken, even unbeknownst to anyone else, he will take a penalty that could literally cost thousands of dollars in prize money. That's the honor in the game of golf. These players manage to compete at the highest, most intense level, and still embrace the integrity of the game. Golf has always been that way and hundreds of years later the proud rules of the game are followed. Present day professional golfers speak with reverence of those who came before them. They know the history and the individuals who created that history.

Baseball is, and has always been, a little trickier. Baseball has never held itself to that much honor, although it started as a game of high integrity. For kids, it has always been a game of fun. Unfortunately, that fine line between honor and winning in baseball is not only fuzzy but also completely undetectable. Honor has made its way to "good sportsmanship" which, has made its way to winning, to winning at any and all cost…even at seven and eight years old. Depending on one's interpretation and motivation, sportsmanship may be completely confrontational to ones goal of winning. We have moved up the rightful progression from fun to winning at any cost and in doing so, have created huge problems in the game. Baseball is the vehicle to not only teach a game, but to teach life lessons. Our concern for winning, especially at very young ages, has created a domino affect that has far reaching consequences. Our failure to teach the correct lessons "between the lines" has done great harm to all.

It is true that the game of baseball, even in its infancy, had rules that allowed for less than honorable actions by its players. That's part of the beauty of the game. That's what makes it special.

For instance, a fielder, upon tagging a sliding runner at a base, hears the umpire call out. Unknown to anyone but himself, he dropped the ball, only to recover it quickly with his glove still hidden under the runners body. He obviously doesn't run up to the umpire and inform him that he dropped the ball, nor does he immediately shout out that the runner should be called safe. As any observer would note, "That's part of the game."

That's baseball. No one expects a player, even someone we hold in high esteem, to be that honorable.

That's a simple example.

But how about the batter that intentionally moves into a pitch to be hit by it, which allows him to advance to first base. That's technically illegal and if you look it up in the baseball regulations, you would quickly discover that it's clearly against the rules. It's definitely not within the rules of the game. So is it honorable, or even fair, to act in this manner? Players of all ages now do this. Professional ball players now wear enough padding on their forearms that being hit with a pitch is not even a momentary discomfort. You now see high school players making this action an art form, throwing their forearm out on an inside pitch. When a batter now gets out of the way of an errant pitch, like the rules say you are supposed to do, you will surely hear the following from the bench and bleachers, "Come on, take one for the team." The argument for that by an avid fan may be "That's the umpire's call, that's why he's there." In other words, if you can get away with it, then it's not cheating and therefore is within the rules. Is that really good sportsmanship?

You may be right again, but now we're heading down that slippery slope of an attitude of anything to win. Now the same batter steps back just a little and pulls his bat back ever so slightly as the pitcher comes home with the pitch, intentionally swinging in a manner that will make the bat strike the catcher's glove and hence, induce a catcher's interference call. One may once again say that this should be a call by the umpire. That may be true, but it's a step further from sportsmanship, from honor. It is not only intentionally breaking a rule, and hoping the umpire doesn't catch it, it is bringing an opposing player into harms way. Sometimes the reaction to the misdeed depends entirely on the end result, and that is really sad. If the batter is successful in completing this devious task by only glancing the catcher's glove to get a free base, his teammates, upon realizing his intentions, may laugh in the dug out and appreciate his creativity. But on this play, if instead of a gentle glance, it is in fact a direct hit to the catcher's hand, which would assuredly create a broken bone, there would be in all probability silence from his teammates, with possible disdain for his actions.

Opposing spectators would call this dirty playing and possibly retaliate in some manner. Even some fans of his team, which got the free base, may have problems with this type of play. In both cases, it's the same motivation and the same activity, but in one case it is creative, and in the other case it is dirty playing. The only difference is to what extent the catcher was injured. Does that make sense?

Of course, one could debate forever the "bean ball," throwing at batters. Players could be seriously hurt. Nowhere in the rulebook does it state that intentionally throwing at a player is legal or part of baseball. As we all know, though, it is and will probably always be part of the game. Throwing at a hitter sometimes is done as retaliation, to show support for a teammate who was originally plunked by the opposing team. Sometimes it is just done because the opposing player hit a home run off of you. So your opponent makes a good play and instead of showing respect for his performance, you throw an object at his head? That doesn't even make sense. Where's the honor or sportsmanship in that?

If the retaliation resulted in a severe head injury to the opposing batter, it could conceivably result in criminal action if the pitcher admitted to throwing at the batter. So, if you throw at a batter and hit him but he doesn't get hurt, you are considered a good teammate for sticking up for your own player. But if it is the same exact situation and the batter gets seriously hurt, are you still that good teammate? Are you playing the game with honor? Is that good sportsmanship?

If this isn't going far enough, consider the plight of Mark Downs, Jr., a T-ball coach in Pennsylvania. Mr. Downs offered one of his players $25 to intentionally hit a teammate with a ball during a pre-game warm up. This happened on June 27, 2005. The coach offered the cash because he did not want the young boy to play in the game. It seems that the boy was autistic and not considered a good ball player. The boy was only nine years old, but the coach wanted to win so bad, was driven for a victory so intensely, that he instructed a boy to hit him with the ball. When the boy did what he was instructed, the ball glanced off of the 9-year-old autistic boy.

That was not good enough for the coach.

He then instructed the boy him to hit him harder. The next throw hit the boy directly in the face, this time much harder.

The victim of this senseless and unimaginable act no longer plays soccer. He now is in therapy, afraid that this event is surely going to happen to him again. The coach was found guilty of corruption of minors and simple assault. He was immediately sent to prison. This coach had two of his own children on the team.

Baseball is no longer about honor. It is about winning. In a lot of cases, it is about winning at any age, at every age. Recreation has been replaced by "competition with honor" which now has evolved into "winning at all costs". As a young boy who played thousands and thousands of hours of baseball, I always played to win and I never took losing lightly. To this day I can take myself back to a ball field as a nine year old boy and feel the intense disappointment and pain of losing a pick-up game. I can to this day feel the sheer joy and excitement of coming up on the winning side of a game at our childhood field. In both cases, emotions ran high which more times than not, led to nasty words or perhaps a fist fight between players. The competition was fierce and the barbs that flew back and forth were something I would not want my young son to participate in.

We were all about winning. We didn't understand things that I now call "life lessons." No one back then used those words or explained what it meant. But now looking back through adult eyes, the lessons were taught without us knowing. The coaches had in their own way instilled values in us that were more important than a victory. Yes, winning was the only thing that mattered, but we had somehow just assumed that this winning came with its own rules, its own commandments. Certain things weren't done. We didn't cheat… or think about cheating. We picked fair teams. We respected good plays by our opponents. We respected our coaches.

We didn't wine and complain. We always hustled. We always encouraged our teammates.

Today these principles are not communicated, taught, or demanded nearly enough. There's more to the game than the numbers on the scoreboard. There's more to life than winning at all costs.

Sometimes there is nothing that will get in the way of a coach doing whatever he must do to win. I see that much more today than 30 years ago. We seldom had kids sit at the end of the bench game after game and not play, or perhaps play that two innings that was required by the rules of a league or just enough time to say that he got into the game. Sometimes winning at any cost includes breaking the rules which in itself is bad enough. Sometimes it is worse; you may break somebody's heart.

Just ask Joel Roberts.

When a kid starts playing baseball for the high school in ninth grade, the future is at best hazy. No one can play out their next four years in their mind without questions or doubts. Some kids dream about being a starter on the varsity team some day. Some just want to make the team, while others may dare to "shoot for the moon" with their thoughts.

Why not?

I have no idea what thoughts crossed Joel Robert's mind as a freshman trying out for the JV baseball team at his high school. I didn't even know who he was. I only learned the name and the person through watching my son play ball. Joel was a pitcher, and as time went on, became a very good pitcher.

When my son Eric was a freshman in high school, Joel was a sophomore. Joel made the varsity baseball team that year, but wasn't really good enough to contribute a lot to the team. He would come "back down" to the JV and do some pitching, usually in big games against the better teams. There was nothing flashy about Joel, but he was very effective and seemed very mechanical and unemotional on the mound. He could put you to sleep. Every pitch was the same delivery, whether it was a fast or curve ball. Any time I would talk to Eric about Joel, he would laugh and say "His curve is terrible."

As a junior, Joel got a little more pitching time for the varsity. He probably threw "in the low 80's" at this time, and again without much of a curve. For those of you who are not baseball experts, the "low 80's" is not the temperature, rather it is the velocity (mph) in which the pitcher throws the ball, and in this case, is a fairly good speed for a high school pitcher. His pitching on the varsity team as a junior was still somewhat limited. Although a couple of pitchers had graduated to lessen the competition from the older players, he was passed up by a freshman named Tyler Hibbs. Tyler, like we all knew, came on the scene like a "bat out of hell." We all knew how good he was. So it was Tyler, three seniors, and Joel. Through this baseball season, Joel continued to work hard, as hard as anyone on the team.

As a junior, Joel saw his team reach the State finals, only to lose a heartbreaker in the last inning of the championship game. He did not see any action in that game.

In that off-season, Joel continued to work hard. His senior year would be his year. The three senior pitchers were gone and he was entrenched as the #2 pitcher on a very good baseball team, a team who had the potential for another great year. Maybe they could make it back to the finals again.

The baseball season rolled around and as predicted, the team was strong. They started the county season with a ten run "mercy" win over Southern and never slowed down. Other than them stubbing their toe once, against Northeast, they breezed through the county with a 15-1 record, one of their best records ever. Joel was a big part of this winning season. He pitched extremely well. The 1-2 combination of Tyler and Joel was awesome, without a doubt the best in the area. Along with Joel's good control and location, he possessed a decent fastball, and now, a much better curve that certainly made him a very effective pitcher.

The state tournament had now started, and like clockwork, the team was breezing through the opponents. Old Mill, North County, and Chesapeake were knocked off in succession. They then took on the team who beat them in the finals the year before, Quince Orchard, in a revenge game. They avenged the previous year with a sound beating of the previously undefeated opponent. Tyler pitched the whole game, once again throwing very well.

Here they now were ready to play yet another state championship game. Now, because of how the pitching rotation worked out, Joel got the assignment for this final game.

I don't know Joel's dreams as a new freshman baseball player, but could it have been better than to be a very good senior pitcher who now has earned the assignment on the Arundel High School baseball team who is attempting to win an unprecedented 10th state baseball title? This had to be a dream come true. This was a true example of what baseball and hard work was all about. Joel Roberts, a kid with good ability, not great, was depending on nothing more than a great work ethic to get him to this point.

Hard work and a good attitude do pay off for those of you who are not superstars, just good players with a passion to do well. Joel deserved this opportunity as much as anyone. Tyler pitched them into this championship game by winning the semi-final game. Now it's Joel's turn to shine. What a great story!

Joel was not only a good athlete, but very much respected by his teammates. He had an excellent work ethic and was extremely well mannered and respectful of all fellow players.

The championship game was played on a Friday night at Ripken Stadium in Aberdeen, Maryland. It was overcast with the threat of rain. It poured at game time and the start of the contest was put off for about an hour. Lots of people attended the game. Joel's parents were two of them.

The game finally started and as expected, Joel was on the mound for his team. After three innings, the Arundel Wildcats were leading by the score of 3-1. Up to this point Joel had pitched good, not great, but very solid. He gave up one run and he actually appeared to be getting stronger and relaxing a little more. Appearing to be in command, he came bouncing off the mound after the third inning into the dugout.

The team was pumped up and excited. There were lots of "Atta boys" and "Keep it up" going Joel's way. At this point in time, he must have been on cloud nine, living out a dream. His senior year, possibly his most important game he'll ever pitch in his life.

Joel would not be considered a top-notch college prospect. He is a good high school pitcher. This is his time to shine, to go out on top. This is the type of game you remember all your life, the one you tell your buddies or children about twenty years from now. No one deserved this "fifteen minutes of fame" more than Joel Roberts.

Now his focus had to be on the next four innings. That was it; four more innings… take them one at a time. Keep your focus, keep your composure. Just pitch the way you know how. Continue to pitch the way you are pitching. As he reached the dugout, he accepted well-deserved high fives from the teammates. He saw his coach walking toward him and readied himself for any suggestions or support Coach had.

Coach's words,

"Good game Joel, Hibbs is going in."

In hindsight, this was probably the plan all along. Tyler had pitched a few days earlier and certainly couldn't have pitched this whole game. Joel's job was probably to give a few strong innings until they could get to their ace. It makes sense from an "x and o" perspective.

These decisions are made every day by coaches and that is why if you have never coached, you have no idea the difficulty of the job. You have to make decisions and constantly be second-guessed. This appeared to be an easy decision to make by a coach despite Joel's performance. Tyler was the man, the number one pitcher. The coach figured he had four good innings in him, had the lead, what else was needed? Who wouldn't have made this decision? Tyler went in, Joel came out, and the game continued.

Arundel went on to win 5-3 to give them another state championship, their 10th. It was another feather in their cap, another reason for Arundel to be able to puff out their chests. The state championship shirts followed, along with the state championship rings.

The next day the newspaper's headlines rang out in bold letters "Hibbs leads Arundel to State Championship." There was one line at the bottom of the article, which said "Senior Joel Roberts started for Arundel." Almost all Arundel fans left the game that night ecstatic; smiling, laughing, full of pride. They had won another state championship! Number Ten!

But a few Arundel fans left Ripken Stadium angry. Just a few and I was one of them.

Not angry with anyone in particular, just angry at what we had become. I was truly happy for Tyler. No one works harder than him. I don't know if he's slowed down at all since the first time he picked up a baseball and threw it to his dad ten years ago. He is the ultimate warrior, always asking for the ball, never waiting or hoping that he is chosen. Give me the ball, I'm the best, this is my arena, watch me perform. Those words don't need to be said, they're written all over his body. All you need to do is look at the confidence that drips from his body when he is performing. He pitched great that night under pressure, and that's what he likes. I was happy for all the players. A lot of them may never get an opportunity like that again, to play on a championship team.

But I was angry and I still am. Every thought of that tenth school baseball championship is a thought of Joel Roberts and what was taken away from him.

Most people just don't get it. They don't have a clue. They never realized the injustice that was done that night. They were too busy feeling good about themselves and their child's accomplishments. They were too busy basking in the glory of winning, winning at any cost. That is to be understood and expected. Sadly though, once the euphoria wore off, once one had to put the game behind them and look forward, I don't think many people saw the injustice. The final score on the scoreboard isn't the only type of winning that should happen on a ball field.

Perhaps some day 20 years from now, Joel Roberts will be talking to his son about baseball. The topic of high school baseball will come up. Joel will do one of two things. He'll take the high road and explain to his boy all the wonderful experiences he had playing baseball in high school, the good teammates, the close friendships, and the coaches who really cared and taught him so much.

Or he'll tell the truth.

He'll want his boy to understand one of those life lessons, the one about winning at any cost; the lesson that was taught that night.

The wrong lesson.

He'll tell his son that he worked hard for four years to get himself in the position he was in that Friday night way back in 2006. Perhaps one shouldn't expect to have that opportunity, but he was there and fate put him at the right place at the right time and he truly deserved to reap the benefits of his hard work. He'll tell his son that he was pitching really well and was on the verge of finishing off his high school career in style, proving that hard work and dedication means something.

He'll tell him that coaches should recognize that you have earned something and you should be given the opportunity to complete the task handed to you. He'll relate the fact that the coach had enough respect for you to allow you to finish what you started. It was your game to win. It was the crowning moment of your high school career and you deserved it.

But for some reason, the deep unrelenting desire to win at all costs reared its ugly head once again. Fairness did not come into the equation. Compassion did not come into the equation; nor did setting a good example for everyone to see. As Al Davis, part owner of the Oakland Raiders, made famous years ago, "Just win baby!"

He'll tell his son all of this, with the rawness like the game was played the night before. Perhaps emotions that have been bottled up in him for years will once again emerge. He'll tell him that right in the middle of the game that he was pitching so well, that meant so much to him, that he was winning and ready to lead his team to a championship, his legs were cut off under him. His coach told him in so many words that you don't deserve an opportunity to finish the game.

"Joel, I'm not sure you're good enough, I don't think you deserve an opportunity to continue."

When his boy says to him, "Dad, if you were doing so well, why did the coach take you out," I wonder what the answer will be. Which positive, heart-warming response will he pick?

Well, Arundel won the game. There's a real good chance that Arundel would have won that game leaving Joel into pitch. Joel pitched three innings and let up one run. Tyler pitcher four innings and let up two runs.

Technically, Joel out pitched Tyler that night.

He out pitched everyone that night. I guess what he deserved was one line at the bottom of an article, kind of an after thought. We'll never know what the outcome would have been if Joel had received his fair shot to finish the game.

More importantly, Joel will never know.

I hope somewhere down the line Joel coaches his little boy in some type of organized baseball, perhaps when his son is eight or nine years old. The time will come for Joel to make decisions out on the field. Another little boy will be out on the mound in an important game. He'll be pitching really well. The boy's mom and dad will be rooting with all the enthusiasm in the world. With a one run lead in the fifth inning, the boy is so happy and the parents are so proud. Joel wants the kids to win really bad as does all the parents. The shortstop is their star player and best pitcher. Parents are really into this game, two innings away from the little league championship. They are becoming vocal about the fact that the star pitcher has "a good two innings" in him to finish off the game. If the coach moved him to the mound, the chance of victory would probably be increased. Joel thinks for a few moments about possibly improving the team's chance of victory.

His eyes take him to the kid on the mound who is doing okay and trying real hard. He's still pitching fairly well. He then glances over to the mom and dad in the stands who are both smiling and full of enthusiasm. He has a choice to make. Does he increase his chances of winning a bit, or does he give that pitcher the shot he deserves?

Which decision would make him a better coach?

He thinks back to that night 20 years ago, when his mom and dad sat in the stands full of pride, when they were completely caught up in his magical moment. He thinks back 20 years ago when a bunch a fellow ball players were yelling and screaming on the field when they had won the championship, and how happy that made them. These kids, and parents would love to have this championship trophy.

Which decision would make him a better coach?

He calls time and walks slowly out to the mound to talk to his pitcher, and possibly replace him. The parents all want to win and they know what decision gives them the best chance for victory. They're all waiting to see what Coach Roberts does.

The trek to the mound, though only about 80 feet or so from the dugout, seems a lot longer. He walks slowly and it's obvious that his decision, whatever it may be, is not yet clear.

Which decision would make him a better coach?

He takes the ball from the young boy and firmly holds it in his hand. He places his other hand on the little boys shoulder and whispers something to him. Every parent in the stands sits with anticipation, wondering what those few words could have been.

The boy, head down and shoulders drooping, slowly nods his head up and down.

He then takes the ball and places it back in the pitcher's hand.

He has made his decision.

It's not popular.

But it's right.

He leaves the pitcher in. He becomes that coach who doesn't know what he's doing. He upsets a lot of parents who have taught their kids at a very young age the wrong life lesson, that the score of the game is always the most important thing. Just like that night 20 years ago.

Is it really important what unfolded the last two innings of that game? Does it really matter what the final score was on the scoreboard? Or was the correct lesson taught, and learned, when he showed confidence in his young pitcher, believed in him, and stuck with him…. and gave him the opportunity that he deserved?

The final score was …………………..

Well, like I said, it's not really important, because winning should happen in a lot of different ways.

One goes through life and hopefully understands life's lessons. They're all out on a ball field waiting to be learned, to be understood every day. Winning can be taught so many different ways. When one concerns himself with personal accolades rather than teaching a young man a valuable life lesson that can be treasured the rest of his life, there's a problem.

My friend Linda decided to help coach a youth team last year, a bunch of 9 and 10 year old boys. She had coached 21 years ago. I asked her if things had changed from the last time she coached. Her reply—"My first and only other coaching experience was when I was 18 years old. I coached an 8U soccer team. We had a great time. We practiced, we played, and we laughed. They learned basic ball control and dribbling. I'm not sure how many games we actually won, but I do know that it was a fun time for these young boys and girls.

After I coached this time... 21 years later - I was shocked to see how competitive the sport had become. What I wasn't prepared for was the extent of the competitiveness at such a young age..... not with the children as much as the parents! It seemed that the days of playing a sport for fun were long, long gone."

When I asked Linda if she would coach again, the answer was no.

Eric was now 11 years old and I prayed that the fun part of baseball was still out there some where, that our insatiable appetite for victory had not diminished the chance for the kids to have a good time.

At 11 years old, Coach Sheeler was still my little league baseball coach. His son Pete had moved onto Pony League (13-14), but Coach Sheeler stayed with the Little League program. He was the program. It was not about his boy or for that matter, about him. He coached the team before his son got there and after his son left. He never had an assistant coach who I can remember. He was at every game, every practice. A player would coach first base. Parents, especially the dads, would come out to the games and watch. There was never any drama, never a dad in the coach's face, never an outburst by a player that wasn't dealt with promptly and harshly. And most importantly, never did Coach Sheeler seem to place winning over teaching the right lesson at the right time. We all loved him; perhaps not at the time while we were playing on his team. Years later, however, as we moved on to Pony League and Colt League and High School ball, there wasn't a memory of Little League that didn't have a warm feeling, and an appreciation of him.

As my son completed his year as an 11-year-old player, it was hard not to take myself back to my childhood and compare times and events. The biggest difference was the quality of coaching. I knew this now because I was the adult, and therefore possessed the memories. Eric had no clue then what type of coaching he had just witnessed. Like most things in life, baseball included, you only get an appreciation of how good, or bad, something is years later.

Winning, like beauty, is in the eye of the beholder. The scoreboard is only one of a multitude of ways to judge a victory. Someone needs to tell this to a whole bunch of parents and a whole bunch of coaches. Years and years of a "now society"... that I need results today, I need to be the star today, I need to win today, has taken us all further and further away from what is really important.

I do believe that Coach Spellman has been looking down from heaven and watching my plight. I do believe that when I started coaching a slight smile spread across his face. He was too modest to even think he was a great coach, but he was. In his own way, I know that he was hoping that somehow I could relay some of my childhood experiences on to others, that maybe the life lessons that I learned could be shared with others.

I believe that nothing that I learned from playing baseball was more important than putting winning in perspective. I remember the night that I found out that I would be the head coach of Eric's 11 year old team. I remember how I had played as a boy and young man, how driven I was to accomplish one goal: to win. I wasn't sure that I could handle my "winning at any cost" attitude that I possessed as a child; that I could get on the ball field with 11 year old kids and put my strong obsession of gaining a victory in check. I knew what was right, but I knew how I played the game. Could I possibly do the right thing now that I was the coach?

I got my answer the very first game that we played that season. It was nothing that I did, it was how I felt, and how I was led. We were winning 2-0 in the last inning and I had rotated all the kids around the whole game in what I thought were a very fair manner. The other team loaded the bases with no one out in that last inning. Our second baseman and shortstop who were now in the game at those positions were probably the least talented kids on the team. They were in there because it was their turn to play. My head knew that my two best ball players were sitting on the bench and that reduced our chance of victory. My heart knew that these two guys who were out in the field needed to be out there. For some reason, it didn't bother me at all to see two small, nervous players being positioned as my middle infielders.

I don't know why I wasn't upset. That certainly wasn't my make up. At least, I didn't think it was my make up.

Their next batter came up to hit and things certainly looked dim for our team. It was one of their better hitters on their team and our pitcher was not what you would consider a strike out pitcher. The kid was going to hit the ball somewhere. The runner on second base got a huge lead and I yelled out for our second baseman to hold him closer to the base. I'm not sure he even knew what that term meant, but the words just rolled out of my mouth before I realized what I had said. It was a reaction on my part to the big lead that the runner was taking. If I would have thought before I had spoken, the words would have never been uttered. It would have been hard enough for him to stop a ground ball and throw it to first base accurately, let alone hold a runner and cover the second base area. It was said, however, and he followed my instructions the best way he knew how. He ran over to second base, and stood on it.

He was standing on the base. He was still firmly planted on the base as the pitcher threw the ball to the batter. He was way out of position as he just continued to stand statue-like on the base while the pitch entered the strike zone. He was not anywhere near where he should be. The batter swung and hit the ball squarely, about as solidly as one can hit the ball. It was a shot right up the middle that went past the mound area with no chance of the pitcher catching the screaming line drive. It appeared that it was a hit headed toward center field and would probably tie the game and assuredly guaranteed that, still with no outs, they would eventually score the winning run. Everything for that split second looked hopeless.

But sometimes strange things happen on a baseball field. Sometimes the lessons taught are not expected.

My second baseman, the least talented player on the team and the one player who you wouldn't want out there in this situation, was standing right where the ball was coming, right where he shouldn't have been, right on second base. As the ball approached the nervous second baseman, he somehow understood that he should put his glove up in the air, which was done. The ball somehow through what I believe was divine baseball intervention met the glove and disappeared deep into the glove's pocket. The boy, totally unaware of what had just occurred had no idea of what to do next. It didn't matter because he needed to do nothing. The batter was out because he caught it, and the runner at second was out because the fielder was actually standing on second base and the runner was not. It ended up as a double play on a ball that had no right being caught. If the better player had been out there, he would have been in the proper position at the time of the pitch, and of course, would have had no chance of catching this ball. Some people would call this dumb luck. I just call it what it is; a lesson being learned and a lesson being validated.

The next batter was retired on a fly ball to the outfield that under normal circumstances would have scored their third and decisive run. But this wasn't normal and we went home with a 2-0 victory. Sometimes it's just better to be lucky than good.

Perhaps Coach Spellman was looking down at me during the game and without me knowing, was calming my soul and was giving me a lesson on winning isn't everything. Perhaps when I inexplicably yelled out to the second baseman to keep the runner closer to the bag, it was Coach that put that thought in my head and put that second baseman exactly where he should NOT have been. All I know is that I left the field that day feeling that there was more at work than dumb luck that in a way the baseball Gods had once again stepped in and taken over a game.

I never again doubted myself about putting any player in a game at any time, no matter what the situation was. The lesson was firmly entrenched in my mind and soul. Winning is much more than what is flashed on the scoreboard.

Winning isn't everything.

CHAPTER 6
BEING A GOOD TEAMMATE

"Instead of trying to be the best player **ON** the team, try to be the best player **FOR** the team."

—Tom Hatala

Along with Eric and Jesse, Jason Patten was another player that made the trip to Cooperstown. Although eligible to participate on the 11-U team that spring, Jason "graded out" high enough to play on the older team and that's where he competed. He was, and still is, an excellent athlete. When he came home from that week long tournament in Cooperstown, he also turned in his uniform and joined both Jesse and Eric on the new team. Goodbye to Crofton and hello to Gambrills. Like his two new teammates, Jason went forward and never looked back and never regretted the move. The poor coaching, the poor organization, the lack of leadership and genuine passion for the game, was about to become a memory.

It was an experience not to cherish but to learn from.

Before the Crofton experience Jason spent his first years of baseball as a short, stocky first baseman in an organization outside of Philadelphia, Pennsylvania, called the Audubon Recreation Association (ARA). Jason had always liked baseball as did his older brother Ryan.

Jason as a young hurler

A change of employment for Jason's father, Steve, brought the family to the Anne Arundel county area where they bought a house in Davidsonville, Md., in the fall of 2000. When Jason's father and mother, Joyce, tried to sign him up for fall soccer that first year with the local organization, they were told, "Sorry, we're booked up."

"But we just moved here, can't you make room for one more?"

"Sorry, we're booked up …you may want to try Crofton."

A last minute attempt to get Jason in to the soccer program in Crofton was successful and that's where Jason played that first fall. When it came time to play baseball the next spring, the Pattens thought it would be just as easy to keep Jason in the Crofton organization, so that's where he started his Maryland baseball career at the tender age of 11.

Jason's youth baseball career began as one normally does, being nothing more than a lot of fun. T-ball moved into coach pitch, which then progressed to real baseball. Jason was an excellent baseball player and the sport came fairly easy to him. His experience with the Crofton organization lasted only one year. It became obvious very quickly to the Pattens that based on Jason's ability and desire for good competition, a change needed to be made. He wanted better competition and the organization did not want to supply it, refusing to allow a team to play in a more competitive league.

The new association that Jason, Jesse, and Eric joined was located three miles down the road in Gambrills, Md. It was called the Gambrills Athletic Club. Although they never played on the same team in Crofton, Jason crossed paths with Eric Potter more than once during their stay in that association and would now become teammates. Little did I know at that time how valuable and precious this partnership would become!

This new group of players would also disband, but Jason and Eric would be cornerstones of yet another team that played ball at Gambrills, the newly developed 2003 Gambrills 13-U team. By this time Jason was no longer the chubby infielder, rather a taller, thinner center fielder/pitcher.

When the decision needed to be made for attending high school for Jason, it was either public school (South River High School) or a private school, Archbishop Spalding High School. The Patten's older son Ryan had a not so friendly baseball experience at the public school. That may have helped sway the decision to go to Spalding High School, where Jason was joined together with his baseball coach from the Crofton days, Steve Miller. Steve also came to the realization that the program in Crofton was not headed in the right direction for his son's needs, and sent both of his kids to Gambrills to play ball in the summers.

Finally, high school ball met head on with Jason playing his summers at Gambrills. Spalding won out, Gambrills lost.

Jason warming up between innings in one of his Gambrills starts.

Jason's story is mirrored by tens of thousands of youth baseball players and parents throughout the country each year. A player ends up with a group of kids by pure fate. He changes leagues or communities or instructors. He's referred to this coach or this team. Someone's misfortune is his opportunity. If the woman in Davidsonville would have said, "Let me make room for him on this soccer team" seven years ago, then Jason probably would have never been throwing fastballs by hitters at Spalding High School. He never would have seen Crofton, probably would have never met Eric Potter and may have had more friends in Davidsonville who convinced him to go to South River High School in Edgewater, Md. He would have never had the opportunity to play high school ball at Spalding and meet Chris Huisman, who he considers his best teammate ever. Who knows if he would have even stuck with baseball? Perhaps his love of baseball was kept alive by the impact of his teammates in Gambrills. We'll never know...

Perhaps all of this happened because this one woman didn't make room for one more little chubby soccer player. I probably wouldn't have met him, or his parents. Countless dinners with the Pattens would never have occurred and Jason would have never gone on vacation with our family. I would have never had the privilege of working with Jason or hearing his coaching dad say a hundred times, "Put him in the books, and let's get out of here." My wife and I would be minus a lot of good memories, as would countless other parents. The Pattens have always been, and still are, a class act.

At first Eric seemed to have a love for all sports. Soccer took up the fall seasons, basketball the winter, and baseball the spring and summer. As time went on I think soccer was just too disciplined for his liking. It was run by an ex-soccer player whose directions to Eric to play in a certain area of the field didn't seem to interest him too much. The area that he was assigned to was always on defense, and Eric never got a chance to play offense. He never got an opportunity to even try to score. The coach's son always played offense; he was the "go to" player. Get the ball to my son, he's the best player. Soccer lost its luster. Basketball, believe it or not, was the same. Eric played for a coach who would finish every huddle by telling the players to pass the ball to his son because he was the best shooter. I know this because I was his assistant for one season. I listened to these instructions every game. His boy was also the "go to" player and never came out of a game.

Well, I shouldn't say he never came out of a game. There was that one game that I was in charge. ....

The head coach had to miss one of the regularly scheduled Sunday games. He called me that morning and went into detail of what the strategy should be for the game. Every other sentence included his boy's name. I listened very intently and responded at the right times. I am sure he felt that I truly understood his directions to me. They were very clear.

When the game time finally arrived, I had a great pep talk with the team before I sent them out on the court. I stressed teamwork and how they should pass the ball more and always look for the open player. The game started and the tempo of the game was the same as usual. If the coach's son got a rebound he would dribble down court and shoot the ball every time. If he did not get the rebound he would demand the ball from who ever had it. He would then dribble down court and shoot the ball. The opposing coach, realizing what was happening, began guarding him with two or even three boys. There was now no place to dribble to as he had a defensive player on every side of him. It didn't matter, up went the shot.

Gentle encouragement from me to "Pass the ball off" was met with deaf ears. Harsher communication to him from me was met with glaring eyes. I obviously was not being very effective in communicating my desires to him so I called a time out. As the team came into the huddle I told the players that we were going to make some substitutions. The stud superstar son of the coach was one of the boys who would take a break on the bench. He could not believe what he heard, as could no one else. He had never been taken out of a game before this day. I thought he was going to cry and I must admit that deep inside I was probably feeling better at seeing his anguish than I should have been feeling. It was pure delight.

The game started back up. I wish I could tell you that there was this nice, heart-warming end to the story, that we went out there without him and played as a team, and came back from our eight point deficit and won the game. That would be a nice way to finish this story. Well, there was no fairy tale ending; the eight point deficit increased to a 14-point deficit. Every time the other team scored and increased their lead, the superstar brat would say something under his breath from the bench that was not real encouraging or team building. I believe at this point in time, despite the team going backwards on the scoreboard, the kids for the first time were having fun. Players actually were allowed to shoot the ball and throw the ball to an open teammate. They were actually smiling. I'm not sure, but I think the happy faces were for two reasons. First, they were actually allowed to participate in the game and feel that they were contributing and part of a team. Secondly, I think they were enjoying the long overdue reprimand of the coach's son.

About five minutes later, I called another time out. It was time to make substitutions again. As the players came off the court, the players on the bench also stood, knowing it was their turn to go back into the game. I replaced all the players on the floor with all the players on the bench.

Except one.

The coach's son would sit a little longer.

Hopefully, he would learn some sort of lesson. Perhaps he could look out on the court and see that his teammates were actually having fun, the world did not revolve around him, and that this was a team game.

The game went on and on and our team actually started playing a little better. The 14-point deficit fell back down to the original eight point deficit, and at one time was reduced to five points. I finally put the team's star player back into the game. Any thoughts in my mind of him learning a life lesson while sitting on the bench were eliminated the first time he touched the ball. With a player standing under the basket frantically waving his hands for the ball that would assuredly have given us two points, the coach's son felt it was better to launch a shot from about 20 feet away while surrounded by three defenders. The shot wasn't even close. The game finally ended and I told them all that I felt that they played very well as a team and they showed their best teamwork of the year. I knew that each word that I uttered would get back to the head coach. I was hoping so!

That night I received a call from the superstar's father, the head coach. He communicated to me that another father had volunteered to help out with the team. In the most tactful manner he could muster, he informed me that my services would no longer be needed. It was okay. The game, and lesson of that day, will never leave my memory.

Eric lost interest in basketball about that time. I have no idea if it had anything to do with this experience or not. I do know that he did not like the fact that he hardly got a chance to shoot and like most of the other players, was yelled at when he didn't pass the ball to the superstar. The game of basketball was never passionate for Eric; now it wasn't even fun. It was all about the coach's son. He came to dislike going to the games because the coach created an environment that was not conducive to teamwork and fun. Eric continued to play basketball for a couple more years and actually still likes it a lot. It's fun for him to get out and shoot some hoops, but that's all it was – fun, not a passion. Baseball was left as his sport of choice.

Like the Pattens, we were more than ready to move onto another organization after the 11-U spring season had finished in Crofton. Usually it's hard to tell if you should make a change when you have nothing to compare something to. Neither of us knew what the new team was all about, nor had any of us met or played for the new coach. We heard that he was good and had a lot of experience. We knew he didn't have a son on the team. At this point, all we really knew was Crofton and we didn't know how any other organization was run. It didn't matter, we could not envision anything else quite this bad.

So off to the new program we went. Little did we know at the time that we would stay so long!

When Eric moved to the new Gambrills team with the rest of his new teammates they immediately were introduced to baseball at a different level than they had ever experienced. It was clear from the start that the coach had assembled some good talent and he was all about playing some good ball. There was no doubt that he was in total charge. That was made clear from the start. He had two built in coaches that he brought with him. Jason's dad, Steve, was out on the field from day one helping, and became the third assistant coach. That was enough coaches and I quietly, and from a distance, once again became a father. Coaching would have to take a back seat. Although I would have preferred to be out on the field coaching, my only concern at this time was for my son to have a good experience. It was back to biting lips, closing my eyes, and deep breathing, but that was okay.

The next two years were filled with a lot of baseball experiences that would probably be best described as interesting. Eric had an opportunity to play lots of competitive ball and forge many friendships. One of those friendships was with Jason. They had one thing in common, they both pitched. From the beginning, Jason was more the tall hard throwing right-handed power pitcher, Eric more the short, crafty left-handed pitcher. The two of them have always had a friendly rivalry in terms of their pitching. Jason was always telling Eric that he couldn't throw real hard. Eric always countered by making fun of Jason's curve ball that "never broke."

The team did very well, at least in terms of wins and losses. Other than one other local team who was very good, the Gambrills Athletics dominated the league that they were in and regularly beat up on the local competition. Scores of 25-2 and 17-1 were commonplace. It wasn't that they were running up the score, the other teams were just that bad. Although some of the kids and parents may have thought that they were that good, they weren't. I think they could have used Joe Sheeler's lesson a little more, "Always compare yourself to someone better."

The highlight of the team was probably a trip to Hopkinsville, Kentucky, to play in the 2002 National Championship 12-U Tournament. The roster was made up of their 12 players from that spring season:

Eric Chaney
Nick Elko
Ben Ertter
Tylor Hibbs
Cory Jensen
Matt Pace
Jason Patten
Shawn Pleffner
Eric Potter
Al Shandrowski
Matt Skrenchuk
Adam Summerfelt

Four years later five of these players would be on the Arundel High School roster that won the 2006 Maryland State Championship. Lots of their youth base ball games ended up being played at Gambrills. Of the 12 ball players on that roster two of them never made it to high school baseball. Their candles burned out early.

At this tournament in Kentucky the team did okay, but they were over matched in the play off round by better players and better coaches. No one seemed to realize it at the time, but this was the beginning of the end for this team. The coach had attempted to put together a super team, probably getting caught up with the local success of running over the competition. The fact was that the team didn't need another player here or there, it needed teamwork. That's what was missing. They were beat by better players, not so much physically but mentally. Our players were not trained or coached to be mentally tough. That made all the difference.

While the team was bull dozing over competitors earlier that spring, teamwork was falling apart. The team became all about individuals. The coach was having issues with some parents and their child's playing time. Other parents were publicly bemoaning the fact that their son wasn't pitching enough, or hitting high enough in the line-up. The coach didn't handle these issues real well, allowing pockets of discontent to spread. Everything looked fine on the surface, but things were boiling underneath. There were problem parents and the fact that the coach now had favorites was obvious. There was no control and very little respect left for the coach.

As was the case with Eric when he was younger, he once again plodded along, having had enough ability to get a decent amount of playing time. That part of it was fine. He was developing as a ball player and the talent level on the team was a good way for me to monitor his progress and compare him to other player's abilities. Eric was not the best player on the team, and I never had that illusion. He was probably somewhere in the middle of the pack. He played first base, outfield, and he pitched. His dad, back in the day, played first base, outfield, and pitched. Eric was a left-hander. His dad was a left-hander. Eric, at the age of 12, was one of the smallest kids on the team. His dad, at the age of 12, was one of the smallest kids on the team. All Eric lacked that his dad possessed was a terrible temper. Considering this, I believe Eric was ahead of me in his progress. I ended up being a decent ball player and there was no reason to think that Eric couldn't achieve equal success. As for his size, it didn't concern me. When I was 13 years old I grew seven inches and went from being short to being fairly tall. I thought my son had a chance to follow my same growth and that would be great. If he didn't ... he didn't. I was happy that he still loved the game. He didn't play as much as the coach's favorites, but that's part of what every one needs to deal with on a team. He seemed to handle it just fine, and it certainly wasn't enough of a problem to bring up. I learned a long time ago to pick your battles.

The fall of that year became more of what I thought would happen. Things were really unraveling. The team went to a local tournament and lost three games, all by one run. The coach was beside himself... angry, confused, emotional, pretty much falling apart in front of the team. The team started playing worse, the parents were more vocal in their displeasure, and there was no sign of teamwork. Other coaches were questioning the moves and motivations of the head coach. He had lost control. He was all about winning and did everything possible to win every game. Development of players existed only if it paralleled scoring more runs than the opponent. Discipline was non-existent. There were no life lessons being taught.

The season finally came to an end and that was good for everybody. Maybe all that was needed was for the team to take a break and for the coach to do a slow and thoughtful review of the season. It was a long year, starting early spring, going through the summer and a trip to Kentucky, and then running through October. Perhaps the winter break would cure some of these apparent problems. The kids could go play basketball or some other activity and get a well-deserved break from the baseball diamond. The coach could perhaps take some time off and assess the team and where the team was headed. It was obvious that this was a well talented team with kids that loved to play ball; but something was missing.

During the fall season, the coach had asked me to help out with the team the following spring. He said he needed a baseball guy. Perhaps that was true, but I think it was more his frustration in losing control of the team, and in a round about way, blaming the other coaches who were assisting him. I agreed to help him, but I also knew how difficult it is to work with a control freak. I knew I would be nothing more than a coach with a title. That was okay though. Perhaps I could help in some way and contribute something positive to the team.

Actually, I was really excited about getting involved in coaching again, even if it was nothing more than throwing batting practice or coaching first base. I would be back on the field where I wanted to be. The last year and half was difficult to watch at times. The coach knew baseball well. He just didn't know the other part of the game that deals with teamwork.

A few months passed without baseball and I must admit it was refreshing. Although Eric loved the game and I enjoyed watching him play, he needed a break and we needed a break. It was a good time to put things in perspective, get back to basics and re-affirm the value of teamwork.

In January of 2003, the head coach gave me a call one night and wanted to sit down the following Sunday morning and start strategizing for the upcoming season. He had some ideas on making the team stronger. He informed me on a "pick up" he had made of a player and he proceeded to give me the boy's name.

I immediately felt ill. The head coach's excitement over this boy coming to our team was exactly opposite of what I felt this team needed. He started to spew out these superlatives like this kid had just been inducted into the Hall of Fame. I knew the boy and I knew the parents, and I knew the history. I wasn't immediately happy with the news, but as a guy who likes to see that glass half full, I was anxious to hear the coach out and what his rationale was. This player had a reputation for pitching and throwing the ball hard. You just never knew where the ball would go. This was, in my mind, another example of what was wrong with this team, trying to bring in another superstar and not confront the real problem of teamwork.

"Okay Jeff, don't be negative. Hear the man out; I'm sure he has a plan."

We got together that Sunday morning. Present were the head coach, another coach, the new player's father, and me. I was getting ill again. The father is a great guy and had been nothing but nice to me as long as I knew him. I just wasn't sure why he was at this coaches meeting. I soon found out.

About five minutes into our get-together, the father looked at me and said, "You're okay with Eric not playing first base this year, aren't you?"

It took me awhile to let this one sink in. I am sitting at this coffee place on this nice Sunday morning, immensely enjoying their finest brew. We just started our first official discussion of this year's team and I'm very pumped up and excited about what plans, strategies, ideas that we can discuss to make this team solid and productive. I have ideas swirling in my mind that I would like to share with the group. I am the new assistant coach because the head coach wants to take advantage of my baseball knowledge. And five minutes into this meeting I have a father, not even a coach, inform me that his son is going to be playing first base this year. My son will not play first base.

It didn't take long to realize how this arrangement came to be. The head coach, in his infinite wisdom, basically made a "deal with the devil." This particular player had pitched for a few teams before, always throwing hard and always having all the potential in the world to be a star some day. He was not adequate, however, of playing any other position. A few coaches relayed this information to his father, that they wanted him as a pitcher, but pitcher only. He would be a liability at any other position. That was not what the father and son wanted. They wanted a team where the son could play first base also. They found that situation at Gambrills with this coach. If you bring your kid over here as a pitcher, I'll make sure that he plays first base when he doesn't pitch. For me, the meeting was over. The next two hours would have been better served doing anything else. I left that coffee shop thinking that we were in for another long season. Unfortunately, my instincts were right.

This is only one example of what helped bring this team down that particular spring. The team already had two first basemen. Now they had three, one more than necessary. The boy did pitch and did play first base, but did neither especially well. Actually, it was a disaster. It was only one of many things that alienated parents more, alienated players more, and created nothing short of turmoil. What needed to be done the most was done the least. That spring was a season that everyone would simply like to forget. Nearing the end of the season the coach announced that he wouldn't be back. It wouldn't have mattered; no player would have been there to coach. It was a sad ending to a great start for that coach. He had brought together a bunch of kids from a lot of different teams and gave them an opportunity to play some good baseball. He taught the game of baseball very well. He taught the game of life very poorly.

Once again, for the sixth consecutive year, Eric just chugged along with his average ability and average performance to earn adequate playing time. He played enough to continue improving his skills. That seemed to be the routine. Eric just kept moving along, while others got the spotlight. Eric was still small in stature and was never considered a star player. All he could do was just keep honing his skills the best that he could.

More than once, however, during that spring he wanted to quit pitching, primarily because of the head coach. More than once during that spring Jason not only wanted to stop pitching, but to give up playing. The coach's personal skills were not the best, nor did he seem to excel in motivation, discipline, team building, respect, or consistency. He could show a kid how to bunt, or be in cut-off position, or double steal. He couldn't, however, make a player feel good about himself. He couldn't quit making excuses for certain player's poor performances and bad attitudes. He couldn't communicate with the parents and he certainly couldn't get the most out of the players. Little did I realize at this time how much this paralleled what Eric would encounter for years to come; the high school years.

I gave Eric the best advice that I could at the time, "Hang in there...do your best...your time will come...when it does, be ready." I wanted him to remember the saying, "Luck is when opportunity meets preparation"

He didn't stop pitching. Maybe I talked him out of giving up pitching; maybe he talked himself out of it. Maybe he realized the coach was leaving so there were no reasons to quit. I'm glad he hung in there..........

Jason's situation was about the same as Eric, and in the conversations that I had with him, tried to convey the same message of hanging in there. For some reason, Jason got on the coaches "sh_ _ -list" and never got off of it. I think that Jason was close to quitting baseball, the constant verbal beatings that he was taking were influencing him, and his confidence was waning. It was totally unfair the way in which Jason was being treated.

As planned the coach did leave without one tear being shed. Along with him, four of the players left… perhaps because they made the plans before the coach announced his departure. Or perhaps, as one player did, they left because I was becoming the new coach. This one particular player absolutely did not want to play for me. The feeling was mutual. Although he had as much talent as anyone on the team, he had an attitude. I wouldn't have put up with it and he and his parents knew that. To this day, he has a tremendous amount of talent. To this day, he has that attitude. Like the coach who left, every coach, including his high school coach, since that time was willing to accept his attitude as long as he hit home runs.

Sound familiar?

Once again, a team breaks up, implodes, whatever you want to call it. The reasons are endless, but there are a few key elements that seem to be present. The most important one is teamwork. This team had no teamwork and had no one trying to create it.

Now the kids were 13 years old and officially teenagers. As we started practicing as a new team there did not appear to be any problems left from the old group of players or parents. The four players who left the team were the four players who should have left the team. I now wouldn't have to listen to those parents quoting the worst line that I have ever heard on a baseball field, "Come on, be a hero."

If their son was up to bat in a close game with runners on base, this is what they would do… yell for their son to be a hero. Be a hero? Is there anything that would build teamwork less than pushing a player to be a hero and emphasize you, rather than we? We don't need heroes on the field, we need good teammates. Of course we all know that baseball and all sports are moving away from the concept of being good teammates, but what we needed as a team was to build together and support each other. I felt that the best way to do this was to have a goal of ensuring the fact that all players received ample playing time. I decided very early on that all players would sit their share of the time and all players would play their share of the time. That's not how it was done the two previous years. Hopefully, everyone would get on board with the new program and understand the long term benefit.

Our first competition as a newly formed team was a local tournament. We played in the tournament and won all six games… and never looked back. In the next 18 months we won six tournaments. In most cases, the starting line up in the championship game was the nine kids that had played the least in the tournament up until then. That's the way it was. They all seemed to get better and really play some good ball. Eric, like all the years before, found himself right in the middle of the pack. He was probably the #3 pitcher on the team but found himself a distant third. Jason Patten and Tyler Hibbs were the top two hurlers by far. They both threw a lot harder than Eric, who had to rely on location and control to get by. He was still small in stature and in the shadows of better ball players.

Tyler Hibbs was one of them. He played for GORC (Gambrills-Odenton Recreation Council) his first couple of years of baseball. Although the organization did a fine job of giving all boys an equal opportunity to play ball, they did not provide an avenue for the kids who wanted a higher competitive standard. Tyler was a kid who wanted, and needed something much higher. Good competition became non-existent and therefore, once the 11-year-old spring season was completed, Tyler moved on to this newly organized team in Gambrills to become teammates with Jason and Eric.

Tyler is a tremendously talented ball player… always has been. He gets that from a combination of natural ability and a strong desire to win. Most people think there are two types of ball players when the pressure is on, one who hopes the coach *doesn't* give him the ball, and the other who hopes the coach *does* give him the ball. Tyler is the third type.….he doesn't hope for the ball, he goes and asks for it. Tyler is as competitive as you get. You don't take credit for coaching Tyler, because the quality of his play is not because of you. Just sit back and enjoy the ride. It's not that Tyler doesn't have his shortcomings, because he does. He has a temper and occasionally will let you know it. He also has the potential at times to let the boy in himself come out. No one, however, is more tenacious than Tyler Hibbs on a ball field.

When Tyler entered his freshman year of high school, he was going to play fall ball for the school, along with staying and playing some games with Gambrills. He wanted to play as much ball as he could. He went out to the first few practices at Arundel and his reputation preceded him. That was probably my fault. Every time someone asked me about Tyler and how good he was, I told them what I thought. Tyler was probably the best infielder Arundel High School would have that coming spring, even as a freshman. That didn't seem to go over well with everyone, especially the fall coach. A conversation very early, I believe the first practice, went something like this;

Coach: "Tyler, there's lot of infielders out here, you're going to have to learn to play the outfield."

Tyler: "I don't play the outfield."

Coach: "What, you think you're better than all these infielders!!!"

Tyler: "Yeah, I do."

The coach reacted to this response in a manner in which I guess he thought was the most productive. He tried to embarrass Tyler. While the entire team watched, he put Tyler at shortstop and hit him countless grounders; basically hoping that Tyler would screw up so he could put him in his place. That strategy didn't seem to work real well.

The more grounders that Tyler fielded cleanly, the harder he hit the balls. The more hard hit balls that Tyler fielded cleanly, the more balls were hit further away from him, until it was apparent to everyone there that the only goal of the coach was not being proven. More effective coaching!

I believe the coach didn't understand and comprehend the fine line between arrogance and confidence. If you don't know Tyler real well, you will misinterpret that his total belief that he is the best may come across as being way too cocky. Backing up what you say isn't being cocky, it's being confident. It didn't matter because Tyler decided not to play fall ball for Arundel. There was a conversation that took place between Tyler's dad and the head baseball coach. The coach to paraphrase basically told Tom that Tyler did not have to play at Arundel in the fall. As long as he was playing good ball somewhere, that's all that mattered. Tom as politely as he could told the fall coach that Tyler was not going to play anymore fall ball.

The rest is history. Tyler started on the varsity as a freshman and has gone on to become one of the best-known high school ball players in the state. After his junior year, after the Junior Olympics, the trips to Venezuela and Florida and Panama and Missouri, after all the accolades and after breaking just about every school record, Tyler signed a letter of intent to the Florida State to play baseball.

After all of this, Tyler is still confident and tenacious and he still has that boy in him. He's still Tyler.

Al Shandrowski started his baseball career in the Brooklyn Park area. He soon moved to GORC (Gambrills Odenton Recreation Council) where he played for a couple of years. He also moved to Gambrills with the others to start a new 11-year-old team. He stayed with the team for a year before the coach basically told him, "You need to move on, you're not good enough." This is one of the moves that the previous coach made, taking a little bit more talent over a lot more teamwork. It was a big mistake. Al went and played for the Metro Orioles in the Baltimore Metro League for a year before they too fell apart. He came back to Gambrills to play on our new team, the Gambrills 13-U team.

I remember Al showing up for the first workout. He looked a little nervous, perhaps not knowing his status on this newly formed team. I remembered Al playing with the team previously and I remembered him being the model teammate. He should have never been sent away. I was only a spectator at that time, now I was the coach.

Al and his dad walked up to me and we went through the formalities of re-establishing our acquaintances. I then said to Alan, in front of his dad, "Al, you're my left-fielder and my lead off hitter until you show me that you can't do it. And I don't think that will ever happen." He turned away and hustled on to the field. It's now five years later and he hasn't stopped hustling.

Al was one of the hardest workers I have ever seen on a ball field. He had no choice as his talent alone would not be enough. He had a below average arm, average swing, good speed, but a huge heart. He was extremely respectful and well liked by teammates. The former coach at Gambrills was attempting to put together one of those "super teams." He had a lot of good ball players and he thought that he found someone who was a little better than Alan so he had the boy come out for the team. He had Alan share time in left field with this player. Instead of making both kids, and sets of parents, happy he managed to upset everybody. I guess at the end of the season he thought the other kid would turn out to be a better player. He was bigger and stronger than Alan and could throw a ball really hard. He just wasn't a baseball player. Alan was a baseball player.

A few years ago we were playing the last tournament of the year in Clarksville, Md. It was the first weekend in November and it was extremely cold. We were playing in the championship game and everything was going our way. We were ready to "mercy rule" the other team. In the last inning they had a man on second base with no outs and we were ahead by 12 runs. Alan was playing left field. The pitch was thrown and once the ball got past the batter, Alan took three quick steps toward the left field line. Another pitch thrown, and again, once the ball got past the batter, Alan took three quick steps toward the left field line. Two batters later, the man is still on second base, and now there are two outs. Nine times in a row, Alan took three quick steps toward the left field line once the ball got past the batter. Nine times in a row, just in case that in the possibility that catcher for whatever reason throws the ball to third base, he would be in position.

Alan, and all outfielders, was taught that if there is a man on second base your job is to back up the play when the ball gets past the batter. That way, if the runner for any reason breaks toward third base, you are in position. If you wait for the catcher to throw it or wait for an over throw, it's too late. Be ready and in position before something happens. Here is Alan, with the score 12-0, backing up every single play like it's a tie game in the last inning.

It's called work ethic. He did it enough times that it was second nature. I have never seen another outfielder on any other team do that. They're not taught that. I guess it's too much work.

I've known Alan since he was 11 years old. You can't watch him hit two or three times and then make an assessment. It could be painful. He doesn't have what you would consider the proper stance, he doesn't run the proper way, and he doesn't have a text-book swing. You could easily dismiss him, like that former Gam-brills coach did. You need to put Alan in the top of the line up the first of June and put him there just about every game. Then you need to look at the averages when the summer is over and Alan will be near the top. Most coaches don't like hitters like Alan. He doesn't swing correctly and he doesn't hit for power. He just produces, if he's given a chance. He led our team in hitting one summer.

Conrad Weibler is the main reason that this Gambrills team was put together with so many good ball players and so many good baseball families. He was the general manager of the team. He scheduled games, attended meetings, ordered uniforms and equipment, handled the umpires, reserved hotel rooms for tour-naments, and everything else in between. My job was to show up at games and coach the kids. His son was Derek Buehler. Some people may think that his son had the inside track for playing time because Conrad did so much for the team with his contribution of time, money, and effort.

Think again.

Because Conrad was so much in to work ethic and discipline, it was easy for me to be tough on Derek. Conrad's demeanor re-minds me of the good old days, of Joe Sheeler and Coach Spellman and most of my other coaches. Back then, when the coach yelled at the kids, the dad yelled at his son again. When I gave Derek grief about something within earshot of his dad, I would immediately get a visit from him.

"What did Derek do?"

"Was he talking back?"

"Was he not hustling?"

As bad as I gave it to Derek, he heard it twice as much from his dad. There was no favoritism there. Derek played second base and he pitched when he came to our team. He did both well. He was the glue that kept the infield together. With him at second base and

Tyler at shortstop, there was no better double play combination around.

As with a lot of the players, high school baseball in the summer was an obligation and Derek went off to fulfill that commitment. The last few summers he has played for the St. Joes team in the Baltimore Metro League. That, however, has not stopped me from sneaking him over to play six or eight games with us each summer. Anytime he had a hole in his schedule, he would be playing again with Gambrills.

Nick Gioioso came out for our team a week or so later than the other kids. He showed up at the first practice with his dad and appeared to be extremely shy. He was quiet and because of just missing the cut off date of age eligibility, he was almost a year younger than some of the other kids on the team.

Because we had many kids come out for the team, we needed to make some cuts. Nick was on the bubble. Matter of fact, it didn't look real good for him. It appeared that a few other guys might be more talented and would keep him off the team. I really liked him though. I finally made a decision in my mind to cut him and I would need to take action on it the following night. From a skill level standpoint I knew that I was making the right decision. Nick just needed a little more maturity to play at this level.

I went to practice the following night and I knew what I had to do – cut Nick. It would be extremely hard to do; I really liked him and his parents a lot. As practice started that night I watched Nick for what I thought was the last time. I watched him hit, I watched him field, I watched him give all that he could give on every play. I watched his effort that was superior to almost everyone else. I watched myself change my mind about Nick. Actually, I didn't change my mind, he changed it for me.

I didn't cut him. I called his dad (Don) over and told him that Nick was on the team. I told him that I liked his work ethic and enthusiasm and potential and I was glad to have him on the team. I think his dad appreciated that. I think his dad knew that part of Nick making the team was his great attitude.

Nick played for us for two years before his high school (Loyola) summer obligations collided with Gambrills. Like the other players, his departure was amicable. Nick played some great ball for us during that time. He pitched, played some third base, and played the outfield. He did anything you asked him to do. He was the most respectful player that I have ever coached.

As time went on, I had the pleasure of meeting his mother, Joann. She ended up taking over the responsibility of the snack bar and was magnificent in that department. Don and Joann were the perfect baseball parents; supportive, encouraging, funny, and understanding of what we as coaches were trying to accomplish. Don not only supported Nick, he yelled out and encouraged all the players, all the time.

Nick decided this past year not to play baseball anymore. He was the first candle to burn out. It was actually very sad to hear that he had given up the game, but I knew that his experiences were good and he could use some of those lessons learned on the field in his future endeavors.

Kieran Flannery played baseball from the time he was eight years old, making his way through the Columbia Reds, the Metro Orioles and a few other teams before landing with us in Gambrills. At 13 years old, Kieran was a good hitter. Since then, he has developed into one of the purest hitters that I've ever seen. For a while he batted second, then maybe fifth or sixth, then back to second. Finally, it was obviously that he should be hitting third. Once he was put in that spot, he's never moved.

Kieran left the Gambrills team rather abruptly in May of 2006. His father, Mike, said an opportunity had opened for Kieran that they couldn't pass up. They were going to pursue it.

I said good luck.

It appeared to be something that had possible potential, but like a lot of things, it turned out that the grass wasn't quite as green as they had imagined. That sometimes happens when you're chasing something with your heart instead of your head. Kieran is now back where he should be, in Gambrills. Kieran attends Palotti High School in Laurel, Md. His resume as a high school ball player couldn't be more complete. He will enroll in Indian River Junior College in Florida this September.

Chris Ball came to the Gambrills team the same time that Kieran arrived. Two good ball players, two good catchers. Unfortunately, there is only one ball and one plate and one catcher in a game at one time. Something had to give, and it was Chris. They both did their share of catching for a few months, but at a certain point in time I told Chris that Kieran would probably get a little more catching than him. I told him if he wanted more playing time, he would need to learn how to play the outfield. Christopher was very proud and I believe in his heart he felt that he was just as good of a catcher. Instead of pouting or complaining, Chris did just what was suggested – he learned to play the outfield. He did it well and he gave a great effort in learning this new position. To this day he is still a good catcher, but he also became a very good outfielder.

Chris was a player who always loved baseball and played a lot of it, but the competitive level that he was accustomed to was a bit less than most of the kids on our new team. When he first arrived on the team Chris struggled with the bat. He worked hard, very hard, at his game and learned to be a good hitter. He probably improved more as a player than anyone on the team. Over the years he became one of my favorite players.

Chris has spent the last year not only honing his own skills, but spending countless hours working with younger kids and their baseball skills. He has helped me immeasurably with young ball players, teaching them the fundamental skills of hitting, fielding, and throwing. Although not catching regularly on his high school or summer team, he continues to give one on one instruction to younger catchers. Chris will be playing his college baseball at Shenandoah University in Winchester, Va.

Kylin Sims was the one player that almost didn't make it on our team. That would have been a tremendous loss for everyone. It wasn't that he didn't have the talent or the attitude or the drive. It was all an assumption that he and his mother made, perhaps based on their past experiences with coaches in other organizations. He and his mother just assumed that I may not give him a fair chance. I didn't know that they felt that way at the time. It only came out a couple years later in a conversation with his mother, Monica. The perceived problem that they saw was that Kylin played the same position as Eric Potter, my son, and more importantly to them, the coach's son. What chance would he have to make this team and start at first base?

That question was answered, at least in my mind, the first time I saw him swing a bat. It was a thing of beauty. I knew he was on the team right then, but mom needed convincing. She took him to another tryout with another team, only to be told exactly what she feared from me. The coach happened to have a son on his team who happened to play first base. The coach told Kylin that he would need to learn to play the outfield. He turned down that team's offer and came back hoping that he would be treated fairly with this team.

Kylin was in the line up from day one, and he hasn't left yet. Three years ago, in one of the best games that Gambrills ever played, we beat the team who told Kylin he wasn't good enough to play first base for them. The score was 2-0 and both of our runs were scored on home runs. Both home runs were hit by Kylin Sims. Poetic justice is what they call that. Kylin Sims is currently playing baseball at Dundalk High School in Baltimore when he's not playing for Gambrills in the summer.

Matt Pace began his baseball career at the age of six, playing T-ball in the Brooklyn Park Youth Athletics Association. He played for the Reds and his coach was Chuck Potts. Matt stayed with this program for the next five years, moving up through the system from one coach to another coach. In 1998, at the age of nine, Matt broke his arm about three games in to the season. He was being a typical kid running through some water sprinklers. He fell, and to protect his head, he threw his right arm down and broke it. Once he realized he could not play ball for a while, he cried. That didn't stop him, though, from putting on his uniform and sitting on the bench for every game that his team was scheduled to play.

Matt's mother usually took him to the games. About five weeks into the injury, his mom could not take him to a game because she was sick. So dad had to take off work and go to the game. When they got to the game that day, it seemed like they would have to forfeit the contest. They only had eight players. The team had not lost a game all season but they were looking straight down the barrel of their first setback. One player short, and of course Matt sitting there with a cast on his arm.

It didn't take dad long at all to weigh all the information and determine that the best course of action would be to volunteer Matt's services as a one handed right fielder. The deal was Matt could stand out in right field with his broken arm so they wouldn't have to forfeit. In return Matt promised his dad that mom would never find out. Out goes Matt in right field, cast and all. Some where in the middle innings a line drive was hit to Matt and despite wearing the cast, he managed to not only come up with the ball, but also throw a runner out at home.

The promise to not tell mom was superseded by Matt's enthusiasm for his accomplishment. Despite the coaching from dad, as soon as Matt walked in the front door it was, "Hey mom, guess what I did at the game today."

In 2001, Matt followed his good friend Al Shandrowski to Gambrills to play on a new competitive team and the two of them are still there. Matt considers Al his best teammate ever. Matt's position at Gambrills has always been third base and he never left the "hot corner." Matt was the starting third baseman for three years at North County High School and now attends McDaniel College, where his baseball career continues.

A year or so ago, Matt made a decision to leave the Gambrills baseball team. For some reason, I felt myself a little more worked up about this than any other player who decided to try a new team. At first, I didn't know why. It just seemed to bother me a lot. I have seen countless kids come and go, but what was the deal with Matt?

Then it hit me.

Matt was the one player on the team that was me... that took me back in the day to when I played.

The following e-mail sent to many of my baseball parents says it best about me and Matt.

When I took over as coach of a bunch of 13-year-old kids at Gambrills a few years back, I was blessed with a bunch of kids that had a lot of talent. Talent goes a long way, but as we all know, you need more than just talent.

One of the kids on the team was Alan Shandrowski. I've told you his story, how he was asked to leave the 12-U team because he wasn't good enough, how he came back when I took over the team, how he became my lead off hitter, how he was one of the hardest workers who I have ever seen on a ball field. He is now a senior at North County High School and as of last week was hitting .322 and having a very solid final year of high school baseball. He's still at Gambrills. I am so proud of him.

Alan lives in Brooklyn Park, and from the time he could throw a baseball, has been a teammate of Matt Pace. Matt played in Brooklyn Park and came to the Gambrills organization, like Alan, as an 11-year-old ball player. When Alan left as a 12 year old for a year, Matt stayed. When Alan came back, Matt was still there.

They both started with me on the team that I took over as 13 year olds. Their personalities are as different as two could be. Alan is quiet and tends to hold things in. He would think before he reacted, especially in an angry fashion. Matt is fiery, reactive, and has a temper that perhaps equaled mine as a kid. Perhaps that's why I like him so much. Talent wise, Alan always had to out work every one. Matt had the natural ability and was always big and strong.

When we were a 14-u team, we were playing a tournament one weekend in Allentown, Pa. We had won the first two games and were now in the single elimination part of the tournament. Matt came up in the first inning, and his "at bat" did not meet his expectations. His helmet paid the price as it was slammed in to the bench. I believe a few expletives followed from his mouth.

Matt spent the remainder of that very important game, the next seven innings, sitting beside me on the bench. I put in our back up third baseman that, let's just say, everyone took a deep breath when any ball was hit to him. We ended up winning that game 1-0. That experience was an example of the contentious relationship that I have had with Matt over the years. It has never changed.

I have been harder and tougher on Matt than any ball player who I have ever had (I will keep my son out of this discussion). I have yelled at him more, challenged him more, and probably confronted him more than anyone else. I have seen anger from him that has taken me back to my youth.

At the end of last year's season, Matt made it pretty well known that he was leaving the team. I think he felt that he needed a change, perhaps the ride at Gambrills should come to an end. All I could do was wish him the best and move on. I told him to do what made him happy. It would definitely be hard to replace Matt: his bat, his glove, his base running, and the "fire in his eyes." I think he was just tired of me.

Somehow, somewhere, sometime, from the time Matt decided to leave the team, he had second thoughts. He decided to stay. Perhaps he assessed the situation, looked at all the scenarios, and decided that the grass wasn't greener on the other side. It could have been a lot of things. I think it was his teammates.

Our team had some really good athletes and that's why we won games. It wasn't superb coaching with great strategy and perfect managerial moves. We just had better athletes than most teams. As a coach, when you are in this position, the best thing to do is probably stay out of their way and let them play ball. They don't need the athletic help; they need the coach for all the other things with building good teamwork right on the top of the list.

How do you build good teamwork? I am sure there are thousands of books out there that could help all of us in this area. The problem with books is that too many people read them, and then try to teach right out of the book. It sounds "canned" to the recipient of this lesson and therefore the message doesn't seem to get through. Kids are a lot smarter than we think they are. I think sometimes the best way to be effective is not act like you're trying to teach something. Let them learn it without it seeming like a lesson. Be natural, have fun, be creative. Sometimes I tried this. I'm not sure how effective I was, but I had a lot of fun with the attempts and I didn't read any book.

I really enjoyed the day I remember only as the "line up day."

When you're out on a baseball field, any day is beautiful, but this particular Saturday, the weather was also accommodating – a mid 70's springtime morning. It was May 22, 2004, to be exact and it was picture perfect for a day at the park. I had my bat in one hand and my coffee in the other hand, just chilling out watching the guys warm up. The field had just been dragged, the snack bar was being opened, and the warm breeze was pretty much perfect. Life as I knew it was on hold and would be for the next six hours. We were at the ball field and there wasn't room for anything else. Like magic, all life's problems and worries disappeared, at least temporarily.

We were playing a team in the Baltimore Metro League on this day. The Forest Hill Storm was the opponent and they had made the trip down to the Gambrills Athletic Club, our home base. What a beautiful place to play ball. Not many fields nowadays have the old time grandstand where you can sit behind home plate and take in a game like they did 30 or 40 years earlier. That made our field special; and the fact that directly behind the property was a farm with acres and acres of cornfields. That bit of information by itself means nothing unless you know the history of the club and the memories of the cornfields. You would need to know that 60 years ago there were games being played at Gambrills. Old timers will tell you that as kids one of their biggest thrills was to be at the club on a Saturday afternoon and be the lucky little kid who was designated to be the ball boy. Your job was to get every foul ball was hit, including those that went in to the corn field. At the end of the game you were rewarding for all of your hard work. You were handed 25 cents. As one of the old timers told me, "That was enough to get two hot dogs." He then added with a smile, "Doubleheaders were even better."

Most people don't know that The Gambrills Athletic Club once hosted a semi-pro baseball team, once had the likes of Al Kaline and Reggie Jackson playing there. Who knew that Tommy Lasorda played ball there when he was stationed close by at Fort Meade. The history is there.

Just like all scheduled Saturday games in this particular league, this was a doubleheader. Starting time for the first game was 11:00 a.m. It was now about 10:30 a.m. We had gone through our hitting and most of the players were now in the dugout taking a break before we took infield-outfield. I waited for the few stragglers to get their drinks and join the team. The next few minutes were usually set aside for me to make up the line up. As the coach, this is one of the many parts of your responsibility. I take this part of my job very seriously. I usually did the line up myself; but not today.

Today will be different. It's time for one of those experiments in human nature. It's time to have some fun.

Fun is something lacking on the ball fields across this country anymore, especially as the boys get older and especially when the kids are playing highly competitive baseball. Coaches have a hard enough time catering to the whims of 12 or 13 sets of parents while making sure their own kid is being showcased. Then on top of that, the winning at any cost adds additional pressure. Add a mix of parents not paying their fees, whose turn it was running the snack bar that day, why wasn't the grass cut, who set up the umpires, and you may argue that there just wasn't room for fun.

Luckily, we always found time for fun at Gambrills. There was always time for fun. As the stragglers made their way into the dugout, I got their attention and asked them a question that had no correct answer. Who's the fairest guy here?

A few hands went up. I guess these players were voting for themselves. Then a few names were tossed out there, which was followed by some laughing and light bantering back and forth. Finally, one name started coming up more and more and before long, we had a consensus. I walked over to this player, handed him the scorebook and told him that I needed a line up. The only information he was given was the starting pitcher. I did this in front of all the players so that it would get the full impact. Twelve very inquisitive looks appeared on twelve faces. "What was going on?" were the words that equated to their expressions.

I then turned around and left. As I walked around the back of the dugout toward the concession stand, the stone silence of a few seconds ago turned to quiet discussion. Before I walked another 20 steps, the dugout had turned into laughter. It was loud laughter. I smiled. As I approached the concession stand, a father asked, "What's going on in there?" "They have an assignment" I said. He gave me an inquisitive look, so I explained."They need to come up with a lineup."

"That should be interesting" was his response. It was very interesting.

Within five minutes, the player assigned to the task walked toward me at the concession stand and handed me the scorebook. I made sure that I was around several parents when it was given to me, again for full impact.

"All done?" I asked as he approached.

"Yeah,"

"Any problems?"

He answered no with a slight chuckle.

"Were there any problem players?" I asked kidding.

"Just a few" he said.

Now he's in a full robust laugh.

"Do you think that I could guess who?" I asked.

"Definitely" he said, still laughing.

Nick was the guy with the scorebook. Along with my assessment of him being the most respectful player who I had ever known, he probably was the fairest. He most assuredly was the one who I just knew would end up with the book, who would be the player's choice. He was the kid who didn't have quite the talent level, the one who I almost cut. That would have been a huge mistake. He was a part of the puzzle that fit so well.

I looked down at the lineup for a second and nodded slightly as though I was given my approval. It didn't really matter what names were where, that wasn't the point of the exercise. I just needed to see the right amount of names. The lineup was a little different than I would have done, but it was *their* lineup. It ended up being very effective and we won easily; I believe the score was 10-0. We won because we just were a better ball team with a lot more talent. The order of the line –up and who played where were totally insignificant. The players who didn't start got in the game and everyone contributed to the victory. It was fun and it was teamwork.

Once the first game was completed, the scorekeeper immediately gave me back the book, as she (yes, a mother!) always does between games of doubleheaders. She knew that I would need it to put together a lineup for the second game. I was walking with the players toward the concession stand at the time. Our players, along with the visitor team, spent the next ten minutes ordering and gulping down hot dogs, hamburgers, and sodas. More business is done at the snack bar in that time span between games than the other five hours the stand is open. That's always the hang out after game one of a doubleheader.

Once most parents were standing at close proximity of the concession stand, I knew it was the right time once again. I walked up and handed the book back to our scorekeeper and told her I needed a lineup for the second game and I wanted her to figure it out. I communicated to her who the starting pitcher would be and like the first game, that's all the information she was given. Again, it would have been a lot easier to just give the book to her when no one was around.

It just wouldn't have been as much fun.

The best way to describe the scene that followed is, have you ever been at a lake stocked with fish, and watch what happens when you throw some food in the water? Or perhaps you've seen a bunch of ducks on a pond when you throw some bread between all of them. Well, she was the bait, and here come the animals.

About fifteen minutes later, she brought the book back to me and said "Never do that again."

I laughed.

The memory is still etched in my head. The parents hovered over her like a bunch of vultures, communicating to her why their child should be "hitting third" or catching and "You know my boy had two hits the first game." Those 15 minutes really needed to be caught on video. It was like one of those master card commercials ... priceless. Some parents tried to be really cool about it by kind of meandering over to her, while others had no couth at all, explaining their kid should obviously be not only starting, but moved up in the line-up. One of the more subdued parents stood near by quietly, just shaking his head and laughing. My scorekeeper is good-natured and she knew exactly why I was doing it.

The kids and parents took completely different paths to the same destination. What the players did was lobby for a position and tried to influence the other kid making the lineup in a good-natured way. They wanted to start and they wanted to bat high in the lineup. In general they accepted the outcome with very little complaining. They razzed each other in a positive way, lots of chuckling, and lots of kidding. They filled the dugout with laughter.

The parents had a much harder time with the lineup. Poor Sue! There's no way she deserved what I gave her. I watched for a few minutes, but I couldn't any longer. I had to look away. It was painful.

It shouldn't have been difficult to carry out this small request. It shouldn't have mattered who started and who didn't in a game like this. The parents knew everyone would play a lot, especially against a weaker opponent. They should have understood that it's about teamwork. Every player is as important as the next one. There was not a lot of laughing with the parents, or kidding. It looked pretty serious.

Why did the parents have so much more of a problem than the kids, especially after they saw the kids do the first game lineup with so much ease and fun?

First, let me say that I was blessed with a great group of parents. They were beyond acceptable or okay; they were great; extremely supportive of the coaches and their kids and very passionate about the game of baseball. Never was there a problem having the grass cut, the field lined, or hamburgers being flipped on the grill. In general, fees were paid in full and on time and umpires, scheduling, tournaments, equipment were things a coach didn't have to worry about.

Most of us, however, have this particular issue that seems to be a combination of ego, insecurity, living through our kids, and a parent's protection of his young, much like an animal in the wild. For some inexplicable reason, competition brings out a slew of emotions that can sometimes overshadow just doing the right thing.

We all possess it.

When I took the lineup back toward the dugout that the parents had created, I was met by two players.

The one said with a smile, "Let me see it, let me see it," like a little boy opening a Christmas present. I handed them the scorebook and you could see their eyes quickly glance over the names.

One of the players who didn't start the first game was also out of the starting lineup the second game. Both players made that fact clear to me.

I noticed that myself, but didn't say anything. I said to the two players, "I didn't make the lineup, the parents did."

Both players volunteered to sit at the start of the second game so that the player could start. I have a pretty set rule that everyone on the team starts one of two games when we play a double header. It's really not that hard with 12 players. The players knew that. So did the parents, but I guess the parents thought they had a better idea. The two players settled it between them, who would sit to start the second game. I made the change on the scorebook and then made up another lineup card.

This fact was never brought up again. Those two players were never given their proper credit for being selfless. I never made a big deal to the parents of how some 14-year-old kids had more maturity and teamwork than them. The parents, or should I say dads, were too caught up in putting together the strongest lineup, which of course, included their son. The goal should have been putting together the strongest team, building teamwork, and being fair. As my friend Tom, a motivational speaker, made clear to me as I once spoke to him about teamwork, "Jeff, sometimes instead of a player wanting to be the best player *ON* a team, he should try to be the best player *FOR* the team." Wow…that hit home, and as he said it to me, I instantly thought back to these two players. I think both of them at that moment wanted to be the best player *FOR* the team. That's real teamwork.

When I went back over to the scorekeeper I told her that one of the kids "turned his ankle" and couldn't start. The one player who didn't start the first game and wasn't in the lineup the second game was now starting. The player never found out what happened. If he wouldn't have started the second game, I believe no parent other than his own parents would have noticed that he was sitting on the bench at the start of both games.

We played that second game and won. Again, it had nothing to do with the proper lineup or coaching. We just had better players with more talent. Those two victories weren't what we should have left the field with that day, though. Two kids, probably without realizing it, made a very mature and responsible decision. They showed that they were really good teammates. The parents didn't have a clue.

That second game lineup is an example of how we all are. We get so wrapped up in how our son is not getting the proper playing time or pitching enough innings or getting mistreated in some way, that we don't see other injustices that happen to other players.

But the players saw it.

It was just another life lesson that was learned on a ball field. That's the biggest memory I was left with that day, two kids trying to convince each other why he wanted to sit out.

I was really proud of these two guys. One was Kylin Sims. The other was Eric Potter. It was ironic that these two young men would be the two that together were most concerned about playing time for some other player.

Here's why:

When the 13-U team was organizing, we had a lot of players who wanted to play ball on the team. There was way over 20 at the very beginning and we almost made two teams, but egos and pride squashed that idea. So we settled for one team. Up until this time in Eric's baseball background, he had played on teams and as related earlier, received adequate playing time. Probably not as much as he deserved, but as was the pattern, enough that he was not mistreated. The one area, however, that he did not get a fair shake was at first base. For some reason, there were always extenuating circumstances in regards to Eric playing first base, a position he actually played very well.

But this year, this new team, would be his turn to be the starting first baseman. He clearly was the best guy for the job and it would make him happy. More importantly, it would make his mother happy. Mothers are sometimes the forgotten parent out there on the baseball fields. The dads are coaching and the perception sometimes is that this is a men's game, but trust me, moms play an integral part in the development of these players. My wife is no different. She had keenly noticed the last couple of years that Eric's playing time at first base was sacrificed in order to placate a few disgruntled players and parents. She had been fairly level headed about it at the ballpark… she saved her wrath until she got home. Sheryl was not a happy team mom about this. Her displeasure, although controlled, was always right at the boiling point. The end of the season did not come soon enough!

Okay, now it is a new season, Eric is entrenched as the starting first baseman, and I am the coach. Everything looks great! About a week after our team first assembled, we were having practice one night and a new player came to try out. I had heard from a couple of his former teammates that he was big and strong and could hit the ball a long way. He also was a great kid and a very good teammate. He also was a first baseman. His name was Kylin.

As I said before, it took me about five seconds, or one swing, to fall in love with him. His swing was a thing of beauty. His attitude was great. He did everything he needed to do that first practice to obviously be good enough to play on our team.

Did I say he was a first baseman?

How would I explain this to Eric?

How would I explain this to Eric's mom?

This was one of those days you remember like it just happened, and how it happened. I learned a lot about my son that day, things that had no relevance to baseball in particular. It has become one of the three or four moments on a baseball field that I have been most proud of Eric.

Practice was over and we were ready to leave. I got in the car and Eric got in the other side. He looked at me and immediately said, "He's good!"

Eric ready to deliver to the plate as Kylin prepared to defend the first base area. Kylin has the "softest" hands that I have ever seen.

We both knew who Eric referring to as "He". It wasn't what Eric said, it was how he said it. He was truly excited about Kylin being part of the team. It wasn't about him and his position. Eric's mother had more trouble accepting this new member of the team. She was not happy. I told her that Kylin was a really good player and that he was an excellent first baseman. I told her that Eric would still play some first base, but now we had two really good first basemen. She told me, "We really didn't need two good first baseman, we had Eric. Eric deserved the position, he had waited patiently two years and now it's taken away again." Her frustration with me was building.

She finally said, "Eric can play first base as good as him."

I replied, "I know that, but that's really not the point."

It is now four years later. Kylin is still playing first base on my team. Eric still wants him there. Eric has probably played with over

100 teammates on different teams throughout the years. I asked him recently to name his top three teammates of all time. Kylin was one of them.

Eric ended up playing some first base over the years, not as much as if Kylin would have never shown up on the team. He has played enough, though. He has learned so much from Kylin, and Kylin has likewise learned a tremendous amount from Eric. They became good teammates, and then good friends. They pushed each other to be better ball players. Based on their actions on that Saturday morning, and fighting over who would sit out that game, they learned plenty more than baseball. They learned things that they will treasure forever. How to be passionate and a good teammate were only a few.

When I was young, I would <u>not</u> have considered myself a good teammate. That's one of the things I didn't pick up real well. I was an above average ball player growing up and that seems to make it harder in some respects to be a good teammate: at least in the mind of a kid. You feel that your talent alone makes you a good teammate and you should always be in the line up. You contribute more than the others. You're the star pitcher or star hitter while the other players give less. It's hard to comprehend at that age the difference between your God given talent and the ability to see others as valuable as you. It's all about you. As a child my two worlds, "all about me," and being a good teammate hadn't collided yet.

They did on May 6, 1970.

I was a sophomore in high school and I was the #2 pitcher on our varsity baseball team. I was only 15. I was a star and I was on top of the world in regards to baseball. I had just pitched a no-hitter my last start and was written up in the Pittsburgh Post Gazette. That was a big deal.

It was a Saturday morning and we were playing a game against Hopewell, one of our archrivals. They were 5-1 in the league and we were 4-2. This game was for first place. Back then, first place was a big deal. If you wanted to get into the state play-offs, you had to win your conference. Not like today where just about everybody is eligible. I was lucky enough to come from a school, Ellwood

City, that was known back then as an excellent high school baseball program. Western Pennsylvania was big time baseball... Beaver Falls, Ambridge, Aliquippa, and New Castle. On this day, I was the starting pitcher.

I was pretty full of myself.

The game started and it was going fairly well. I pretty much shut down Hopewell for the first six innings and took a 3-2 lead into their last at bat. Both their runs were unearned and I seemed to be pitching better as the game went on.

I took the mound in the last inning and quickly got behind the first batter 3-0. The opposing hitter then took the next two pitches which were both strikes. With a full count on the batter, I threw the next pitch, which was a soft fly ball to the center fielder Chuckie Nardone. He squeezed it in his glove.

One out.

The second batter up in the inning proceeded to strike out.

Now we have two outs and one batter away from victory.

With two outs and nobody on base, I walked the next batter. I then proceeded to walk the following hitter on a full count.

"Okay, get your act together, just one more out."

Two outs, two on, and out of the corner of my eye, I saw Coach Spellman walking out of the dugout toward the mound. Our ace pitcher, Rich Lawson, was closely following him. I couldn't believe my eyes ...he couldn't be taking me out of the game! What was he thinking? This was incredible! How could he possibly take ME out of the game when I was pitching a three-hitter, 11 strike outs, and it was MY game to win? Yeah, I knew I had 11 strikeouts and I knew they only had three hits. Remember, it was all about me.

As he got closer to the mound, my ability to control my temper was failing. I had quite a temper when I was young, but I thought that I had it under control.

I was wrong.

I can't really remember what I did or said exactly, but I believe there was dirt kicked around the mound, a few comments made, and a not so friendly transfer of the baseball from me to Coach Spellman. On top of this, I'm sure that I had no kind words of encouragement for Lawson. I'm sure that I made a rapid exit from the mound and left no doubt with my teammates, my coach, the visiting team, and all spectators that I was not happy.

It wasn't that I didn't know we were still going to win the game, I mean Lawson was an awesome pitcher, one of the best in the state. I knew he would get the last out, but *I* could have gotten the last out. *I* could have finished the game. *I* could have received all the credit and attention. And it was all taken away from *me*.

I do remember sitting in the dugout very upset as I watched the end of the game. Rich Lawson threw the first pitch to the new batter.

Ball one. On the next pitch, which was a strike taken by the batter, Hopewell sent the runners and the double steal was successfully completed.

Now they have runners on second and third with a 1-1 count and two outs.

It's getting a little interesting.

The next pitch was a grounder to Brian Conti at shortstop, probably the best fielding infielder I have ever seen. That would be the last out of the game.

But a funny thing happened.

Brian Conti, who had made a total of one error all year up to this point, bobbled the ball, allowing the runner at third to score. When the runner from second went to third on the play he made a wide turn around third base. Brian, seeing this, quickly picked up the bobbled ball and tried to pick him off.

He threw the ball into the stands. The runner trotted home from third base with what turned out to be the winning run. Brian made three errors that year ...two were on that play. Now insult is added to injury. Not only did Coach screw up by taking me out of the game, now the game got screwed up and we lost. It serves him right.

Coach Spellman wasn't happy after the game. Hopewell had also beaten us in the league opener, 2-1 on two throwing errors late in the game. Now they beat us on this day with four unearned runs. This wasn't the type of baseball we were accustomed to playing. I believe Coach ranted for a while ...I wasn't really focused on what he was saying. He's the one who screwed the game up because he took ME out. He never said anything to me after the game, good or bad.

This was on Saturday.

When I went to school on the following Monday morning, I had an "issue" left unresolved from the week before that needed the attention of the assistant principal, Mr. Magnifico. When I went to see him about my little "run-in" with a teacher, he told me that I needed to go to detention that afternoon. I occasionally had some issues that needed the attention of the assistant principal. He knew me by first name. I accepted my punishment and started out the door.

"Jeff, wait a minute," he said as he picked up the phone.

I didn't have a good feeling. He never had me wait a minute in all of our other dealings. A few seconds later, I heard Mr. Magnifico say the words that I dreaded, "Mr. Spellman, could you come to my office?"

Coach was also a guidance counselor at the school and his office was no more than 30 feet away. A few minutes later, Mr. Spellman came into the office. The assistant principal communicated to Mr. Spellman that I would miss practice that afternoon and the reason why. Coach Spellman, looking directly at me with those awful piercing eyes said, "That's fine, I believe Jeff showed his real character out on the mound Saturday." And he walked out of the office.

In your whole life, there are probably a handful of times that you just want to shrivel up and die that something so embarrassing or humiliating happens to you that it's beyond words. That moment, after all these years, is still real high on my list.

The baseball team, despite that heartbreaking loss two days earlier, went on to win the conference that year. We came back and won our last five games to tie Ambridge for the conference lead, then won a play-off game with them to get into the state play-offs. We won our first two play-off games and lost the next one to be eliminated.

It would be nice if this story had a good ending; something like I went out and pitched some great games in the playoffs and all was forgotten. There was no nice ending.

This was not a made for TV movie; rather it was real life with real consequences. Matter of fact, after that Monday morning discussion with the assistant principal, Coach Spellman went 19 days without speaking to me. I counted all 19 of them ...... not a word.

I never saw the field again that year.

He benched me for the rest of the year because I put me first and I put the team second. I showed him up. He did this because of one little outburst. He never approached me and told me why I wasn't pitching anymore. I guess he knew that I would figure it out for myself. Unless you have played the game of baseball with some real passion and intensity, you would not know what that felt like, basically being ostracized by your coach, sitting and watching players with less talent doing what you should be doing. I wasn't used to this. That was never done to me before. Perhaps I didn't deserve that type of treatment before this day.

One of two things could have happened at the end of that baseball season. I could have given up baseball because the coach didn't like me or didn't give me a chance....or I could have just gone the other route....given an extra effort and hoped that he would give me another chance the following year. I picked the latter and it worked out for me. I guess I realized that he was right and I was wrong. I realized that he didn't need me as much as I needed him.

When I came back as a junior, I was the #1 pitcher on the team and scouted by many professional baseball teams. I had a great year and was voted the MVP in the conference. I won a lot of games and got a lot of accolades. The biggest thing I did my junior year, however, was become a better teammate. I would like to think that I did it all on my own, but the truth was that I had no choice. I found out the hard way that it wasn't all about me. Coach Spellman didn't allow the kids with the most talent to become bigger than the team. He didn't rave about you and go to the local newspaper and tell them how great you were and how you someday would be a star. That wasn't part of being a good teammate. He forced me to make a tough decision. He knew I had a temper and he knew I could have just as easily blown up and quit playing ball, and he would have lost his best player for the next year. That didn't matter to him. It really didn't matter. His attitude was "If you're not a good teammate, there's no way you're my best player." He made me grow up.

Not only did he not put stars on pedestals, he actually tried to downplay their accomplishments. Instead, he emphasized teamwork and hard play above all.

I became a better teammate, and then eventually became a really good teammate. When someone made an error behind me, I would be the first one to say, "No big deal." I started giving other players credit. I quit thinking it was all about me.

Looking back, I may have cost my team a championship my sophomore year. When we got eliminated from the playoffs that year, Coach Spellman had to pitch another kid that wasn't as good as me. Coach showed me how to be a good teammate the best way he could. He may have given up a better shot at a championship just to prove a point. It wasn't all about winning to him. Although he won his share, the titles weren't as important as a player having a good attitude. He would always say, "You become a better teammate, you will become a better person."

Today, you go to a game and watch players swear, throw bats, don't run out balls ... and nothing happens. When they get to first base on a ball misplayed by the shortstop, the player looks into the dugout and says "That was a hit." Players don't hustle on and off the field. They don't back up plays. It has become all about the coach and all about the star players. Teamwork is a thing of the past. Being a good team player is the exception, not the norm.

There are so many ways in which you can be a good teammate, and talent has nothing to do with a lot of them.

You go to a game and perhaps see seven or eight kids strike out as the norm. How many of those kids who struck out take the high road and hustle back to the dugout and communicate to the other batters what kind of pitch the opponent struck him out on? As you know, the choice is usually for the batter to swear, pout, throw the bat, make faces at the umpire, or any combination of those things. Every time a player strikes out and throws the bat and swears instead of letting the next guy up know what type of pitches the pitcher threw, he is not a good teammate. It's all about him, and not trying to help the next batter.

Every time the outfielder intentionally misses the cut off man just to show off his arm and how far he can throw it, he's not a good teammate. It's all about him and not trying to do what's best for the team.

Every time a player roots against the other player competing for his position, he's not a good teammate.

Now that's a tough one...

You're neck and neck with that other guy who wants to be the starting second baseman. You want the job just as bad or worse. You have shared time at the position during exhibition games so the coach can really see who deserves the job. It's the bottom of the last inning and your team is down by a run and of course, the bases are loaded with two outs. Your competitor for the second base position is up to bat. Or should I say, your teammate is up to bat. Do you want him to get the game winning base hit or strike out? If there were 20 teammates on your team with the same scenario, how many would want their competitor to get that hit? Would their mothers and fathers want that other player to get that hit?

For most players, baseball ends after high school. For some more, it's a couple years later. The hitting and pitching instructions that are engrained in your head are nice memories, but they carry no value out in the real world. Your coach is long gone. Your former teammates have started their own lives. Teamwork, however, if learned properly on the ball diamond, will never leave you and always be a comfort to you.

A business is no different than a baseball team was years earlier. Millions of dollars a year are spent on team building by large and small organizations. Tens of thousands of grown men and women come home every day from work and bemoan the fact that their co-workers don't care, have an attitude, or don't know how to work together or treat people.

I know. In general conversation, I may ask a parent how their week is going. Maybe I won't ask that question again! That's the real world. That's the teamwork we've learned. We go into the work force and continually are inundated with examples of no teamwork. We obviously aren't learning it, we obviously aren't teaching it.

Why not?

Why don't we teach teamwork?

You would think that if there is one thing we have learned as parents in our adult life it is the fact that the ability to be a good co-worker, or partner, or teammate is not only important in life, but it's a necessity. So if teamwork is so important, why don't we teach it? There isn't a class in school (there should be) called teammates that you can take, so where is this skill learned? It's learned on the athletic fields … on the baseball diamonds. At least it should be.

Winning has become the only motivation to a lot of people. That's what we teach …winning. Winning is great but temporary. Teaching teamwork is, as previously stated, forever. You won when you were in high school because you had the best team with the most talent. Coaches need to get a grasp of this fact. Most wins by a coach are because they have the better players. Winning a ball game is nice, but how about succeeding in life? What did that coach teach you about that?

High school baseball is over, and you now go into the work force and you come to a startling realization.

The teams are even.

The talent is well dispersed and you have no advantage like you did in high school. Now you really have to earn your wins. You can't just show up. The easy classes you took in high school, the ones that your coach or parent signed you up for (wink wink, nod nod) do you no good now. Matter of fact, they're kind of an injustice to you. Back in high school, maybe they made you eligible to play ball, maybe they made it easier to get into a certain college, but what did those particular classes really do for you?

You're staring life right in the face and you really have no answers. Perhaps you become a salesman selling computers, or cars, or widgets… it doesn't really matter what you're selling. Let's say that you're selling computers. Twenty other companies are selling computers. How do you get the sale? How do you differentiate yourself from all of those other guys and gals?

What did your coaches teach you as a young man that you can now use to succeed out in the real world? Forget about that other salesman in the office showing you anything. That's a noble thought, but that's really funny! Remember back when you were the star in high school. How many times did you go over to the new guy, the underclassmen, and help him? How many times did you grab that guy and take him out to shortstop with you and show him a few tricks to make him better? How many times did you take that freshman catcher and work on blocking the ball, just the two of you? Right, you didn't.

Now you're the new guy. You're in a sales office and your fast ball that you used to throw past hitters isn't going to help you. Your 400-foot bombs are a thing of the past. I mean, why would this other guy in the office come to your assistance? You're the enemy, you're the competition. Why would he teach you so you can take a sale off of him? Isn't that why you didn't help that sophomore in high school? Weren't you afraid that he was the competition, that if you helped make him better, he would take your job?

Now when you really need some teamwork, it's not there. It wasn't a priority on that awesome 14-under team that won the league. It wasn't a priority in that showcase league, or that legion team or your high school team. Just win baby! Your mom and dad aren't there now to make everything better, to make a phone call and put you on a different team because they don't like your situation.

There isn't another team.

You're just trying to get on A team. And when you do, you'll be the bottom player looking up at everyone else who has absolutely no motivation to help you. They're not good teammates; they didn't learn the right lessons. They learned to win, not share. Pretty scary stuff, it really is.

It is very scary.

It is scary ….unless, of course, they were taught the right lessons as a child and a young adult. They understand teamwork and being a good teammate. They understand how important it is to utilize one's talents to help whoever they can. When you don't help, it's nothing more than a character flaw.

That's all it is.

Now you remember back. You were always the star. Things came easy on the baseball diamond. You worked hard, but it was all to make YOU better. You never really gave a second thought to making your teammate better. How many times have you ever heard a coach get mad at players because they are not helping their teammates enough? Seldom will you hear those words communicated to a player.

Listen to coaches speak at practices and before and after games. They scream about not covering bases, not hustling, not being in the proper position, not watching the signs, anything and everything you can imagine on a ball field.

Have you ever heard them screaming or even talking or ever being upset that a player did not help the other player enough? We don't teach kids to be selfless. We don't teach kids that it is more important to get ahead by how good you are, not how bad somebody else is. You shouldn't root for that guy to strike out who's trying to beat you out of your position. You don't want that position by him doing badly. You want that position by you doing well. You want to earn it, not have him give it away.

Be a builder, not a destroyer.

You really needed a Coach Spellman in your life.

A good coach should always use the following verbiage somewhere, sometime in a talk to their team.

"You as players have responsibilities. Every one of you has a talent out here on the ball field that can be used by other players. You all are better at something than most. Maybe you can bunt better, get a better jump when you steal, know how to get a running start when you catch that fly ball so he can throw the runner out that is tagging, hit to the opposite field, or maybe you have a way of kicking second base when you take the throw from the second baseman on a double play.

You have something that you do better than the next guy. You need to share it. If you're not working with each other and helping each other, shame on you. That's the easiest way to improve your game. That will make you a better player and a better teammate; and a better person."

Every one should hear that speech. Maybe not those exact words, but some comments closely related to that.

Coach Spellman taught teamwork. You needed to be part of a team. You needed to help the other players. He had a way of making all players "check their egos at the door." He was toughest on the stars. Lessons learned from Coach Spellman are still used today by former players ... and remembered.

The following is from the Spellman book.

Dave Blazin has such memories.

Dave was one of the catchers in a long list of top receivers at Lincoln High School in Ellwood City, Pa. He was sandwiched in (1968) between two other pretty good catchers. I should know because they were both my brothers. My brother Jim graduated in 1966, and after Blazin started for two years, my brother Rich came along to start for two years before graduating in 1970. Yes, it is the same brother Rich, who six years earlier walked to Robuskys on that July day while Pete was getting a life lesson from his dad.

After graduating from Lincoln High school, Jim attended Marietta College, the school that Don Schaly became head coach at, the same Don Schaly that graduated in 1956 from Lincoln High school, the same Don Schaly that was pictured in the book on Spellman's first high school team, and became one of the top coaches in the country. Rich, upon graduation, attended Gulf Coast College in Panama City, Florida and played for Bill Frazier. Yes, the same Bill Frazier who also graduated from Lincoln High School and was a high school teammate of Don Schaly. Bill Frazier also went on to become one of the top college baseball coaches in the country and also is pictured on Coach Spellman's first baseball team at Lincoln High school. Both coaches learned baseball under Coach Spellman.

Dave Blazin, like all three Potter brothers, had a passion about baseball and would have loved to play professional baseball. It didn't happen. After an impressive high school baseball career, he moved on to the University of Iowa to continue his baseball dream. Reality hit home and that was the end of the line. All dreams come to an end.

Dave then joined the Navy. He went into the officer-training program with the hopes of becoming a pilot. The film, *Officer and a Gentleman* took place at that school - in Pensacola, Florida. The movie came out while Blazin was in the Navy. "I saw some of that stuff that happened in the movie" says Blazin. "When you see people DOR-ing (Dropping on Request) – out of 35 in the class, by the time the entire program was finished, we only had eight left. The physical requirements that we had – we were drilled by Marine drill instructors – and the physical training was quite intense. But maybe being an athlete and growing up in the auspices of having to really work hard to get something certainly made a difference. I saw guys that would fall out on runs."

Blazin became a pilot assigned to aircraft carriers, one being the U.S.S. Nimitz. This was in the mid 1970s.

Meanwhile, a teammate from Lincoln High School, Jerry Bukac, became a welder. He and Blazin had worked together closely under coach Spellman. They were actually the battery mates (pitcher and catcher for you non-baseball experts) in Ellwood's championship win in 1968 at old Forbes Field in Pittsburgh. Bukac moved away to Virginia – got a job at the naval station in Virginia Beach. A special project had begun. The Navy was hiring welders to teach welding to crew members for when they would be out to sea. Bukac was hired to do some training. He boarded an aircraft carrier that was headed for the Caribbean : The Nimitz.

One day, Bukac was walking down one of those narrow hallways below deck. Somebody was approaching from the other direction. Bukac couldn't believe his eyes.

"I get on this ship with 5,000 guys", says Bukac, "and I'm walking through the hallway one night, and here's Dave Blazin."

The happy reunion was not just about two men being from the same hometown. It was also a reunion of young people who had experienced Bill Spellman. They had shared the rigors of being driven hard – working hard – pursuing a level the coach goaded them to reach, and once they got there, they understood it all. Few others their age stood where they stood.

That is a connection that had become Spellman. Others, too, certainly figured in the lives of young people from Ellwood City, but Spellman was the rock. He called on young boys to rise to a higher level. When young people agree to participate - when they accept the challenge – that becomes part of their character. When playing days are over, if coaches have done their job, if sport has served its purpose, the character has been set in place. Teammates take on a whole new meaning. It's no longer a pitcher throwing to a catcher. Those days are gone. But the character had been set in place. Now, as Blazin and Bukac met in the narrow hallway, it's two men from different lives acting in a new realm of possibility. That's a connection at the deep level of character, and Spellman helped build that.

How many high school coaches do that? How many summer coaches, or youth coaches, or travel coaches, do that? Or did they keep reminding you of how many wins they had, how they had a player that would make the majors, or how they could recruit the best players? Did any of them emphasize how important it is to help each other, teach each other, push each other, motivate each other, and respect each other, to be good teammates?

Coach Spellman was the finest man I have ever known. He was classy. He was selfless. He built character by building teamwork. It wasn't about him. It wasn't about the star players. It was about the team.

It all starts with that T-ball coach who instills teamwork. He shows the kids that baseball is fun and everyone gets a chance to hit and pitch and run. Then the kids move up to coach pitch and the coaches begin the process of teaching fundamentals. Get in front of the ball when you field it, follow through when you throw it, keep your eye on the ball when you hit it. And be a good teammate.

Before you know it, the kids are pitching on their own. The games seem like real games. Coaches don't need to participate. All the parents are there, cheering on everybody, encouraging them to be good teammates. Everything seems good.

All of a sudden, you turn around and your boy is 12 years old. The better players are now known. The cream always rises to the top. There are travel teams with players now getting cut from teams. Reality has taken hold. The merry-go-round has started. You have two choices, hang on tight and try to enjoy the ride, or get off.

It has started. Coaches now have already lost sight of what the goals should be. Almost all of the coaches are dads, either by choice – to protect and highlight their own son – or by necessity, because no one wants to be responsible. Lots of dads will help out, but few have the time for the commitment of coaching. A lot of dads who take the job as head coach do not have the qualifications to do the job. They do their best, they try their hardest, but in that small window of time, our children have gone from these small kids having fun to this competitive juggernaut. The coach tries to keep up with all of this competition. The parents have started to let their competitive juices take over.

And before you know it, being good teammates, like the art of bunting, has been lost. Bigger priorities have taken over, like winning. Coaches don't seem to know how to do both, win and develop good teammate skills.

Some people don't think it's really that important that you need good coaches at this level.

It is not only important, but critical. This is the time where these young kids build their foundation as players... and being good teammates. You need a coach who is fair and honest and under-standing and a good communicator and a good motivator and have the respect of the kids and the parents. That's a lot to ask for in a coach; but it's that important.

You need a Coach Spellman.

You need someone who insists on individuals being good team-mates. You need to surround yourself with good teammates. Most players can become very good teammates. They just need the proper environment and the proper coaches. Some players will never be good teammates. That's the lesson that took me a long time to learn. There are individuals out there that never care to be a good teammate. Their parents don't get it. They are all into themselves and the world should revolve around them. It's all about their kid. The best thing to do is get away from them and get as far away as you possibly can. You may think that their talent makes up for their lack of team building, but it's just the opposite. Because they may be extremely talented, they feel that is enough.

I was fortunate to coach not only a lot of good ball players, but be in the presence of a lot of good parents; parents who taught their kids the right life lessons; or allowed the coach to teach the right life lessons without jumping in to protect their child.

My son was blessed to be around so many good people.

In regards to ability, Eric finished the summer season as a 13-u player the same way he started the season; right in the middle of the pack. Tyler probably had the most talent and was without a doubt the most intense player on the team. Privately, I felt that Jason was the best athlete. He was tall, strong, and had the perfect pitcher's build. He could run fast and had potential "written all over him." He would one day be a star. Eric hadn't seen a growth spurt yet and his small stature kept him from being looked upon as a top player. What it did, however, was make him focus on the things that he could do well. He had a good bat, made good contact, was an excellent bunter, and knew the game. His pitching was average, but he knew how to pitch, and not just throw.

As we moved into the fall season, the Gambrills team only got better. Because of summer vacations, football, and other commitments by players, we managed to keep all 15 or 16 players with sufficient playing time. The fall season, however, brought all the kids out at the same time and it became obvious that there were too many kids to play together. An attempt to make two teams failed, and after a few tough cuts, we were left with a very solid ball team.

Fall also marked the time that players moved up in age and now they were playing as 14 year-olds. Eric had just started his freshman year of high school. There was no discussion of whether he would play at Gambrills or for his high school team. To be honest, I am not sure why. Perhaps it was what I thought, that no one had put anything out from the school notifying us of fall ball. Or maybe I wasn't looking for anything, that I wanted him to play for me and therefore, I made no real effort to find out what was going on. In either case he stayed at Gambrills and as I have learned over the last few years, that certainly was the right choice. Little did we know at that time how disappointed we would be in the program at Arundel High School. Little did we know of how many life lessons Eric would be faced with at that school.

The Gambrills baseball team was loaded with talent, and it was reflected in the manner in which we rolled over much of the competition that fall. When the next spring arrived, the team didn't miss a beat by winning a few pre-season tournaments. When the regular season started, the team played in a very competitive Baltimore Metro League and finished third against some very good area ball teams. One of the disappointing aspects of that spring was the fact that Jason Patten had to go without pitching for most of the year with a growth plate issue, and therefore was shut down as a pitcher immediately. Any chance of winning the league was probably removed by this injury as he and Tyler were a terrific one-two combination.

Eric missed a few early spring games as he was one of three players who were in ninth grade and playing baseball for their respective high school JV teams.

Yes, high school ball had started. This was the career that really counted. High school was the real deal. That is where you got your real development and life lessons and exposure to even bigger goals like college ball. This is where you were taught discipline and good work ethic and teamwork and all of the other great things. Our hopes were so high because we had heard so many good things about this program.

Nothing could have been further from the truth.

It was all a bad dream, a very bad dream.

High school baseball, at least at this particular location, was not what we had envisioned or hoped for. Disappointment is way too nice of a word to describe the experience. Because Eric was playing JV ball, that's where I would go to watch practice that first year. That's where Eric quickly picked up his nick name that still galls both his mother and father to this day:

Little Eric Potter.

That's where Eric was told that he couldn't play the field or hit because he didn't lift enough weight. That's where Eric, like so many other kids who didn't have the physical stature, are beat up by the coaches and thrown away. That's where 28 kids constantly had practice with one coach. That was the start of high school baseball.

About three weeks into this season, I stopped down one day to watch the coach run a practice. The coach was hitting infield and outfield... to those same 28 kids. He would hit a ball to the right fielder who would throw it in to a base. The coach would then stop practice and yell at the player for who knows what. He would then pick up the bat and hit a ball to the next outfielder, and once the young boy threw the ball into the infield, he would once again walk out and talk to him about his miscue. I watched this go on for 45 minutes. Those two boys never got another ball hit to them during that time. The coach failed to hit a ball to all of the players yet.

It was painful to watch.

Once he took a break, I had to go talk to him. I offered my services, saying that I would do anything he needed; hit some fly balls, grounders, throw batting practice, etc. He told me that he would let me know if he ever needed some help. Twenty eight kids, standing around in freezing weather doing nothing and he would let me know if he ever needed help!

Eric did get a chance to pitch twice his freshman year. He won both games and did fairly well; but he never got a chance to hit or play the field. The spring was basically a waste of time. That routine happened for the next few years, digressing during the school year, getting better during the time he was not associated with the school and out with his summer teams.

Eric went out that first summer and led his team in hitting. He couldn't wait until the summer. He wanted to be back out with real teammates, the guys that supported each other, pushed each other to be better, and enjoyed each other's company.

We hoped that the first year of high school would not be duplicated in the future.

It turned out to be wishful thinking.

CHAPTER 7
BE EFFECTIVE – NOT RIGHT

"Good teachers are costly, but bad teachers cost more."
—Bob Talbert

Fiddler on the Roof is a great production. Many years ago I saw it at a movie theatre and years later, I saw it as a play at a dinner theatre. On top of that, it was actually the selection of our senior class in high school when we needed to choose a play to perform at the end of our school year.

There are many, many great scenes in the play. One of them had to do with two neighbors who were in an argument about a horse and a mule. The dispute went before the neighborhood "official" who dealt with such disagreements. Both parties were given the opportunity to give their version of what truly occurred, and then the official would make his finding. As usual, several onlookers were present to watch the proceedings.

Neighbor #1 gave his side of the story. The official thought for a minute and said, "You're right."

Neighbor #2 then gave his side of the story. The official once again thought for a minute and said "You're right."

At this point one of the onlookers who was intently listening to both sides of the argument, and to the peacemaker's assessment thus far, said to the official, "They can't both be right." The official thought for a few minutes, then said to the onlooker, "You're also right."

Being right just isn't what it's cracked up to be.

Some of us are always trying to be right. I believe that my wife feels that is one of my worst virtues ... being right. She is constantly saying, "You're always right, you always need to be right." I used to like the fact that I could in most cases prove that I was correct in my position. Now being right has lost its luster. We know more than the next person and are so eager to let him (her) know that.

We always need to correct somebody. We always need to have the biggest and best story and we always need to deflect blame and misunderstandings away from ourselves. I was the worst. As I have been told many, many times in the middle of a disagreement, "You should have been a lawyer." It just made me feel so good to be right.

Then I realized something.

What does being right really accomplish other than fueling our personal egos and making us feel good about ourselves? We should already feel good about ourselves! We shouldn't have to worry about always being right.

Instead of being right, try being effective.

Try to say something to somebody where the result is they actually listen to you and do what you say, instead of coming back later and saying, "You were right." I don't want to be right anymore. I would much rather be effective. That's what is really important, whether it be in life in general… or on a ball field.

Some people just can't be wrong, even when they are. They are so concerned about people believing them and listening to them, that they lose sight of the bigger picture. You can never improve your personal skills if you can't accept the fact that you are sometimes wrong, and more important than being right, figure out what you did wrong, why you did it wrong, and then maybe you won't do it wrong the next time. It is what it is. By always being right, you'll never be effective. People will stop believing you (even if you can't see it) and lack of belief will lead to lack of trust and then lack of leadership skills.

What's this have to do with baseball?

Everything.

The baseball field is just another place to try to be effective. I'm struggling to be effective as a coach. Every coach is struggling to be effective whether they want to believe it or not. It is so much easier to be right. It's so much easier to sit the players down after the game and tell them everything they did wrong. You sprinkle a few "atta boys" in there, but by the time the talk is over, you completely understand that you as a player were wrong and the coach was right.

How many times after a game in one of those meetings at the mound or out in left field or behind the dugout has the coach spent most of the talk telling everyone what he did wrong? Very seldom I'm sure. He is right. If you would have just done things the way he taught you, he showed you, you may have won. I'm as guilty as the next person.

Coaching is hard work. It should be. A good coach will try to be effective, to get through to the players so he doesn't have to be right. Being right isn't important. Being effective is important and very few coaches are consistently effective.

Whether I am out on the field coaching or in the stands watching, there are literally hundreds of situations during a game where you can see that a coach has been ineffective. Every time he yells, he has obviously been ineffective about something.

Every time my team plays a game, no matter how well they played, there are handfuls of examples of me being ineffective. You can never rid yourself of them completely, but it is something that you need to strive to improve upon.

For instance, you may see the batter come up to the plate and there's a good chance he may bunt. You yell out to the third baseman, "Never know, watch the hands" which of course means ... he may bunt and if you see the hand come up on the bat, you need to be charging so you can field the ball quicker and there will be more chance that the bunt won't be successful. The third baseman nods at you, letting you know he heard what you said. He moves up a few baby steps, enough to, in his mind, make you happy. Now he looks a little more prepared than he did a few seconds ago, before you barked out your words of wisdom.

The pitcher goes into his wind up and as he is set to release the pitch, the batter extends his hand up the bat, a split second before he begins to swivel his body around, the obvious indicator of a bunt. The third baseman, once seeing the apparent "squaring" of the body comes rushing in. The bunt is placed down the third base line, rather hard. The third base man comes in, fields the bunt, and directs his throw to second base in an attempt to get the lead runner. He is successful. You hear the parents say "Great play."

It was not a great play, not even a good play. I was right, the batter was bunting. However, the third baseman should have known this. I shouldn't have had to tell him to watch the bunt. I shouldn't have had to tell him to watch the hands. He should have reacted when the hands went up the bat, not when he started to square away. We got the lead runner because it was a bad bunt. A good bunt would have advanced him to second, primarily because my player did not react in the way he should have. I was right, but unfortunately not effective.

Four innings later, our team is in basically the same situation. I as a coach say to myself, do I say something to the third baseman and remind him to watch the hands? Is that being a good coach? Or do I say nothing and hope I was effective and he learned from the time before?

I say nothing. The batter puts a bunt down the third base line. The unsuspecting third baseman comes dashing in too late, comes up firing to first base, but the runner beats it out. This time you hear the parents say, "That was a great bunt." It was great because the third baseman allowed it to be great. If he would have done everything perfectly, if I would have been effective as a coach, that batter is out.

The week before this game the same thing happened. He didn't learn the right lesson and the batter put down a bunt and beat it out to first base. Was I happy that I was right and I knew more than the third baseman? Or do I wish I would have been effective and the third baseman listened to me and learned? Was there any solace in being right? Again, being right isn't what it's cracked up to be. Being effective is much more important.

Thirteen times in a two week period the other team bunted or attempted to bunt in games we played. Four times we did an adequate job defending the bunt. We appeared to do a good job in this area, but that was only because the other teams were doing worse bunting than we were doing defending. Another one's ineffectiveness doesn't make you effective.

I am very ineffective as a coach in this instance and in a lot of other instances. I haven't motivated my third basemen to do what it takes to defend a bunt on a consistent basis. I could tell you I was right 13 times and the player was wrong seven times and look how good of a coach I am because I am right! I could yell at the third baseman after the game as we get together as a team. I could make it look like I am so smart and he is so dense and I am so right and he is so wrong.

The truth is, I'm very ineffective.

I want to be effective.

There are hundreds of times during a game that little things could be done right or wrong, that by me being effective with the players, our chance of winning is better. The more effective I am as a coach, the more times I have influenced a player to do the right thing, the more chance of success of the team. The more times that I am right means nothing.

Anytime during a game, I could go over to the bench while one of our batters, or the opposing batter, has been up to bat for several pitches and say to each and every player, "What's the count?"

Most players couldn't give you a correct answer. I know because I've done this 30 or 40 times in the past. If a player doesn't know the count, he isn't focusing on the game. If he isn't focusing on the game, our chances of success have been reduced. If he doesn't know the count, how on earth would he know what the pitcher's tendencies are in terms of pitch selection on particular counts?

If I asked every player at this time if they would be better off if they knew the count and were focusing on the pitcher, every player would say, "Yeah coach, you're right."

There's being right again…

As a fan, you may watch certain coaches, perhaps your high school coach, yell a lot at the players. He may berate them and scream and give them a hard time about all the things they aren't doing right. In general, the perception is that the more a coach yells, the better the coach he is. He expects excellence and he isn't getting it. The players are not performing to the expectations. The reality is that he's screaming and yelling not because the kids can't do it right, but because they're not doing it right.

It all makes sense.

But the truth is, isn't that coach really yelling because he's not effective? That's certainly why I yell at my players. Sure, I want them to get better and develop and improve. They are not performing at the level that I want them to perform.

But I'm more frustrated with myself than them.

I am frustrated because I am not effective. When the team doesn't hustle out on the field the coach has not affected them in a way to hustle out on the field. All of this yelling is only masking a coach's acknowledgement that he may be right, but certainly not effective.

I meet a lot kids and parents through baseball. Some I meet because they are looking for a team to play on and they think they may want to play at Gambrills. Others I meet because they are referred to me as young ball players who may need a little help and are not sure what to do. They want to play ball and have some talent, but perhaps they cannot find the right type of help. They may need a little jump start or a little attention. In a lot of cases the scenario is that they have had lessons in the past, but perhaps aren't making the type of progress that they would like, and to be honest, aren't sure the lessons are helping.

On the other side of this scenario, I am sure there is an instructor who gave this player lessons. If I were to go to this instructor (I have in the past) and ask about this particular player not making progress, his answer has usually been that he doesn't have the talent, he doesn't listen or he doesn't want to work hard enough. Those are the three that I have heard. Not once have I heard, "I just wasn't effective as an instructor." Instructors seldom take responsibility for a player not making progress. It's always the kid who doesn't make progress. When the situation reverses itself, though, and when the kid makes tremendous progress, what do you think you hear? In this instance, the instructor usually lets everyone know how HE made the ball player the player he is today. How often do you hear, "Well, the player deserves all the credit, the player worked hard." Poor instructors are no different than poor coaches – take the credit when you do well, lay blame on the players when they do poorly.

Let's be more effective!

Two years ago, I met one of these kids who had gone to an instructor and the progress made would be considered not very well.

Someone who thought I may be able to help with the boy's develop-ment referred him to me. He was a pitcher, a left-handed pitcher. He loved baseball and he wanted to get better. I got a "scouting re-port" on him – terrible control, can't throw strikes, doesn't throw hard. Again, he had lessons, and I was not sure by whom and I don't really care. If his parents still has the instructor's address, they probably should send him a seven word note that says:

Please return the money I paid you.

I really wish this type of situation was the exception to the rule.

It is not.

It is very common to have players take many lessons and spend much money with a result that is not only unacceptable, but also very costly. There are more reasons than I care to write on why the proper progress was not made. Let me give you the one that is never uttered, but should be on top of the list.

The instructor was not effective.

This may sound a bit harsh toward instructors, but aren't they the professionals? Are they the ones who are being paid, that in most cases are marketing themselves as experts?

Unfortunately, kids are never too young to be the object of paid instructors. It is not uncommon to see 10 and 11-year-old kids watching an instructor intently speak of radial deviation, hip rotation and weighted balls. There are hundreds of little tricks and drills for the willing ball player. Just come in, plunk down your money, and someone will make you feel good about yourself and your child.

Kids love the fact that they are taking lessons and getting at-tention. They are engrossed in the whole process. Mom or dad, or both, are standing no more than 30 feet away and taking every word in, how their boy really has a lot of potential. Most of us have been through it and have bought into it. Like most other good salesmen, the instructors tug on our heartstrings. It becomes very emotional. You want your child to have every opportunity that he, or she, can possibly have in life; including these high priced lessons.

I'm not an expert in the field of instructors, but I've spoken to well over a hundred parents on this subject. I've also taken a few different surveys which are shown below. One of the questions in this particular questionnaire was "In general, what is your opinion of the value of personal lessons and paid instructors?

Listed below were the responses:

	Number of Surveys	Positive	Neutral	Negative
Parents	22	3	5	14
Players	27	5	4	18
Coaches	16	4	4	8
Totals	65	12	13	40

Less than 20% of all involved people believe that instructors and lessons are a valuable experience. Eight out of ten people did not have a good experience with this.

Why?

That was broken down also. The reasons were as follows:

	Parents	Players	Coaches	Total
Total Responses	14	18	8	40
Charged too much money	5	2	0	7
Instructor insisted on too many lessons	1	2	1	4
Instructor lacked proper knowledge	3	3	3	9
Instructor insisted on doing it his way	1	5	2	8
Instructor poor communicator	4	6	2	12

This certainly isn't an exhaustive look into the world of base-ball instructors. There are plenty of teachers out there that do wonderful things.

The good guys know who they are and know what they are doing is the right thing for the right reasons.

One of my personal concerns with instructors is a philosophical one.

The student never graduates.

The student never completes the class.

Kids go to high school and eventually graduate. If you want to be a real estate agent, there is a class to take, and a graduation. It's the same thing with a bartender, bricklayer, financial consultant or a fireman. Take your classes, learn from your classes, pass your classes, and go into the world and improve upon the skills that you learned in the classes. It sounds pretty clear-cut.

Now we come to the baseball player.

When does he pass the class and go on to the real world and hone his skills? Doesn't he leave the instructor and go play on a team with a coach whose job is to make sure he is the best player he can be? Are we saying that all of these kids who go to instructors are playing on teams who have coaches without the credentials to make sure the skills they have learned already can be improved upon?

Is it just too simplistic to say that in a lot of cases, if the student graduated from the instructor, there would be no more lessons and hence, no more money for the instructors.

Isn't that really the deal?

If I charged a young man $50.00 an hour to learn to be a bartender, I guess I could forever show him how to make different drinks, or learn more about certain wines, or how to flip bottles to put on a show for the patrons. But at some time, don't you just say, "I've taught you the basics (fundamentals), now you will get better by going out and doing what you've learned here. Get a job as a bartender and every time you work as a bartender, you will get better, and learn more. You will learn by your mistakes."

Or should I bring him in to my place every week after he has landed a job, and have him practice mixing a rum and coke or a sloe gin fizz? For that refresher course, he can give me another $50.00.

Does that make sense?

We don't do that. I have personally taken many classes in life that varied from sales to management to finance to real estate. There is a starting date and an ending date. There is a cost along with an expectation. The instructor covers the course. That's it! He isn't there a month later to have you come back in and pay him more money for the class he already taught.

Can't we use that same logic with baseball players? An instructor shows and teaches a student how he can best hit. He works on weight distribution, leverage, hip rotation, radial deviation; hands threw the zone, getting the barrel of the bat out, and all of these other neat things. He finds out what works best for the student and then sends him on his way.

Do we really need to keep charging him money week after week, month after month? In all seriousness, once a player has worked with the instructor for a few months, couldn't the instructor get together with the player's coach and the player, go over what he has taught him and how he has taught it, and let the coach kind of monitor the progress? Why don't instructors put a player in a course that lasts a specific amount of classes? Certain things should be taught or developed in that time frame. The parents then would know what the charge would be and more importantly, what the expectations would be.

Instead of this rather logical plan, we get caught in a vicious cycle.

The instructor keeps telling the student how well he's doing, but he's never doing well enough to graduate. Keep coming back … keep giving me money. If a student never graduates, how effective has the instructor been? Even if the instructor, for months, has been teaching the right things but the student is doing the wrong things, he apparently hasn't been effective.

That's not to say that there aren't great instructors out there. There are many, many good individuals who do a great job working with kids.

I just haven't seen many.

Besides that, I certainly haven't seen many graduations.

When was the last time you heard an instructor say, "Congratulations, I am done with you. I have taught you all the basics. You don't need to come back anymore and give me more money. If you do need to come back perhaps for a refresher lesson, I will be more than happy to do it free of charge."

Wouldn't that be nice to hear just once?

To make this whole situation even messier, it is a fact that in most cases, when a player goes to an instructor, he has been to a different instructor already. Someone in the players past has taught him a certain way of hitting or pitching. Invariably the new instructor will tell that player that everything he was shown in the past was wrong, that he (new instructor) will have to start all over, "break him down," and teach him the right way. Translation...lots of lessons, lots of money

Dad, just open your wallet.

Three individuals who played for me at Gambrills for three years went to a local instructor a few years ago. The gentleman was putting together a team to play in the Junior Olympics in Florida a few months from then. These players were going to try out for the team. It was a great opportunity to play in this tournament, lots of exposure, and lots of scouts. The instructor was going to take a look at them and determine if they were good enough to make his team.

The three players batted third, fourth, and fifth for me in our lineup. All of them were good hitters. Perhaps though, the instructor may be able to "tweak" them a little. Perhaps he can see some sort of minor flaw that he can improve on, and make them just a little bit better.

The first player went to the work out, hit some balls in the cage, and was told by the instructor that he had a "hole in his swing." The second player went to a work out a few days later and he too did some hitting in the cage. The instructor's assessment was he had a "hole in his swing." The third player went through the same time type of workout, and once finishing the batting part of it, was given the assessment, "Young man, you have a hole in your swing."

But there was good news for all of them. With some help, he (the instructor) could "break them down," start all over, and put their swing back together for them.

What a great guy!

It would however, take a great deal of patience and determination, and yes, lessons and money.

The first two players went to the workout with their mothers. There is an obvious perception that mothers don't quite know as much as fathers about baseball and the intricacies of the game. In general that may be correct, but plenty of mothers are pretty keen on the game of baseball. This particular instructor ran into one of them. No reason to use the expletives that she used to explain how she felt about the instructor, but they certainly weren't words of gratitude. Let's just say that she didn't completely agree with his assessment and she certainly wasn't appreciative of his solution.

The third player went with his father. The conversation went something like this:

Instructor: He has a major flaw in his swing

Father: What are you talking about?

Instructor: The swing isn't right, he can't handle certain pitches

Father: He has played against all kinds of pitching and has never had a real problem handling any type of pitcher.

Instructor: Yeah, but with his swing he'll never hit the long ball.

Father: He makes great contact, strikes out very seldom and hits the long ball occasionally

Instructor: Scouts look for the long ball, it doesn't matter how good you hit.

Father: I think we'll stick to what we're doing, I'm pretty happy with his situation.

There are a couple of things to note regarding the third player:

He wasn't there for lessons and certainly wasn't asking for them.

The instructor never had seen him hit in a game.

The instructor never asked him if he currently had another instructor.

The instructor never asked the father for his baseball background.

Matter of fact, none of the kids was there for lessons and never requested them.

This last player attends Palotti High School in Laurel, Md. The only reason he did not start on the varsity as a freshman is that the coach didn't believe in putting freshmen on the varsity. He started as a sophomore for his high school team, hit .450 and led the team in home runs with five. Matter of fact, he led his league in home runs. This is from someone who will never hit the long ball with his swing. As a junior, he was voted on the Washington D.C area all-met team, which is quite an honor. He is one of the best high school hitters in the State of Maryland… and he still has his senior year. He has already accepted a full athletic scholarship to Indian River Junior college in Florida. He went down last winter for a personal work out. That's all the coach needed to see. Recently he was selected to represent the state of Maryland in the national home run hitting contest this past January in Tampa, Florida. Perhaps I should send that information to the instructor.

The first player went out and started as a junior (he also started as a sophomore), hit .380 and led the county in doubles. In his senior year in high school, he hit .420 and set a record at his high school for runs batted in for the year. He is currently playing college baseball.

The second player started as a sophomore at Dundalk High School, hit .365 with three home runs. In his junior year, he hit .405 with four home runs, leading his team in hitting.

I am sure that the instructor saw things that he didn't feel were right and in some way felt that he could help. How can you help someone who you've never seen hit in a game, someone who wasn't asking for help, someone who actually wasn't having a problem hitting? I would have to assume that if my three best hitters all had "holes in their swings," then the other hitters must have had bigger holes in their swings. I guess all 14 of them needed personal lessons.

I have another pet peeve.

Instructors have a way of taking credit when a student does well. He goes to games and lets everyone around him know that he instructed that player and made him the player he is. Yet when that same player doesn't do well, you don't hear that instructor tell everyone that he is the reason the student struck out twice. All of a sudden, the student isn't doing things right, the student isn't listening. It's the student's fault.

If an instructor is going to take credit, he should certainly take the responsibility of failure. That gets back to being effective. If a player isn't doing what the instructor showed him, then the instructor wasn't effective instructing the student. Instead of blaming the student, perhaps the instructor should work on being more effective, and being responsible.

Almost every player I have ever coached has taken a lesson from a paid instructor: pitching instructors, hitting instructors, fielding instructors, and running instructors. There is an instructor for everything. You want to work on your slow twitch muscles, great.

I have the instructor for you.

Or perhaps radial deviation in your swing is your weak spot. No problem, I will get you a "radial deviation" guy. How about "soft hands" instructors for those infielders who need help? That's an easy one. I'll hand you and your buddy some wooden paddles and have you toss balls back and forth using the paddles for half an hour. When you're done, both of you can hand me $50.00.

Please!

My son has taken a few lessons, not many. Most of his lessons were not requested by me, or Eric. They were usually someone else taking lessons and they wanted to know if Eric would also go to split the cost of the hour or fill up a class. Eric always wanted to attend and always enjoyed them. I always encouraged him to go. The few classes that Eric has been involved with in the past were excellent.

Steve Lombardozzi, an area baseball guy who played professional baseball for the Minnesota Twins, ran one of the classes. Eric was 13 at the time and the classes involved fielding. They were set for four weeks and there was a flat fee. That's it…a starting point, an ending point, a fee, and I discovered the first 15 minutes of the first class exactly what he was attempting to accomplish with each kid. He was excellent with the boys, speaking on their level and explaining every action with good communicative skills. Never did he attempt to impress the players. It was fundamentals 101…. get your body in position, keep your glove down, and see the ball into the glove. One of his personal drills was to have the kids not only look at where they are throwing the ball, but to actually say out loud where they were throwing it. So you would see these kids fielding ground balls, come up ready to throw, and as they released the ball they would yell "To the chest." I thought that was a good drill, and the students certainly had fun doing it.

He would then get some wooden paddles out and have the players field grounders with the paddles on their hands instead of gloves, teaching them to have "soft hands" and to pull the ball up to their body as they received the ball. He didn't just hand them some paddles, though, and tell them to go use them. He actually showed them with hands-on instruction. He taught the basics and he made it fun. I thought he did a great job. The following year he came over to Gambrills and spent a couple of hours with the guys as a team. It was well worth the money.

Another time Eric took a few lessons from Joe Palmer, another local instructor. Joe was somewhat unorthodox in some of his teaching, along with having a very sharp tongue that at times would spew out words that may offend some parents. That was Joe, though, and that's how he taught. I would sit and watch the lessons. Kids were standing there with big beach balls between their legs and kids were hitting heavy basketballs instead of baseballs. Kids were doing warm up drills that I had never seen before, or since. Kids were being yelled at and called names.

"Don't be jackasses" was one of his favorite sayings. I don't think it offended many people, certainly not me or Eric.

The kids were having fun. Again, there was a starting point and an ending point to these classes. There was a flat fee. There were expectations. In both cases, the instructor was involved, actually doing the drills with the players.

The drills made sense and both instructors showed the players why the drill would help them in the long run. That is so different than many of today's instructors who have these fancy drills where the long term effect is not apparent.

One of the more popular drills for pitchers is the "towel drill." Take a towel and extend out with it to help you follow through, get your arm a little further out and release the ball six inches closer to the plate. We have all experienced the towel drill. It is extremely popular. Lots of high schools, and paid instructors, use it.

Tell me again exactly what this does.

Tell me what long-term benefit it has.

I had a new player who was coming aboard on our summer team two years ago. He was a pitcher and I discovered upon general conversation that he was taking private pitching lessons. I noticed that when he was pitching in winter workouts (before he started playing for me) that he was struggling. His dad agreed. Before saying anything to the pitcher, I asked his dad if I could go watch him work out with his instructor. I wanted to see what he was being taught and how he was being taught before I got involved with him. It was fine with his dad so I made arrangements to attend a work out and observe.

The pitcher started his work out by throwing 40 or 50 pitches. Of course these pitches weren't thrown to a catcher; rather they were just thrown to a tarp with a circle on it. The instructor wasn't really watching because he was talking to the dad at a table about 30 feet away. The conversation was quite interesting, talking about all of the instructor's success stories in baseball from the time he was ten years old to the present, 68 years later. It would have been nice, though, if the instructor had been instructing rather than reminiscing. Once the student finished with the throws, he informed the instructor that he was warmed up.

The well paid instructor then walked over by the mound where the student was standing and placed a bucket just out of the reach of the student's follow through. He handed him a towel and told him to hit the bucket with the towel.

Oh goodie, I'm going to see the towel drill again!

This is the drill that most instructors use for pitchers. I never understood its significance, but perhaps tonight I would get some additional insight. I watched intently as the pitcher took his wind up with the towel in his hand, followed through with the towel extending out toward the bucket and… yes, the towel missed the bucket.

"Okay Rob, try it again" encouraged the instructor.

The student once again went in to his wind up, full of determination, extended his arm toward the bucket and …for the second time he missed it.

"That was better, do it again," the instructor blurted out.

Rob did it again … and again… and again … and again.

None of the attempts hit the destination.

Finally, before the seventh attempt, the instructor yelled out, "Come on, get your body out there and hit the bucket."

On this attempt, Rob hit the bucket with the towel. The instructor said, "That's the way to do it." The pitcher smiled knowing he had accomplished his task.

There was only one problem.

By making such an effort to hit the bucket, the pitcher had completely forgotten that he was a pitcher and basically lunged for the bucket in a manner that had no relationship to a wind up. The instructor was so enthusiastic that the "towel drill" was successful that he either didn't notice what had happened or didn't care what had happened. I stood there in amazement as both instructor and student were smiling with so much satisfaction. I could not believe that the father could possibly think that this instructor earned the money that was handed to him about 20 minutes later. It was the most ridiculous thing that I have ever seen. For an instructor to believe that he did this kid some good and taught him something that night astounds me. There's no way that the word effective could be considered for this night's work.

When I ask high school pitchers what they think about the towel drill, they invariably say "It's stupid." Thousands of kids are doing the drill. Very few understand it, even less think it's helping them. It's nothing more than another ineffective drill that a coach learned at a conference or watched on some video.

So you get your arm six inches closer to the plate, maybe?

Do the math.

Six inches closer from 60' 6" and exactly what do you pick up? If you throw 80 mph BEFORE you begin this exercise and after perhaps six weeks you perfect this feat, guess how fast you are now throwing from 60 feet rather than 60 feet, 6 inches? Well, if you round it off to the nearest mph, you are still throwing 80 mph.

Do the math.

Now take these 40 or 50 hours that the pitcher is out there looking like a fool and put the time to better use by working on balance point, hip rotation, or how to "open up" during your follow through. Or maybe use all this time to run some serious sprints to strengthen your legs, or perhaps work on your pick off move. Perhaps this may do more good.

Does anyone really think this silly towel drill does any good? Does anyone really think that a pitcher really uses this in a game? He basically does this drill because he is told by his coach that he must. If by learning to actually do this drill, are we sure it doesn't have an adverse affect on some other part of his delivery. The pitcher is focusing so much on the towel drill, is it possible that he is losing proper mechanics and form to accomplish the task of swiping a bucket with the towel?

My son spent a lot of his afternoons last fall going to the high school baseball field and meeting up with a few of the other baseball players. They were all starters on the team and two of them were pitchers. They would do a lot of long toss and get in the cages and hit quite a bit. They would run. They went to the field for months and obviously did what they thought was important. A few times I drove down and watched them from a distance. They always spent part of their time throwing. Not once in two months did one of them whip out a towel and start doing the infamous towel drill. I see other kids working out and I talk to other parents of pitchers. There is lots of long toss, lots of indoor throwing.

I never see them with a towel.

If the players really thought that these towels were helping them, wouldn't they use the drill all the time, or a least sometimes? How effective have these coaches been in convincing these players that the towel drill is good for them? The answer is absolutely not effective at all. Sometimes to accomplish nothing but to get a big chuckle from one of the pitchers at the school, I will ask him while he is working out, "Where's your towel?"

The pitcher will always laugh.

Where exactly do instructors go to get their instructor's certificate? Is there such a thing? Who instructs the instructors? What actually is the definition of an instructor? Is it someone who teaches…. and is paid for it? If you are a coach, you obviously teach. Are you an instructor? If you charge for your services, does that make you an instructor only, or have you now elevated yourself to a *professional* instructor?

When I was growing up, I never had the experience of working with what today would be deemed an instructor. In other words, I never paid for help. All my coaches helped me, my brothers helped me, and my teammates helped me.

I'm not sure because it never happened, but I believe that if I ever would have gone to my high school coach and told him that I was going to a paid instructor for help, he would have been both upset and embarrassed. He was the instructor. He was the mentor. He was the person who knew baseball, knew you, and was there to make you the best ball player you could be.

Jeff Meehan, a teammate of mine in high school, tells the story of being down at the park in Ellwood City hitting balls one day as a young kid. Here comes Coach Spellman, who just happened to be riding by the field. He worked with him for over an hour. He worked with countless kids for hours and hours. It was his passion. When you put a price on helping a kid be a better baseball player, it usually is no longer a passion. It's a business. When you don't put beginnings and ends to paid lessons, it's a bad business.

I was speaking to one of my favorite dads, Tom Hibbs, one night. Tom and I have known each other for some time now and we've shared a lot of discussions about baseball. We agree on most things, and I'm sure there are things where our opinions differ. That's what makes it fun. His son, Tyler, is one of the best ball players around. We were up at the local high school field one night two summers ago watching a ball game. The batter up at the plate had our attention. He seemed to be having some difficulty with his plate appearance. He looked real tense and completely without confidence. His stance appeared to be awkward and we were almost in pain watching him swing.

First pitch, he took for a strike.

The second pitch was a curve ball. He swung and missed it by what looked like a foot. Tom looked at me with that look. No words needed to be said. As mentioned before, baseball dads can speak without uttering a word. The batter, now appearing very discouraged, slammed the bat into the ground. I looked back at the field waiting for the next pitch. The batter dug in and from a distance of about 50 feet away, I could literally see that his knuckles were white from squeezing the bat so hard. I said in a low voice that only I could hear, "Please don't throw another curve."

The pitcher obviously did not get my vibes. The pitch came in, the batter bailed out, and the ball curved right over the plate. The batter once again slammed the bat into the ground and started toward the dugout even before the umpire motioned strike three. I turned my head and looked at Tom, who shaking his head said, "You know, he's been taking lessons for three years."

I asked, "From the same guy?"

"Yeah, his dad loves him." Tom replied.

I say, "Yeah, I'll bet the instructor loves him."

Perhaps the instructor is good, and perhaps the instructor has explained the boy's limitations, and perhaps he has explained to the dad that he can only do so much with some limited abilities, perhaps everything has been explained in the most professional manner.

Perhaps not.

All I know is that based on the manner in which the boy was approaching the ball, he would never be a hitter. And this is three years in to lessons?

I then said to Tom, "I'm not really big on instructors"

He countered, "You know, here's my philosophy on hitting: See the ball… hit the ball."

He continues, "Not that some kids don't need a little help, but it's really pretty basic, see the ball, hit the ball."

The going rate for an instructor is around $60.00 / hr. Some are a little cheaper; some are a lot more expensive. A lot of instructors want to impress you with their credentials. I played "professional baseball," I was an all SEC pitcher, I played in the ACC, I was drafted by the Minnesota Twins, I was a teammate in college of Roger Clemons, my roommate in college dated the cousin of the pitching coach somewhere, etc.

Forget all of that.

It may be impressive and it certainly does not discount them from being very good, but it also does not guarantee effectiveness and success. If you are dead set on getting lessons for your son find the right person, not the right title.

You will know when you see the right instructor. He will make you feel at ease. He will explain expectations, and he will not charge you for the first session.

When you and your son go to an instructor and hear the words "Everything you have been shown in the past is wrong," you need to run away.

Run away and run fast. And while you're running, hold on to your wallet.

What he's telling you is that there are lots of lessons necessary and lots of money will need to be shelled out.

What you need to hear is, "Bring your boy in for an hour … **there is no charge for the first hour.** I will take a look and see if I can really help him. I will give you an honest assessment of what I can do for your boy. Then you make a decision if you want to continue with some lessons."

Back to the boy who I had met two years previously.

He played on a high school JV team that spring. He didn't get a lot of pitching time. The friend of mine asked if I could work with him. We were actually playing our last game of the fall season the next day. I told him to get the pitcher out to our game the next day. We would throw a uniform on him and let him pitch a couple of innings.

He came out to our game, and although extremely nervous, did a very good job for two innings. I asked if he wanted to pitch more and he said, "No, that's about all I can pitch. I haven't pitched more than two innings this year." I said okay.

A week later we were starting some indoor pitching classes. I asked if he wanted to come and throw with some of the guys, and he said yes.

He threw for two weeks and there was a world of difference.

He didn't need a pitching "guru" or a high paid instructor.

He needed someone to spend just a little time with him to "fix" his pitching mechanics. Not "break him down and start all over" (although I could have used those words and I'm sure his dad and him would have bought off on it), but just show him a few basic things.

When he went into the very first part of his wind up, he was twisting and turning his whole body backward. Because of this, he was forcing himself to throw "around his body." He not only was twisting badly backwards, but his leg was not tucked near his body and was "flailing" out. When he attempted to come forward toward the plate, he could not bring his right leg around enough and it was landing about two feet to the left of where it should have been landing. He was throwing against his body, instead of with his body. Although he had a very smooth fluid motion, the mechanics were terrible.

That scenario would have had some instructors absolutely salivating. That had big bucks written all over it. I mean, his high school team who would play together the following summer had basically already told him that, "We're not interested in you playing with us." He was messed up and probably short on confidence. This was ripe for the taking.

I can just hear it;

"You really have a lot of problems. I think with a lot of work I can get things fixed, but I will need to break you down and start all over."

What the young man needed was for someone to tell him the obvious. Any coach should have been able to help him with his basic mechanics issue.

I relayed to him the basics. He was then instructed to go home and practice what was related to him. His dad also told him to practice the obvious.

He went home and practiced. He came back the next week and was doing better. I worked with him a little more and forced him to not twist his body when he started his wind up, to keep the leg more tucked in, and to land approximately two feet further to the right so his body was square with the plate and he was not throwing against and around his body.

There was probably a total of one hour to correct about 90% of his problems. At this point in time, an instructor would have been fine, but what he really needed was a coach who would engrain this information into him every time he pitched and would work with him on a continual basis.

In one hour he graduated.

No charge.

Most players do not need to be paying lots of money to instructors. Where are their coaches? Where are their high school coaches, and summer coaches, and youth coaches? Didn't they work with them during the season?

I know this sounds really far fetched, but let me give this a try.

How about the teammates?

I know that may sound crazy, but back in the day that's how we did it. When one of our teammates wasn't hitting well, we worked with him. We helped him. He helped us. We watched each others swings. We understood hitting. As pitchers we worked with each other, talking about using your legs to push off, balance, where to land. We helped each other with pitches, location, and movement on the ball. We were forced to understand pitching, not throwing. Coach Spellman actually made all of us instructors. It didn't usually get that far, though, because Coach Spellman straightened us out first. After working with him, the high school coach, it would have been silly to go anywhere else. He knew as much as anybody.

Why aren't high school coaches doing this now? Why can't a player play in the spring for the high school, then take what he has learned there into his summer league? Shouldn't a high school baseball coach have as much knowledge as one of these instructors? If all a player is doing is taking the high school coaches instruction and using it in the summer, then why the additional instructor? Are we saying that high school coaches do not have the knowledge to instruct, or is it that they do not have the commitment to instruct? Neither answer is real good.

So your high school coach, for whatever reason, is not giving you everything you need in terms of hitting or pitching help. You turn to an instructor. I'm not saying that instructors aren't fair and ethical people, but what you have created is a situation where an instructor's motivation is not to cure you but to perhaps string you out. I know that doesn't sound good, but he gets paid every time you go back to him. He doesn't get paid if you graduate.

You may say, "No that's not true, his incentive is to improve everyone because that's how he gets referred to other customers."

I will say to you, bull crap. I've seen players go to instructors for YEARS, week after week, and the parents love the instructor. The instructor obviously loves the parent. They feel comfortable with him. They feel he really cares about the player. Maybe he does.

In general, we as parents do not have high enough expectations for instructors.

Let's take the following example.

If you wanted to do work on your house to improve it some way, you may need the expertise of a contractor. This person may know best what changes were necessary to do to improve your house. You may even give the contractor carte blanche, or free reign, in terms of ideas for your house. But even in giving a contractor complete freedom in ideas, would you ever let that contractor start work in your house not knowing how long the job would be and what the total price would be? Would you allow a contactor to say to you, "I'll just get started and I'll bill you every week, and every week I'll tell you that there is improvement in your house, but I may never finish your house because there is always improvement that can be made. Just keep paying me money and I'll keep coming back to your house. And, oh by the way, your house is really looking better."

Of course you would never have that conversation with a contractor.

Then why would you let an instructor do that to you? I understand that it may be difficult to know what improvement that player will make and how long it will be, but shouldn't an instructor tell a parent up front what the expectations are, and if that instructor can not get the player to those levels, then perhaps he (instructor) isn't being effective, and perhaps classes should terminate if improvement isn't being made.

Why would you reward someone who is ineffective?

Parents should be instructors.

Coaches should be instructors.

Teammates should be instructors.

None of that costs any money.

If all fails, then find someone who will give you a free hour and a real strategy with goals and time lines.

That's a true instructor.

Find someone like Butch Adams.

I had the pleasure of coaching against Butch for a couple of years when our teams competed against each other in the Baltimore Metro League. His team, the Westminster Titans, was always well coached and well prepared, just not well talented. When we played them we won but coaching had very little to do with our victories. We just had ball players with more talent. Butch always got the most out of his kids. You could see him talking to the players as they came off the field, explaining in detail why something did or didn't work. He seemed to be big with fundamentals and discipline and continuously encouraged the players to give a complete effort.

A couple of years ago, we went our separate ways. When I started writing this book, I contacted him, asking him for some assistance and input. That is when I found out that he started working with younger kids, like he had done years before. This time he started giving lessons. When he e-mailed me to tell me how he approached kids as an instructor, I was once again given hope that there are people out there with the right motivation. His e-mail is shown below and I have been tempted many times in the last few months to forward this e-mail to every instructor I know. Some of them have the same thought process, but very few.

"I started doing it for money last year (2005). I had three fathers who insisted on paying me. A couple of well-known instructors in the area were doing it for $40-$45 a half an hour. The fathers said that they would pay that but I couldn't accept that. I suggested $20 a half hour and we settled on $25.

I laid out ground rules from the start. Don't come here unless you want to work on getting better and give me 100% focus for each session. I always gave "homework assignments" and always asked for recaps of our previous lessons. I gave them a timetable on what we would do and about how long it would take to get there (about 8-10 sessions). We would not go into their season. Once their teams were practicing outside, we would be done. I can't see trying to work on a player's swing while they are in their season. Breaking down and correcting problems should be done in the off-season and should have a stopping point. I have a different philosophy working with kids during the season. A major overhaul of their swing or pitching mechanics can only be done when you can control all of their opportunities for reinforcement. They will go back to the way they were doing it before unless you control that.

I basically have three phases of hitting I like to work on. I let them know when they will complete each phase and ask if they want to continue on to the next phase. I think parent's expectations are too high. We live in a generation that believes that money is the key. Everything can be had if you have money. Parents will seek the easy way out to get what they, or their kids, want. And above all, they have an out. If their kid is not the next Cal Ripken, they have someone to blame. It's never their fault if the kid is a lousy ball player; it's the people who coach him. That's why I ask for control of their mechanics when we first start. If they continue to throw from their hip, or won't keep their hands above the ball, then I say they will never be a successful ballplayer. There are places they can continue to play the game and have fun, but they will never be able to go to the next level of competition if they continue with these basic flaws. I have always invited my parents to attend my practices to help reinforce what we work on. They spend more time with their kids than I do. I say the same thing about their coaches. Bottom line is to agree to work on what benefits the player.

My biggest reason for starting private instructions is these kids need help at the younger levels. I'm finding it harder to work with 14, 15, and 16 year old kids because they are too head strong about changes. They are convinced that they were stars in their local recreation leagues, and that is enough. They are the ones who are most crushed when they don't make a high school team. I'm trying to give the 10, 11, and 12 yr. old kids a good foundation and a better chance to play high school ball. In my seven years of coaching high school, it still amazed me that every year, a left-handed kid would try out for middle infield. Somebody has to be honest with these kids a lot earlier in their careers. I guess I nominated myself to be one of these people."

More good baseball people like Butch need to nominate themselves to be good instructors and coaches. Can you imagine how much better it would be for all these kids if every instructor approached lessons in this manner? I can't find one thing wrong with what he says.

My own son has never gone to an instructor, at least on an ongoing basis. He has had a few fielding lessons, a few hitting lessons, and yes, has attended a few seminars on pitching. Along with this, he has gone to a few camps and workouts. He's not, however, been the recipient of a group of lessons from an instructor. He has never shown the interest to have lessons, and I have never had the interest to provide him lessons. He is now seventeen and I do believe that all the lessons in the world would not have made him a better pitcher than he is right now.

His lessons have occurred on the ball field. I have coached him for a few years now, and when I didn't coach him, I watched his ball games. I always looked at his baseball journey as just that, a long journey. I never was interested in him being the star or the best pitcher. I always was interested in the end result. When he was young, I was concerned with high school and what abilities he would need to play high school ball. When he entered ninth grade my concern was varsity, and when he became a junior in high school, my focus was on college. What does he need to do to make the step to the next level? I really have never thought much about where he was, always looking at where he was going.

He always was a pitcher who had to depend on location and change of speed. He did not have the physical ability to throw the ball terribly hard. Therefore, very early in his career he learned to pitch, not throw. He had to, he had no choice. If he just threw, he would have been clobbered every game. So he learned to change speeds, change pitches, move the ball around, come up with another pitch. He had to learn early to be mentally tough. He was not a strike out pitcher so he had to depend a lot on his defense. He needed to deal with errors more than those power pitchers who could strike out a bunch of batters.

As I coached him and worked with him, it was apparent to me that I was no different than any other dad. Kids will listen to their dads last. They will listen to anyone else before they will take the advice of their dad. What does a dad know? As a young kid, if it ever impressed Eric that I was a pretty good pitcher in my day, he did not disclose that information to me. He didn't want my advice and didn't mind showing me that I really couldn't help him with his pitching.

I would give him advice and he would not listen. It would not work his way and I would be more than happy to communicate that fact to him. I was right. In the early years of his development I was finding myself being right a lot. It made me feel pretty good being right so much. Man, I must still have it! Look at me; I'm helping my kid be a better ball player, look how often I'm right! I know so much, I'm so good at baseball!

It took me a while to, as my son now tells me, "Get over [myself]." I was so impressed with me, that I hadn't realized that I was not helping my son. I was being right, but certainly not effective.

It took a long time to learn how to be effective. I'm still working at it… every day. I still struggle tremendously with being effective, but the one thing that I feel I have improved upon is the fact that I now understand how important it is to be effective. Being right does nothing more than stroke your personal ego. Every coach, every person, struggles with being effective. It takes a lot of hard work to improve in this area.

I've improved.

I stopped worrying about being right.

I came to realize that being right is so little of the whole equation. Naturally, you can't be effective by not knowing what you're talking about but it's what you do with that information and how you communicate it that's important. A lot of it is psychology. A lot of it is motivation. A lot of it is hard work. I've learned through the coaching process to use all the tools at my disposal to be effective. You need to understand that each individual is unique and therefore is motivated by different things. Sometimes, complete opposite strategies need to be used to get the desired results from each ball player. I worked hard to be effective with my son and I do think that I have made good progress. There's no right recipe, just a lot of perseverance.

While I waited for my 18-u team to finish their high school season this past year and play in the summer, I coached a 14-u team. We had a practice one night and my plan, or goal, for that particular evening was to be effective. We still hit and fielded and threw like any other get-together, but I wanted to incorporate some of the mental game into the work out. I had no idea how I was going to do this but I figured it would come to me.

It did.

We were just about finished with batting practice as the last batter had started taking his swings. All other players were out in the field. I called three of them in by name. They jogged in and now out of breath, were standing in front of me with gloves in hand. They were waiting for instructions. The fact that they ran in the whole way meant that perhaps effectiveness was already present in some capacity. I pointed at a yellow pole across the complex which was about 500 feet away. I then said to them, "Do you see that pole?"

They all looked at the pole and then looked at me, nodding their heads.

I said nothing else. For a few seconds there was silence, only the noise of them still panting from their sprint. Finally, one of the players said, "Do you want us to run to the pole?"

I told them, "That would be nice."

The three players, almost in unison, threw down their gloves and started toward the destination.

As they took off toward the pole, I then called three other players in by name. They, too, hustled in and were standing in front of me. This time, I simply looked at the pole. All three of them threw down their gloves and start running.

I looked at the four or five fathers standing next to me, and said, "Let's have some fun."

Without another word being said, they all started to laugh. One father was getting more of a kick out of this than the others. He didn't know what was coming next; only that something was coming. Since he is not only a father, but also a motivational speaker by trade, I was glad he was standing beside me. He would have without a doubt been much better at finishing the project that I had started, but he just stood and took in the adventure. Over the last couple of months, I had talked to him and taken in his professional wisdom. He talks to large companies on a regular basis about leadership, teamwork, and management, and yes, effectiveness. That's what it's really all about; being effective. I have had lunch with him several times and had no real objective other than to pick up some nuggets of information and possibly learn something, anything, which would help me be a better coach. You need to learn something every day. I was glad he was there.

The first three runners now had arrived back.

I asked all three of them if they gave a full effort in their running to the pole and back. With slight nods of their heads, they all acknowledged that they indeed gave their best. After approximately 30 seconds of conversation with them, I had convinced all of them that they had not. I may have also suggested that they could do it again much more effectively.

One of the players then asked, "Do you want us to do it again?"

I answered him with a question, "Do you think you should do it again?"

Off they went on their second run to the pole.

At this time the other eight kids had just finished with the batting practice and came jogging into the area in which I was standing. They were awaiting further instructions.

I said nothing and only stared back at them.

A few seconds elapsed, and almost in unison, they dropped their gloves and began the run to the pole.

The second group had now come back, and I guess seeing that the first group was running again, decided that they also should repeat the process. Off they went. Everybody was running yet no one was really instructed to take on the task.

The first three players now were arriving back, and they have now run to the pole twice. This time they ran in faster and were breathing a lot harder.

I focused in on the same player that I had asked the initial question about quality of effort in the first sprint. I asked once again, "Did you give a full effort this time?"

"Yes sir" he answered with a slight smile, while still breathing heavily.

"Are you sure," I asked again.

He again answered with the same strong conviction, "Yes sir."

I looked at the father next to me, the motivational speaker, the individual who I am quite sure could have taught an even better lesson than I was about to attempt. He could hardly look at me, obviously afraid of laughing out loud. He didn't know what I was about to say but he certainly knew that a lesson was about to occur.

He was right.

"Okay, if you feel that was the best you could do that's great, but I have a $10.00 bill in my pocket."

The boy's immediate response, "I think I can do better."

All parents laughed in unison, a few saying that *they* would be willing to run for the ten dollars.

No, I don't think that the best way to motivate young kids to do better is to put money in front of their face and no, that probably wasn't the most effective way to inspire that boy to react in a way that he did.

It doesn't matter.

The point was that everyone can be motivated under the right circumstances. Anyone can be more effective with people under the right conditions. There is a thousand ways to be more effective. Some involve the proper motivation. Some involve trust. Some involve respect. Some just involve not caring about being right, but instead being selfless.

It's not even important that another boy immediately said that he would race him for the $10.00 and that the original boy did in fact run again and did win the $10.00.

He would have run again for nothing.

Find your child a coach ...a really good coach. Instead of looking for the guy who has all the answers and is always right find someone who would rather be effective.

CHAPTER 8

THE MOST IMPORTANT PLAY IN BASEBALL

"The idea of coming together – we're still not good at that in this country. We talk about it a lot. Some politicians call it "family." In moments of crisis we're magnificent at it – the Depression, Franklin Roosevelt lifting himself from his wheelchair to lift this nation from its knees. At those moments we understand community-helping one another.

In baseball, you do that all the time.

You can't win it alone. You can be the best pitcher in baseball, but somebody has to get you a run to win the game. It is a community activity. You need all nine people helping one another.

I love bunt plays.

I love the idea of the bunt.

I love the idea of the sacrifice.

Even the word is good. Giving yourself up for the good of the whole. That's Jeremiah. That's thousands of years of sacrifice. You find your own good in the good of the whole. You'll find your own individual fulfillment in the success of the community – the Bible tried to teach you that and didn't teach you.

Baseball did."

—Mario Cuomo

Here's a man who is known throughout the world and he compares the world, the country, and the community to baseball and specifically to the bunt.

If you're under forty years old, it would be very difficult to appreciate how these few words carry so much passion. I'm just guessing, but although his words may say bunt, his message is much bigger, much deeper. It's everything that the bunt represents.

When you turn on ESPN and watch baseball highlights, you may go a month before you ever see a bunt. Home runs, strike outs,

diving catches, fights on the field, arguments with umpires.......
You will see all of that.

Where are the bunts?

That's kind of a rhetorical question as we all know that a bunt is not considered a meaningful part of the game anymore. It used to be important.

But those days are gone.

The most important play in baseball hardly has a life. No one wants to see someone bunt anymore. Hit a home run, yes. Even strike out, absolutely. Bunting is boring. Bunting doesn't sell tickets. We all want to see the 9-8 game, not the 2-1 game. We all want to see more offense and less defense.

Baseball, like most other sports, has changed its game to get more offense, to be more "fan-pleasing." You can blame Don Drysdale, Bob Gibson, and Sandy Koufax in the 60's for having the mound lowered. Then you had the live ball, followed by the smaller parks, and then unfortunately the steroids. Everything was changed to make the average fan happy. ESPN and BASEBALL TONIGHT is where the kids go now. The all-star game has a completely different night for a home run derby.

Could you imagine setting aside a completely different night, televised to tens of millions of people, for a bunting contest? Wouldn't that be exciting? Wouldn't we all like to see Barry Bonds square up, bend his knees, and place the bat in front of him to bunt a ball? Nowadays, you give a kid the bunt sign and he stands there and literally lets you know of his disappointment that he doesn't get to hit away. He's too good to bunt; it's just not fair to make him bunt!

Bunting used to be exciting. It used to be fun. Players and coaches bought into the fact that this was the ultimate play, the act of sacrificing for your team and teammate. Now kids don't even know how to bunt. How can that be? How can kids go through years and years of baseball and not have a clue on how to bunt a ball?

I've tried to understand the reasons why we have disrespected the game of baseball so much by practically eliminating the use of the bunt. How we have taken the simplest, most fun, purest, most team building action in baseball and turned it in to nothing more than a necessary evil, something only attempted under dire circumstances. I've tried to understand how men with 30 and 40 years of baseball knowledge and experience could literally eliminate the one play that is the basic fabric of the game. I've tried to understand how we arrived at where we are now.

I've asked countless parents and coaches where the bunt has gone. No one seems to have the answer. Every one acts as though they are the victims, not the cause. This spring I got involved with coaching a new baseball team at the 14-u age group. They were all new to our organization and I thought I would be helpful by going over some basic information regarding the game of baseball at Gambrills. I e-mailed some information to the parents about bunting and asked them to respond if they had any questions.

One mother responded to my email in the following manner.

"Jeff, I have forwarded the article about bunting to Joey (her son). I am sure he will read it as well. I don't believe he has ever bunted."

I e-mailed her back and said simply, "He's never bunted!"

She e-mailed me back about an hour later and said, "No, he's never bunted, but he says he will try it."

He's 14 years old and has played in a baseball program for five years, and he has never bunted a ball.

Who's to blame?

Let's lay some of this blame on the "system." I'm not sure how the system became what it is today...that would take forever to figure out, but it's here and it isn't going anywhere. Like a lot of other things, I have a feeling that the system is driven by money and power and ego. So what does all of this have to do with the bunt?

Let me explain.

Hundreds of thousands of kids in the country show up every year early in the spring at high schools for the first day of baseball tryouts. Some schools are earlier, but this date is pretty set in a lot of places. It's circled on each coach's and player's calendar. It's THE Day, excitement aplenty. All the kids show up with high expectations.

It's lots of kids and very little time.

There is little time because when that hallowed day arrives, the best a coach can hope for is something dry and warm. You can be assured that it won't be warm, but if it could just be a little dry, we could at least get out in the parking lot and throw the ball around. Even if it isn't raining on this day, you know it has been raining sometime in the last few days; hence the ground is wet and soggy. It is usually cold and rainy. A few inches of snow are not out of the question. The field is usually not in shape for baseball. Bottom line, it's a mess and all one can do is their very best.

All these kids are trying to do is make a team and impress the coach. Time is critical because there just isn't much of it. Games will be starting in a couple of weeks and we haven't had the first practice. There could be anywhere from 25 to 100 kids, depending on the quality of the program at that particular school.

What's a coach to do? How does he sort this out in the limited amount of time that he has?

So the coaches do what they can to sort the players out as quickly and efficiently as possible. Again, there are lots of kids and very little time.

Most of the coaches focus on three things:

how fast he is.

how strong he is.

how hard can he throw a ball.

By doing these three things, coaches have, in their minds, pinpointed the best athletes or the players with the most potential. It must be considered an effective tool because most coaches do this. I would imagine it separates the kids as quickly and efficiently as possible, determining skill levels in the quickest possible time.

The coaches will work these kids out the first few weeks, primarily inside. If good weather occurs, that's great. If not, and that's usually the case, they revert back to their contingency plan.

There is lots of batting practice, lots of throwing, and lots of running. That's how it's done.

You could go weeks and weeks and never hear the word bunt. If you do hear that word, it's usually the obligatory "Bunt one" before you hit away. When the team finally gets out on the field, there is so much to do! Again, bunting isn't one of those things. It is a lost art. It is gone. It is not important to anyone.

High school baseball is only a microcosm of all youth baseball.

Now, let's go backwards for a moment.

High schools want to see you throw, run, and lift weight in their tryouts. That's how one gets graded. That is how one may make a team or be cut. At my son's high school, he was graded in this manner. As a freshman he graded out terrible and as a sophomore a little better. He was still small compared to most other players. Weight lifting was far from his mind.

Everybody knows the system. Summer league coaches, little league coaches, instructors, parents, and yes, the kids all know that their future on a high school team will probably hinge on how well they do these three things.

That is ingrained in everyone's mind. When you get to high school, sometimes at the raw age of 13, you need to be fast, strong, and throw hard to be noticed.

A player doesn't need to know how to bunt. A player could be the next Rod Carew with a bat, coaches would never know or care.

Run a 6.9 sixty yard dash or bench press 265 lbs., that's enough.

So now we're back with the 10 year old kid who loves baseball and obviously is looking forward to high school baseball. Believe it or not, that little 10-year-old boy will be in ninth grade in three years.

Sadly, it's not that far away. He needs to get ready for the future. Hit the ball far, throw the ball hard, and run fast. Therefore, why would a coach of 10 year old boys teach bunting or spend any time on bunting, if when the player gets to high school, it has no value? Everybody seems to be on the same page. Unfortunately, it's just the wrong page.

High school coaches are sending terrible, terrible messages to youth baseball players and their parents.

The high school coaches who bemoan the fact that 80% of the kids coming in to high school aren't prepared for high school ball because they haven't been taught the proper fundamental of baseball, are in a way the problem. They complain about kids not having a clue about how to really play the game, but they are the ones sending the wrong message. They are the ones saying," Be big and strong and fast, we'll mold you into a good ball player if you have the basic athletic abilities" That's the primary message being sent. Go to a high school tryout and see how many coaches are grading the kids on fundamentals. They don't have time for that, there is too many other things to do. So although the high school coach is in complete dismay that so many kids aren't taught the basic skills, they (the coaches) are the ones who are sending the wrong message.

Like how to bunt.

That message basically says fundamentals would be nice, but they are secondary. Your kid's good fundamentals will only be looked at if he gets through the first stage of being graded on the "BIG THREE." Youth coaches are vilified by people for not teaching the proper fundamentals of baseball. And in a lot of cases, this is justified. There are some really bad coaches out there.

But look at the message they are being sent. Kids 10 and 11 years old are being "gunned" to see how fast they throw. Kids are going out for ten year old "travel teams" with a stopwatch on them. Seeing who can bunt, among other things, is not a priority. Therefore precious time is not wasted on it. There are other things a lot more important.

Because kids can't bunt by the time they get to high school, it's really too late to teach them. There are too many other important things to teach. The high school coach is aggravated that the player can't bunt. A lot of high school coaches do not like to bunt anyway, so you add to that fact that the kids can't bunt, there's no incentive to bunt.

One can see why it has become a lost art. Why try to bunt in a game if you're giving up an out AND there's a good chance it won't be successful? If a kid hasn't learned to bunt by the time he is 14, why should I try to teach him now? Someone didn't teach him the fundamentals!

You may say, "So what, what's the big deal?"

The fact is that the actual act of bunting isn't the only thing that is so important here.

It's what it represents.

Bunting represents basics, fundamentals, work ethic, and sacrifice. It represents what used to make baseball fun and team building. Bunting represents hustle and base stealing and backing up and cut offs and everything else that used to be the core of a baseball player.

Coaches used to look for these qualities first in a ball player; the power and speed only complimented the basic core skills. Now it has flipped-flopped. The core values and work ethic and hustle and passion for the game are only used to compliment the player with the God given ability. Bunting is a microcosm of baseball. It is a microcosm of life. It is the very heart of what baseball used to represent. Now it's considered a nuisance, something you do at certain times because you basically have no choice.

You will hear coaches say, "All a bunt does is giving up an out, why should I give up an out? So the coach doesn't give up an out. But then when that coach really needs a bunt, that kid can't execute. So he tries to bunt, unsuccessfully, and the coach ends up giving up an out anyway. But now he gives up an out and he DIDN'T advance the runner. A bunt usually occurs in a really important part of the game and is usually important to the outcome of the game.

And that's when we're going to practice bunting!

Two years ago, my son's high school accumulated a record of 15-1 in their county league. The bunt may have made them perfect. One year ago, basically the same team accumulated a 16-0 record in the county. The bunt may have cost them the state title.

But why bunt?

There only loss in the county play in the 2006 season was to Northeast High School. They were playing at Northeast. The game went into extra innings. In the top of the eighth inning, Arundel got the lead off batter on base. Up came the next batter who I believe was hitting sixth in the line up, probably a fairly good bunt situation. I know Arundel, like most teams, don't like to bunt: especially in obvious situations. They tend to bunt more out of the element of surprise. They don't believe too much in bunting and giving up an out. In general, when they bunt, they're looking for base runners to be safe.

Well, here we were. Bunt situation, but a predictable bunt situation. I didn't think they are going to bunt. It's fun to be "Joe the fan" and get to watch and guess and then ultimately second guess the coach. We all do it, whether it is on TV or at a local high school game. Everybody is good at that, including me. We're all perfect "Monday morning quarterbacks."

I looked at a player's father who is standing beside me and said, "You know, he really should bunt." He managed a very small smile on his face. We had been through this a hundred times at games, talking out loud about this play or that play. This time, I got the smile, the look. I also knew what the smile represented. "Yes Jeff, I agree, but no Jeff, he probably won't bunt" is what it meant. We communicated a lot by not saying anything. We've known each other for a few years and we love talking baseball, even if it's in silence sometimes. Both of our heads now pointed forward to the field.

The first pitch came in.

The batter swung away and hit a perfect one hopper to the shortstop that had double play written all over it, but the shortstop bobbled the ball and everyone was safe. The father then looked at me and gave me that look, that "I'd rather be lucky than good" look. The bunt was the play, but it didn't happen.

Who cares, we had two runners on and nobody out. This was really cool. It worked out. The fans were happy. Most of them didn't have a clue.

Okay, now we had runners on first and second base and nobody out and the seventh batter was up to hit. Under normal circumstances with a normal team a bunt was called for. Surely they would now bunt and move both batters up. They certainly wouldn't go against the odds again and hit away. Another conversation took place between me and the father. We get to second-guess the coach again. We were good at this.

"Bunt?" I say to him.

He looks back and says, "Yeah, he's got to… doesn't he?"

We both laughed. We were laughing because we were lucky to see five bunts a year. We knew he doesn't have to bunt and probably wouldn't.

Our heads were once again facing the field.

The first pitch came in.

The batter swung and fouled the ball off. We're now both chuckling, knowing that we figured all along a bunt wasn't coming. The batter fought the good fight, but four pitches later he went down on strikes. There was never an attempt to bunt the ball. The father looked at me and just shook his head. I asked him once again sarcastically, "Is there a rule that bunting isn't allowed anymore? We both laughed once again. The next batter hit a sharp grounder to the left side of the second baseman who made a nice play to get a force at second.

Now, if there would have been a successful bunt, they would have had runners on second and third, the infield would have been playing up and the ball probably would have got through for two runs. That didn't happen, however, and now they had runners at first and third with two outs. Well, maybe they will put a play on to get the runner home. Maybe they will steal second or get in a run down or something. Nope.

The next batter grounded out.

No runs, no hits, no bunts.

Northeast came up in the bottom of the eighth and won the game on a passed ball. They were that close to a perfect record in the county.

But why bunt?

In the first round of the 2007 high school state playoffs, after compiling that perfect county record, the team saw themselves down 1-0 in the bottom of the seventh and final inning. The first batter, the fifth batter in the line up, walked to lead off the inning. As like the year before, we now had a bunt situation. We fans were all once again wondering what the coach would do. Bunt, or hit away? We never got the chance to know as the next batter was walked on four straight pitches. We now have runners on first and second base, nobody out, and down one run. Surely we will bunt!

The instructions were given to the next batter. He was told to take a strike. Then, once he took a strike, he was to bunt. It sounded like a strategy that some coaches may have taken, considering the fact that the pitcher just walked both men he faced in this inning.

There was a little problem with this strategy however. If the batter took a strike, and it's well known that you do not bunt with two strikes, he was only going to get one opportunity to put that very critical bunt down to advance the runners. The total amount of times that this particular batter was asked to bunt all year was zero. He was never asked to bunt before this particular moment in time. Now remember back to the bunt, and its insignificance in most high school coach's play book. Lots of coaches, including this coach, don't put much emphasis on the bunt, and therefore don't practice it very often. So this player was asked to do something he hasn't done all year, in the most crucial moment of the year, and it's not practiced, and we're going to make it twice as hard on him by taking a strike away from him.

Well, maybe the opposing pitcher will walk another guy! Then it would have been a good strategy. Unfortunately, he didn't throw four more balls. He threw a strike and the batter, as was instructed, took the pitch. Now he got that one chance to do something that before today wasn't important. Now, it was crucial and the pressure was on. The pitch came in, it was a strike and the batter failed to execute a bunt. Now the coach was screaming from the dugout, "Hit the ball, hit the ball." The batter, with two strikes on him and all the pressure in the world upon his shoulders, struck out.

Now, with the runners not advanced, there is no choice but to hit away. The next two batters do just that, but unfortunately ball never meets bat, and the pitcher ends up striking out the side and preserving that 1-0 victory.

But why bunt?

Earlier that spring, I had been down to the teams practice one afternoon. The head coach had huddled the players around home plate and proceeded to talk about bunting. He now had my attention as I wanted to hear for myself his thoughts on what I consider the most important play in baseball. I would finally hear for myself perhaps the logic in not bunting.

The coach explained to the players how as a young ball player he was a very good bunter. He bunted so well that his coach called on him to do this feat quite often. Matter of fact, more often than he really felt was necessary. He approached his coach and asked him why he had to bunt so often.

The coach replied that he asked him to bunt so often because he did it so well. This coach then said something to all of his players that to this day I can't really believe was uttered. His words were, "From that point forward, I became a poor bunter."

Yes, he just told 30 kids that he was an excellent bunter, but because the coach asked him to bunt more then HE wanted to, then HE decided that He would do what was best for HIM and not what was best for his team.

What a great lesson to teach your kids!!!

Pretend you can't bunt so you get to hit away more often. Don't be a good teammate. Do what's best for you, not the team.

And two months later, in the most important game of the year, at the most important time of the game, this same individual is screaming at a kid that couldn't put down a bunt!

At one of the practices for my summer baseball team we were working on bunting. At the time, it was a very good 16-u baseball team playing against mostly 18-year-old teams. It was immediately obvious to me that the work was necessary. I grabbed a bat and demonstrated how to put down a sacrifice bunt; square up, bend the knees, slide the hand down on the bat, and loosely hold the bat in your hand. I even showed them how to deaden the ball when and if necessary.

It didn't take long for one of the players to straighten me out.

"That's not how we do it Coach he said "We're not taught to square up."

I knew that.

Trying to act as confused as I possibly could, I asked, "So what are you taught to do?"

The player took the bat and demonstrated the proper way to bunt.

He stood at the plate and did his little half turn of the body that really looked so much more professional than the archaic squaring up that I displayed. Some of the other players nodded their head in agreement. A few mumbled, "Yeah that's what we were shown."

Others said that they were never shown anything.

I'm sure it was the proper way and I know people a lot smarter than me come up with this stuff, these changes in bunting techniques and styles. I know you don't square up the body anymore. Instead, you kind of just turn your body a little and kind of bend your knees. It really does looks nice and my player did a great job of exhibiting it. It looked great and he looked professional.

It just doesn't work.

All I know is that I had 15 guys on the summer team. Four of them could really bunt well and they squared up. None of the other guys could consistently bunt and they didn't square up. I guess my question would be;

When the high school coaches taught these kids the modern way of bunting that looked so much nicer did they bother to see if it was effective?

I noticed a couple of problems.

First of all players presently usually aren't taught the difference between bunting for a hit and bunting for a sacrifice. They kind of try to do both and end up doing neither. It's awful. No one has really sat down with them and explained to them what to do in what situation. Because they are given the bunt so seldom, they just assume that they are to just get the ball down somewhere. Most players said they were never shown, even in high school, different ways to bunt for different situations.

It was just a bunt.

Secondly, players don't want to bunt. They don't like to bunt. They don't see the significance to bunting. They don't practice bunting. How can you possibly be successful doing something with that many things going against you?

Two summers ago there were 92 bunt signals given to my hitters (Yeah, I really do track this stuff). Of the 92 signals, 16 signals were completely missed by the batter. Of the 76 remaining "situations," 18 bunts were not attempted because the pitch was a ball; but 14 times the hitter did not attempt to bunt it and it was called a strike (back to this in a moment). That left 44 actual attempts to bunt a ball and out of these 44 attempts, 16 bunts were put down success-fully to advance the runner. Eight additional bunts went for base hits. Twenty times it was unsuccessful. The fourteen times that the player made no attempt to bunt a called strike was because fourteen times he gave up on the pitch. Just gave up on it. One of the reasons that I believe that batters give up on a pitch is the fact that they are only turning their body a little, their head never goes toward the ball and therefore their perception of the pitch is not up close. They just give up on the pitch altogether, especially curve balls. If you square up, and bend your knees, and bring your eyes down to the ball, it will be successful more often. On a sacrifice, who cares if you square up and have less chance of beating out the bunt?

It is a SACRIFICE. You are SACRIFICING yourself. What hap-pens to you personally is secondary. Remember, it's supposed to be about the team.

Another problem is, especially for a left-handed hitter, bunting in this manner does not protect the runner. When a left-hander at-tempts to bunt like this and misses, he leaves the runner wide open to be picked off. When a left-handed batter squares around and missed the pitch, his body blocks the vision that the catcher has of the runner and helps protect him.

Nothing infuriates me more than watching poor execution of the art of bunting. A couple of years ago, my team was in a close game against an excellent team in State College, Pa. We were trail-ing 4-3 in the sixth inning. The lead off hitter got on and I realized that the next batter couldn't bunt. I've asked him to bunt four times during the season, unsuccessful every time.

So what do I do?

Do I say, "Well, he can't bunt, so why ask him to try?" Or do I say, "Play the game the way it's supposed to be played, it's a bunt situation, so bunt." Or do I say basically, "I want to win and I don't think he can put down a bunt, so the best scenario is to hit away." Or do I say, "Damn it, he needs to learn and if it costs us a run, or even a game, for him to learn, then that's the lesson we're all going to learn out here today on the field." I guess we're getting back to that winning vs. developing thing. That's a lot of stuff to think about in ten seconds.

I thought it over and gave him the bunt sign. He popped it foul. Strike one.

Now, if the other team had any doubt that he may bunt, they don't now. Here comes the third baseman in about ten more feet. Forget any element of surprise. Now what do you do? He doesn't know how to bunt! To make matters worse, he's not real fast. So a grounder to the infield is a good chance of a double play. We couldn't afford that. Man, I'm screwed!! In the next six seconds, I needed to make a decision. He was going to be looking down at me and he would be looking for a signal. I'm now pissed off at him, his high school coach, his last summer ball coach, his dad, his hitting instructor, ESPN SPORTS and anyone who has ever written an article about hitting where they didn't give bunting the emphasis it should be given.

To make matters worse, I'm not even confident he will put the bat anywhere on the ball. If I knew he could at least bunt it anywhere fair on the ground, I could send the runner. When you send the runner, a bunt doesn't even have to be good; you just need to get it down. If I sent the runner, though, and he missed the ball, or popped it up, or took a strike (which he has done twice this year before this at bat when given the bunt signal), the runner is a sitting duck. So what do I do?

I gave him the bunt again.

Again he bunted it foul. Now, I'm just frustrated. Part of me in a much distorted way wanted to give him the bunt with two strikes and hoped that he bunted it foul. And he would be out. And he understood that he let the team down. And I don't care about winning this game as much as I care about him having enough motivation to learn to bunt.

Most parents don't get this. They would look at this and say, "Why would he have him bunt with two strikes?" That is stupid, he's no coach, and he doesn't understand what he is doing. Those parents want to win. Who doesn't want to win? Who likes losing? Now once again, I'm mad at everybody. Against my better judgment, I give him the signal to hit away.

He struck out.

That was bad enough, but on his way back to the dugout he kind of gave me this look, "Thanks a lot Coach; you put me in a two strike hole by giving me the stupid bunt sign." He didn't say anything; he just gave me that look. Like it was my fault he couldn't bunt. We ended up not scoring that inning, and we lost the game 4-3. The next batter up that inning got a hit to left field that would have scored the runner if he was sacrificed to second. But he wasn't. With guys on first and second, the next batter hit the ball hard, but right to the shortstop, who turned the double play. It was game, set, match, all because a kid couldn't put down a bunt; all because I was ineffective as a coach.

If a player takes the time to really learn how to bunt, he will do so many other things successfully. That is because bunting is nothing more than hand-eye coordination. Listen to all these instructors talk about everything under the sun and all the impressive drills they know, but nothing in hitting is more important than hand-eye coordination.

Absolutely nothing.

Watch the ball, hit the bat. Bunt the ball. Watch the ball hit the bat. Bunt 500 times and 500 times watch the bat hit the ball. Now take 500 swings, watch the bat hit the ball. Now take 500 grounders, watch the ball go into the glove. Every time, watch the ball go into the glove. When you bunt, you bend your knees and bring your eyes and bat closer to the ball. When you field a grounder, you bend your knees and bring your glove and eyes closer to the ball.

Bunting is the basic drill, basic talent that everything else can be learned from. Have an eight year old kid learn to bunt and bunt correctly, and he will be a better hitter, and a better fielder. He will understand the concept of hand-eye coordination the rest of his life. He'll never lose that. And he'll never learn anything more important in all of his years of playing baseball. He will learn muscle memory, which is absolutely vital. Because of muscle memory he will make the plays more often, he will hit the ball more often, he will lay down a bunt more often, and when he's pitching, he will hit the "black part of the plate" more often. Muscle memory comes from hand-eye coordination, which can be learned the easiest from one simple thing.... the bunt.

Eric did learn to bunt at an early age, and he did it well. We worked on it a lot. It was important to me that he knew how to bunt. In his first couple of years of baseball it did not come in to play much. When Eric moved over to play ball at Gambrills, the coach loved to bunt. That made me happy. The coach would bunt, fake bunt, bunt in all different situations. In a lot of cases, all of this bunting that the team did turned out to be very effective. Eric was one of the better bunters and exhibited very good bat control. This coach had many faults regarding the mental and emotional part of the game, but on the field, he was excellent in making the other teams make plays. In other words, he was always keeping the defense on their toes and forcing them to execute well. In most cases, they did not execute well. That was the effect of the bunt. I enjoyed watching baseball played in this manner. It took me back to when we were kids and the bunt meant something. When I took over the duties of coaching at Gambrills, and coaching my son, the bunt remained a very important part of out arsenal. It wasn't the fact that I wanted to bunt all the time, I just wanted to know that if we needed to bunt, we could. We worked on it a lot, but not enough. Over the years, the failure to put down a bunt cost my teams many games.

When Eric began his high school career at Arundel High School, his ability to bunt meant nothing, nor did the fact that he was well versed in running the bases, playing good defensively, "drawing a walk", getting on base a lot, knowing how to execute a run down or cut off properly, or a multitude of other skills. The ability to pitch, not just throw hard but actually pitch, also had no bearing on the coach's assessment of his value to the team.

What was important to the coach was the fact that he couldn't hit a ball 300 feet or run as fast as most kids. He did not "grade out" high on their rating system and he became known to the coach as "little Eric Potter." From the perspective of high school ball, fundamentals became non important. Bunting became non-existent. As a father and a former baseball player, my initial thoughts of the high school program were ones of shock and disappointment. Once having the opportunity to actually see and understand the workings of the system, my assessment changed. It became TOTALLY shocking and TOTAL disappointment.

Baseball is not the game it once was, but too few seem to care. When push comes to shove, and major league baseball had an opportunity to decide on the integrity of the game or money, they chose money. Steroids were rampant, but with drugs came home runs and fans and excitement and …did I say money?

Every coach should teach kids how to bunt. Every dad should take his kid out to a ball field and make him bunt. Everyone should reinforce the bunt. Communicate the value of the bunt to kids every day, every practice.

It isn't just the bunt that they, and you, will come to appreciate. It is everything it represents. It is what baseball should be all about. It is all the things in baseball, and life, that we've managed to devalue. Hard work, hustle, focus, teamwork are great attributes to have and should have a higher priority with all coaches. It's sad that they don't. It's sad that a lot of coaches have decided to evaluate the kids with a radar gun, stopwatch, and barbell only. That shows no coaching.

Bring back the bunt. Bring back the basics. Bring back the coaches that really get it. Some high school coaches really do get it; most don't.

What I would give to be back in the day!

On the evening of October 13, 2006 I was sitting in my uncle's living room watching a baseball game on TV. It was game two of the National League playoffs pitting the Mets against the Cardinals. Both teams had taken care of business the first round of the play offs and this was to advance to the World Series.

My brother Rich was also there, just the two of us. Yes, the same brother who over forty years ago was on my team the day Pete Sheeler was taught his life lesson, the same day our perfect season came to an end. My Uncle Jim was out in the kitchen going through some papers. He had been out there for a while, but at 86 years of age, I guess everything takes a while. My aunt, his wife, had just passed away four weeks before this. For the first time in 55 years, he was by himself. He probably had a lot of personal papers to go through.

Although I seldom see my brother, when we do get together we have a good time, laugh a lot, and always seem to go back to the good old days. The stories tossed around are generally the same ones, but it doesn't matter.

They're that good.

We tell a story and then laugh. Then we tell another story. Once in a while we actually throw in a new one and occasionally I find out something I didn't know.

On this particular night I asked Rich how his son Davis's high school team did that past spring.

"Not real good, we got knocked out of the playoffs in the first round."

I asked if the coach was pretty good. That's all it took.

"The coach wasn't good at all. These kids don't know the fundamentals of baseball. It's terrible. They don't know how to bunt. I don't know what these coaches are thinking about. I mean a guy on first and second in a close game, nobody out and the bottom of the line up, and he doesn't bunt! I mean, it makes no sense. We lost to a team who just played good fundamental baseball. The other team threw the ball to the right base, put down bunts. No more talent than us. They just did the fundamentals."

Finally, he came up for a breath.

Then he started again.

"They just don't do these things anymore. I remember at Alabama my first year, they brought in this coach who did nothing but work with us with fundamentals, putting down a bunt, coverage's on a bunt, suicide squeeze, sacrifice. We had this play where we were stealing from first, the guy would put down a bunt, and the runner would get to third base. We ran that play a lot."

He takes another breath.

He ends with, "It's just terrible."

At about this time, the Mets had a two run lead in the eighth inning; the score was 6-4. The Cardinals had runners on first and second with two out. Scott Spezio was batting for the Cardinals and Guillermo Mota was pitching for the Mets. The first pitch came in.

Strike one on a nice change up.

The second pitch was thrown.

Strike two on another nice change up.

As I almost always do when watching a good game with someone who appreciates baseball, I started coaching.

I said to my brother, "Where's he going to put this 0-2 pitch?

Rich said with a laugh, "Probably down the middle." Rich is not real impressed with a lot of these major leaguers who are making millions and considers a lot of them "knuckleheads" who really don't know the game. So he really wouldn't be surprised to see a pitch down the middle, the one cardinal rule a pitcher doesn't do with a 0-2 count.

The pitch came in and it was a fastball that was basically grooved. Not right down the middle, but way too good of a 0-2 pitch. Spezio turned on the ball and hit it deep into the right field seats ... foul. If he had not pulled it so much, it would have been a three run homer and a Cardinals lead ... on a 0-2 pitch.

Immediately the catcher went out to the mound. I looked at Rich and said, "Wonder what they're talking about?"

We both laughed.

The pitcher and catcher probably talked for 20 seconds or so. How long does it take to say, "You're an idiot. Don't groove THIS pitch like you grooved the last pitch. You have the batter 0-2. Be smart."

The catcher then left and jogged back to the plate.

I looked at my brother and said, "Where do you think THIS pitch will be?"

He laughed and once again said, "Probably right down the middle."

We both laughed again.

Mota once again went in to his stretch, delivered the ball, and the pitch was RIGHT DOWN THE MIDDLE. Spezio swung and hit a triple high off the right field wall. Two runs scored. Tie game.

This time Rich and I looked at each other and couldn't even manage a laugh. It was far too ridiculous for that. We both just sat there shaking our heads.

Needless to say, the Cardinals, after tying the game in the eight with that triple went on to win the game in the ninth inning. Now the series was tied 1-1. I have no idea how the Cardinals scored in the last inning to win. I quit watching the game after that pitch.

As it turned out, the Cardinals won the series 4 games to 3 to get into the World Series. Perhaps that pitch cost the Mets the league championship.

Maybe, though, it was in the very last inning of the last game in that series. The teams were tied three games each. St. Louis had just hit a two run homer in the top of the ninth inning to take a 3-1 lead. It looked like the Mets were finished, but in the bottom of the ninth the first two hitters singled. We now had the tying runs on the bases with no one out. All we needed to do is move them up in scoring position and have two shots to tie this game. Even the announcers are suggesting that they probably should, may, bunt.

No such luck. The batter struck out and the runners weren't advanced. They end up not scoring.

In the first example, it's not the fact that the pitcher made a mistake. It's the fact that those two pitches were a microcosm of baseball and what has happened. In the second example, it's not the fact that they decided to hit away. It's the fact that fundamentals no longer count. The bunt is a lost art. Perhaps the manager thought he would get a hit. Or maybe, just maybe, the manager never asked this player to bunt all year, and maybe he had very little confidence that he could put down a bunt, and maybe, just maybe, if he knew that million-dollar player could put down a bunt successfully, he would have asked him to. How stupid would he have looked, however, if he asked that player to put down a bunt and he couldn't? They may have still lost, but the whole scenario of having runners at second and third instead of first and second may have changed everything. A base hit would have tied the game then. How can you not bunt in that situation?

I was watching a different game on TV one night last year. One of the teams was Houston; I can't remember the other team. Houston had a runner on second base and after a pitch, the catcher tried to pick the runner off of second. The runner slid back into second base. The ball got past the infielder who was trying to make the tag and the ball went out into centerfield.

I like plays like this. I like to see if any outfielders at this level of play back up the proper way, the way you should be taught at 9 and 10 and 11 years old; the way you should do it from that age until you stop playing baseball. I wanted to see if the outfielder broke toward second base when the pitch went past the batter, just in case the catcher threw down to second. If he didn't do that, he would have at least broken toward second base when he noticed that the catcher appeared to be getting his body in position to throw to second. And at the very least, he would have hustled his million dollar legs toward second base when he saw the ball leave the catchers hand for a possible pick off. I mean there is very little chance that if the ball went toward second that it would end up in centerfield anyway. We have million dollar catchers and million dollar sets of hands by the infielders. The ball will never get into center field. And if the ball does somehow inexplicably end up in center field, surely the base runner will not attempt to go to third.

So I watched. The ball left the catchers hand, and amazingly found its way by the infielder and into centerfield. Now my interest is heightened because the runner was actually going to try for third base. This was going to be great because he was going to run on an outfielder's arm. As he started toward third base, I was watching the television where the picture shows a scan of short center field where the ball is headed.

There was no center fielder yet.

Well, it now appeared that there would not be a play at third base. I guess the center fielder was playing fairly deep and didn't get to the ball quick enough or something like that. The shot now went to the runner approaching third base. He's getting close to the base, but he's not slowing up.

He's rounding third base!!!!!

He's going to try to score. He started down the third base line and never slowed down. There wasn't even a play at the plate.

This wouldn't have happened to Al Shandrowski or Jason Patten or Chris Ball or Eric Potter. They would have been backing up the play. Hopefully, they wouldn't have waited for the ball to be thrown. Once the ball went past the batter, I am sure that they would have taken two quick steps toward second base, like Al did in that game years ago with a 10-0 lead. That way, if there was a play at second, if the catcher did try to make a play on the runner, they would have been in position to back it up. When they then saw the catcher preparing himself to make the throw down to second, they would have continued to run, as fast as they could, to back up the play. That's good baseball. That's teamwork. That's hustle. That's how they were taught.

I don't see that in high school anymore. Outfielders will make moves like they're backing up a play when it is obvious that there will be a play, but I've never seen a high school outfielder back up a play before there's a play. Take those few steps toward the left field line after the ball gets past the batter, BEFORE there is any sign of a play. That's what a good outfielder does.

Now that's seldom taught and obviously not reinforced. I don't think that center fielder came off the field and was "reamed out" by his major league manager. I don't think that these players are held to any high expectations of hustle. What's sad is that hundreds of young boys could have been sitting watching that game with their dads. Probably no one would have noticed that the center fielder wasn't hustling. It's not part of the game anymore. Even when youth coaches attempt to teach this, all you need to do is go to a typical high school game and see that the expectations have been lowered. As the runner went across the plate at that game on TV, the announcer made a comment about the runner's hustle, but never a comment about the fielder's lack of hustle. It's not expected anymore.

The lack of hustle reminded me of a story relayed to me by a friend of a scout. It spoke volumes about the subject.

The strapping young man came out to the on deck circle, swinging two bats fairly effortless. Standing 6'2" and a rock solid 220 lbs, he appeared to be the real deal. It was the first inning and he was the team's #3 hitter. Matter of fact, he had batted third on every team he has played on the last seven or eight years. Now a high school senior, his future looked bright. He would either play baseball for a very good college team, or if things went right, get drafted.

The second batter of the inning hit a fly ball to center field and now there are two outs in the bottom of the first. The lead off hitter had grounded out. Up steps the star hitter. After taking a low and away curve ball, he took a swing at a sweet fastball over the plate. He hit it sharply, but right at the shortstop. The fielded handled the hard two hopper effortlessly and threw the runner out at first. End of the inning and as one team came off the field the home team hustled out to their positions. No real action in this game up to this point.

That is, to the average spectator.

The keen eye of the real baseball fan saw plenty. As the superstar third hitter uncorked the blistering ground ball to shortstop, this real fan did not buy into the comments from some of the parents of how "If we would have got that ball up in the air" it would have been a home run. He was too busy watching something much more important. He realized that the batter must have been thinking the same thing, about the potential of that hit if it would have been airborn. He left the batter's box in a manner more resembling someone out for an afternoon walk, not like a runner with a goal of running down the first base line as fast as he possibly could. As he started down the line, his speed didn't accelerate. Matter of fact, he actually slowed down even before the ball was caught by the first baseman. No fans commented about his seemingly lack of full effort. The coach certainly didn't appear to have a problem with it.

Only one person seemed to have a problem with what happened. Sitting in the bleachers on the third base line, in the midst of several visiting spectators was a middle-aged man who quietly closed the notebook he had sitting in his lap, stood up and headed toward his car. Probably no one had noticed the two trips he had previously made to this high school field in the past. This was his third trip. There would not be a fourth.

The man had one objective that day, to give a final assessment of that hitter who had jogged down the first base line. He was a major league scout. The player was a prospect on their "hit list."

Not anymore.

No one ever found this out; not the player, not the coach, not the player's parents. Nobody. The scout drove 80 miles to the high school to watch a prospect showcase his talents for a total of about five seconds. Then he got in his car and drove back home that 80 miles.

It happens more than just once in a while. This is not a cutesy story to let you know what possibly could happen if you don't hustle. This is real life and this stuff really happens. Years of hard work, time and money can be lost by one jog down a base path, and you'll never know it.

Every time you step out on to a ball field, you need to give a full effort. It doesn't matter how much talent you have, that will only take you so far.

Hustling every play is what baseball used to be. Like the bunt, hustling is a lost art. I would so much love to take a high school baseball team back to 30 years ago and plunk their butts on our high school field and let them practice for a week with Coach. It would only take one player to not hustle one time to get everyone else in line. Let the kids "run the poles" for one practice. Let them look into Coach Spellman's fiery eyes one time. Let them pretend that they were a star player, and therefore special just one time.

Back then you wouldn't dare pull the stuff that happened at my son's school the last few years. It's just not the same now.

Back in the day, when the coach told the players to wear a tie the day of baseball games, you wore a tie. You didn't have the star players snub their nose at the coach over and over by not conforming to the dress code.

When you went on a trip, any trip, you were on time. If you weren't on time, the bus left without you. When you were on time, but not dressed properly, you didn't make the trip. When we had our end of year baseball banquet and were told not to wear jeans, no one dared to challenge the coach.

But I guess times have changed and kids not only challenge coaches now, but they laugh behind their back while doing so. So many things have changed.

Like the bunt.

Please bring it back.

CHAPTER 9

THE PRICE OF SUCCESS

"Progress always involves Risks. You can't steal second base and keep your foot on first."

—Frederick B. Wilcox

I would no longer categorize Eric's ball playing as an experience, it now has the feel of a career. It's not that I necessarily look at him as a professional baseball player some day, but I do see things that are very heartening to me about how he approaches the game of baseball. I see him staying with the game for a long time. Who knows if he will ever have an opportunity to make it to the next level as a player? It's a tough, tough road. There is no doubt, however, that he has the qualities of someday being a good coach. He loves the game of baseball and he treats it with respect. He understands teamwork and why it's important to develop every player on your roster. Most of all, he knows the danger of winning at all costs and life lessons on a ball field seem to have made an impact on him. If he stopped playing ball right now, his journey would have been successful. He would leave baseball having learned so much more than just throwing and hitting a ball. Who knew at this time that just a few months down the road he would learn his biggest life lesson on a ball field, something that would change him forever! Who knew at such a young age that he would confront something, or somebody, so arrogant and shallow that would force him to face the sacrifice needed to be truly successful.

Life has a way of having a beautiful balance. For every success that you encounter, the opportunity for failure, or to be humbled, is lurking around the corner. For every negative person that you encounter, there is opportunity to learn and become stronger. Life gives you chances to learn on a daily basis, to improve yourself as a person no matter what is thrown at you. The baseball field is a beautiful place to learn these lessons and to realize how boundless the gifts of life are.

The price of success is great.

It needs to be or one would never appreciate its value. It's about passion and hard work and respect and selflessness. You need to have all these attributes. As a coach you need to communicate and teach these qualities. As a young baseball player, or youth in general, you need to understand how important these traits truly are. They work together so well. When you do manage to get a hold of all four of these redeeming values, you can navigate the waters so much easier. Then you can have a whole new appreciation of how much time, energy, and effort goes into being successful, and sometimes the sacrifices that need to be made. Nothing in life is easy.

In a nutshell, it's all about risk and reward.

When I was in high school there was always a group of students who smoked. I mean smoked in the school. It was, of course, not allowed, but it happened all the time and there wasn't a whole lot the school could do about it. When I think back to high school and some of the funniest moments, one of them was watching the representatives (teachers and administration) of the school trying to enforce the "No Smoking" policy and how the students tried to get away with it.

Back at Lincoln High School in Ellwood City, Pa. we had three minutes between classes. Once the bell rang pronouncing the end of a period, the guys would literally flock to the restrooms. A few of them really had to go to the bathroom, but most of them were part of the "system". The system was an intricate set of signals that the guys used so they could catch a quick smoke between classes without being caught. One guy was at the door, another one was in front of the stalls and the smokers were taking their puffs in the stalls. When an employee of the school would approach, the signals began. It was either touching your belt meant a teacher was approaching and clenched fist meant it was cool. The lookout by the restroom door always kept his left arm straight down by his side with the hand sort of curled behind him. When he quickly wiggled his fingers on this hand, it was "May Day," get out, emergency… whatever you wanted to call it. It meant that there were serious problems such as the principal approaching. If a teacher, or the principal, were on his way toward the bathroom, cigarettes went flying, toilets were flushed, and everyone made a mad dash out of the smoke filled bathroom. The teachers would yell, scream, and threaten, but they were helpless to do anything. The school policy stated that a student had to be caught with a cigarette physically in his mouth or in his hands. If this did not occur, the teachers could do no more than throw around idle threats.

On the other hand, getting caught was a big deal. You could be expelled from school. The guys had a great system, but the teachers got creative. They recruited "student spies" for one thing. That didn't last long though. Once these spies were found out these kids were ridiculed or better yet, beat up. No one likes a snitch. The administration thought better of this idea and went back to their other bag of tricks. Another little ploy they used would be for a teacher to go in to a stall before the bell rang, right before the end of the period, lock the door and pretend he was a student going to the bathroom. He would wait for the smokers in this hiding place. When this failed to capture any smokers, several teachers would "bum rush" the bathroom at the same time. Again, failure always seemed to be their destiny.

Then they got permission to start searching the students with what they at the time called "probable cause." They tried it all, but almost always it was a daily effort in futility by the teachers. It was a blast to watch, however. Most of us didn't smoke and the smokers were generally considered losers who would make nothing of their lives. Back then, very few girls smoked. That has changed!

Ray Foley was the cool teacher back then at Lincoln High School. He was young, single, and as the girls said, "He was cute." Another reason that he was so popular is that if you took his class, U.S. History, even the most unmotivated student was assured of a good grade. His class was extremely easy. The week before the finals he would go over the test with the students, question by question. Everyone liked Ray Foley.

Mr. Foley never went into the bathroom between class changes because he never wanted to catch anyone smoking. He was cool and really enjoyed being the teacher who everyone liked. He, therefore, steered away from the activities that he knew were happening. By doing this, he was even cooler. That is until the day "Cool

Ray" went into the bathroom when he thought everyone was back in their class.

Sitting in the bathroom were Bob Maine and Tony Pertile, enjoying a couple of puffs of a cigarette. Bob and Tony were big football stars on the football team and that week they had their huge game against an archrival. There they were, guilty as can be, sitting on the toilets enjoying a cigarette and staring down at them was Ray Foley. I believe they were all pretty uncomfortable with the situation that presented itself.

Ray Foley had a major decision to make. Should he tell the football coach, Bob Timmerman, what he just witnessed? I mean he wasn't TRYING to catch them smoking, he was just at the wrong place at the wrong time. Bob Timmerman and Ray Foley went way back. Matter of fact, they were teammates on the very first little league baseball game ever played in Ellwood City, way back in 1950. Ray Foley has the distinction of being the winning pitcher in the very first little league game ever played in Ellwood City. They knew each other since they were nine years old.

Most of the teachers went way back, back to the day. People from a small town knew each other, played sports with and against each other, married in to and divorced out of families. Now they're not out on that little league field, though. They're teachers and coaches who are looked up to and entrusted by parents with their children. They needed to set the example, teach the right life lesson.

Ray Foley made what I would consider the right choice that day. He told Coach Timmerman what he had witnessed. Coach Timmerman, in turn, also made the right choice and suspended both players for the big football game. From that day on, Ray Foley was not considered cool by quite as many students. He lost the respect of some kids, but I am sure he gained the respect, unknowingly, of a lot of parents and co-workers.

Lots of life lessons were present that day. There was the lesson of doing the right thing, and the two teachers passed that test with flying colors. It would have been so easy for Ray Foley to have walked into that bathroom and upon seeing the two star football players puffing on a cigarette, just walked out. No one would have ever known. Or he could have just said, "Get out of here" and kept his mouth shut, kind of "Look the other way." Again, it would have been between the three of them. I can think of some coaches today, upon seeing two of their star baseball players doing something wrong, perhaps decide to look the other way. There's that thing about winning at any cost, and unfortunately as we all know, some coaches think the only winning is on the scoreboard. Matter of fact, I am pretty confident about some coaches looking the other way. I have seen it more than once. It is an ugly, ugly character flaw.

I think the bigger lesson, however, that day was the one about risk and reward. Everything in life is risk and reward. If you don't think it is, think again.

When you march into your boss's office demanding a raise, it's risk and reward. You may get fired, so why take the risk? If you don't take the risk, you may never be paid what you're worth, so where's the reward?

How about when you drive faster than the speed limit? That's the perfect risk and reward. Obviously the speeding is worth the risk of the reward, which I guess is getting somewhere a little quicker. When you go to a baseball tournament and stay up half the night and play ball on four hours sleep, it's risk and reward. And when you try to sneak a cigarette, it's the same thing ...risk and reward; the bigger the risk, the bigger the reward. I know both Bob Maine and Tony Pertile's fathers ... I would not have wanted to be either of those guys that day when they went home. Some risk is more than the reward.

Like life, baseball is all risk and reward.

If you're a runner on first and want to steal second, there is risk and reward. The reward is second base; the risk is being thrown out, or picked off first. The bigger the lead off first base, the bigger the risk....but, the more chance you will be successful stealing the base, the reward. If you take very little risk, such as a very little lead, you're chances of the reward (stealing the base) are less.

When you play the outfield, if you never "go for that fly ball," you'll never get it. No risk, no reward. Play it safe and catch it on one hop every time. Of course it's a risk to dive for the ball. It may get past you. Oh, but what a reward when you stretch your body straight out, airborne, and that ball ends up in your glove!

That's what baseball is... thousands of risks and rewards. The risks are the hard work and focus. The rewards are making more plays.

When you play baseball the right way it is the best feeling in the world. It is with maximum effort and incredible passion. It makes the average or even good player look silly. You don't jog off the field, you run off the field. You're never the last one off the field. It doesn't matter what position you're playing. You don't run off the field to the lines, you run in to the dugout. You set the example. You run on to the field before the other team can run off the field. You're ready to go on the field. You have your glove and hat and ball.

You're prepared every pitch like it was the most important pitch of your life; because it is. Every pitch ...right now ... is the most important pitch and you're ready. The only risk you are taking by being ready and prepared every single pitch ... is effort. Is it worth the effort? The only reason a player would not be prepared for every single pitch is that he has convinced himself that it is not worth it. I guess there is not enough reward, or chance of reward. It comes down to nothing more than that.

Let's say I'm a shortstop. Here's my job. Before every pitch I see what the situation is and I am ready to respond to whatever comes my way. If no one is on base, then I get prepared as the pitch is being delivered. I do my little "defensive ballet" or whatever you want to call it. I know the count, I know the batter's tendencies, I know where the outfielders are playing, how fast the batter runs, how many outs, what the score is, what the inning is, etc. If someone is on first base, I know all the above things PLUS I know who's covering second base on a steal, who's covering second base on a bunt, who's covering second if the ball is hit back to the pitcher, how fast the runner on first base is, how big of a lead the runner has, who's backing up the throw back to the pitcher from the catcher EVERY PITCH. etc. The list goes on and on. That's a lot of effort to make just in case I happen to be involved in a play. A player looking at this objectively may think that the reward is not worth the risk.

I mean this is a hell of a lot of work to do every pitch. If I do none of this I still may make every play I have to. I'll probably only be involved in five or six plays a game. Does it really make sense to do all this work for the reward. There may not even be a reward! What if I can make every play without doing all this preparation? What if I never have a play? I did all this work for nothing! I may have to think about ten things before every pitch. If there's 150 pitches in a game, that's 1,500 pieces of work that I have to do. If I'm involved with 15 things during the game, then my ROI (return on investment) is 1%. That doesn't sound real good. Who works with a 1% return on investment?

Most players may not think this all out, but somewhere in their subconscious they have calculated risk and reward. They have told themselves that it is absolutely crazy to do all these things that, even if I am involved in a play, may not help me. They tell themselves that nobody else does all this stuff. Our stud third baseman doesn't do all this stuff, nor does our star catcher. They convince themselves to give less effort. There just isn't enough reward.

Wouldn't it be nice if we could play the game of baseball without wasting our time with all of this preparation? Wouldn't it be nice if we knew when the ball was going to be hit to us? It certainly would save a lot of effort.

Perhaps we could just daydream most of the game and then when the ball is going to be hit to us, we could make an announcement and say, "Left fielder, the next pitch will be struck by the batter and will be a fly ball in your vicinity. You will need to advance 22 feet forward and 13 feet to your left to properly catch the ball. It will take exactly 3.2 seconds to get to you from the time contact is made. Based on the depth of the hit and the runners speed at third base, there will be no attempt by him to tag up, so you really don't need to worry about throwing the ball home with any type of urgency. So perhaps, once you catch it, you may just want to lob the ball into the infielder because that may be a little easier on your arm. Third baseman, based on this information, you don't need to line up the throw and get into cut off position because the runner's not going to try to score and that would be a whole lot of wasted energy for you. Catcher, no need to throw off your facemask, line up the third baseman, and prepare you for a play at the plate. Again, we wouldn't want you to use any wasted energy."

Wouldn't that make this game of baseball a lot easier? Pitchers would be told what batters are going to take the first pitch. That way they could just focus on getting the ball over the plate and not worry about changing speeds or hitting the outside corner. That is a lot of energy that could be saved. Save that energy. That way everyone could give a great effort when they knew the ball was going to be hit to them.

Kind of like a salesman only making a sales call when he knows that someone was going to buy something. Or a fireman going to work when he knew there would be a fire. Or the security guard who works at the bank and only comes in when a burglary is in progress. Why do we have to deal with all this wasted energy? Wouldn't that make the game of baseball a lot more fun knowing what was going to happen? So much effort needs to be put out for the unknown. I can see where a lot of you so called baseball players don't think that the risk (effort) is worth the reward.

But here's another option for the real baseball players.

Be like the archaeologist who goes out day after day, week after week, knowing that there is very little reward on a daily basis, but willing to work and work until the reward comes through. Be like the surfer who will paddle out into the ocean perhaps 300 times a day to catch that one perfect wave.... to get that one ride, and be prepared for it. That one perfect ride! The bigger the risk, the bigger the reward. The more you're willing to be prepared and give effort, the more plays you're going to make.

And the real answer of course, is that there is no risk because there's no real effort. When you have a passion to do something, all the mental and physical effort isn't work. It's fun and easy. It's not effort to do something when you love doing it.

Just ask the surfer.

You can see it in high school player's faces. You can see the passion, or lack of it. You can see the kids who are out there for a social outing, out there to please mom and dad, out there because they have too much talent not to be out there. Then you see the guys who have the passion. It is not always the talented ones. It is the ones who have learned to respect the game, respect their teammates, and respect their own abilities. It's the ones who will ultimately make it. It's the ones who will take the proper risk for the reward.

In high school at the present time, there are 455,300 kids playing baseball, with 130,000 of them being senior athletes. Of those senior athletes, about 25,700 will become an NCAA baseball athlete. That is a little over 5 per cent, or 1 out of 20. Of this total, 5,700 will make it to their senior year as a college baseball player. Of this total, 600 NCAA senior athletes will be drafted into professional baseball. From high school to professional baseball, you're talking .5%, or 1 out of 200.

That's just to be drafted, not making it to the majors.

Most of those drafted never make the big time. They usually linger in the minors. Not a real bright picture for all these baseball hopefuls and certainly not a proportionate number to what propaganda is being fed to us by high school coaches, college coaches, and instructors. Talent alone is not enough. The road can be hard and lonely. One misstep, one cement wall, one twisted ankle, one wrong response to a coach can send you home with nothing more than a bunch of broken dreams. You need your four qualities.

It's the price of success.

Tens of millions of dollars are spent annually by individuals and businesses to find that secret of success. How can I be successful in an organization, in my job, at home, or even on a ball field? We've all read the books on success. Our companies have sent us all to the seminars, hoping we would come back to the office as a new person with a newfound positive attitude. Or we would sit and read 300 pages from a superstar's biography and in some manner, try to fathom ourselves being that person; like we were going to wake up the next day and all of a sudden be a great athlete.

It doesn't happen too often.

Seldom do you go back to your place of business and change things in a positive manner because you went to a "feel good" class. Seldom do you finish that "Sports Psychology Positive Thinking" book and turn your life around, become a better player or for that matter, a better coach. They almost never work, at least not on a long-term basis. I'm certainly not ridiculing anyone for buying into this, though, since I am the biggest proponent of inspirational sayings and positive attitude books. I am the guy who notices these things on the internet and orders them, sight unseen. I am the guy who always has a saying, always making an analogy, comparing something in life to that ball field.

All of this literature is good, motivational and uplifting. It makes you feel like a new person which is a great emotion, but you need to realize it is someone who is basically trying to make you feel the way you should already feel. All that this marketing provides to you is nothing more than a temporary fix. When you come off that euphuistic high, you realize neither you nor life has changed. You are the same person. Too many people invest in this stuff hoping it will change them to be a better person or better athlete. What this positive-generating literature should do is VALIDATE THE PERSON YOU ALREADY ARE, not re-create you. We invest millions of dollars in trying to change ourselves. We should invest some time just feeling good about who we are.

In a smaller circle, we all try to do this on the ball field. We purchase tapes on the mental part of the game, the emotional part of the game, being a thinker, improving your attitude, being a better teammate. That's all well and good, but the best way for you as a ball player to be more positive and improve your chances of success is to surround yourself with positive, successful people. It's really that simple. No person in any book or on any tape can help you attain your goals as much as that coach or teammate or parent out there with you on the ball field.

Back in the day we didn't have all of this help. We had something that we realized was much more important. We had each other.

Everybody has a philosophy of how they coach, what's important to them and what they want to accomplish. Along with this, they have a formula of how to best be successful as a coach or as a player.

Here is mine.

Follow the four steps below and I believe they will help anybody accomplish anything, even, and especially the player out on the ball field. I think about the people who I know that I happen to really admire. They have these four traits. That's why I think these traits are good, not because I came up with them through mind provoking years of thought or that I am some sort of guru. Far from that! I study people I respect. I study people who inspire me. I watch what they do and how they do it. I try to learn from them.

It all started with Coach Spellman.

I think back to what he offered to people. It was so much and he was so effective in what he did and how he did it. I've talked to people who knew him and people who played ball for him. There's a reverence about the way he conducted himself. Whether it was a ballplayer, co-worker, or local clergy, he had the same influence over everyone. Other coaches have attained a lot more in regards to total wins and championships, but they don't have the admiration that Coach had attained.

Not even close.

I then started noticing what qualities other people had that I admired. They, too, actually possessed the same four characteristics. They are like the four bases on a ball field. If you don't have the one that gets you to first base, you can't go to second base, and so forth. These four traits also work in unison and like a chain; they are only as strong as their weakest link. If one is weak, you have a problem.

First base   -   Passion
Second base -   Hard Work
Third base   -   Respect
Home plate   -   Selflessness

PASSION

Passion is the one trait that drives the others, and drives all of us in general. If you don't have your heart and soul into playing baseball you will never be successful. You may do well, you may even be a star, but you'll never be truly successful. There's a difference between having God given ability and being able to use it to its fullest. Without passion you're just a shell of what you could be. Passion is the motor that drives the car. You can tell when someone has a passion for the game, whether it is a player, coach, or fan. It's a feeling that you get in your gut when you walk on to the ball field. The degree of talent doesn't really have a lot to do with it. Many, many, good ball players have signed contracts to play ball with professional ball teams. They never made it as a player because they lacked that drive that was necessary. In high school, they could dominate because they just were more talented; but then they went away to play with the big boys and talent alone wasn't enough. They all could hit the ball 400 feet and throw the ball 90 mph. You need something else that you feel inside to get you to that next step.

You need that passion.

On the other hand, there have also been hundreds of players who have signed to play professional ball who didn't possess the talent necessary to make it to the big leagues, but they had the passion for the game. Their careers ended in the minor leagues, but they followed their passion and stayed with the game. When playing days were over, they became coaches, managers, instructors, and scouts. Most of your best major league managers are ex-players who either had far from impressive major league careers or never made it out of the minor leagues. The passion to be around the baseball field was still there. Passion doesn't mean just playing; it also means teaching and having the intense desire to show others the beauty of the game of baseball. You can tell the coaches who have the passion and the ones who don't.

When I graduated from high school, I was fortunate to have enough talent to be signed by the Detroit Tigers. I went to spring training the next February. All players go to the same complex and once spring training is over, are assigned to a team. I was assigned to Clinton, Iowa. My coach was Jim Leyland. Who knew back then, in the year 1973, that this coach, who himself was signed by Detroit as a player, would some day be regarded as one of the best managers in baseball? Leyland was a catcher, and from the limited conversations I heard him have with people, came to realize that he was an ex-catcher who in his words "Couldn't hit." I'm sure not being able to hit at a professional level is different than not being able to hit in high school. Anyway, he came to the realization that he would never make it as a player.

Most people at this point in time call it quits. He decided to go in to coaching. He coached with the Tigers organization for a while. Years later, I was watching a ball game on television and I realized that Jim Leyland was coaching third base for the Chicago White Sox. He was still with it! A few years later than that, an opening came up with the Pittsburg Pirates for the manager's job. Tony LaRussa, then the manager of the White Sox, put in a good word for Leyland. Next thing you know, the Pirates announce their new manager. It wasn't a big name guy, it was Jim Leyland. He was managing the Pirates and doing pretty well with a guy named Barry Bonds leading the way. He took the Pirates into the playoffs a few years in a row, only to be knocked off each time by the Atlanta Braves.

Since then, he has won a World Series as manager of the Florida Marlins. Then to add to his impressive resume, just two short years ago he took another team back to the World Series ... that same Detroit Tiger organization he started with. His team played against the St. Louis Cardinals and their manager was, yes, the very same Tony LaRussa that helped him get his first managerial job.

Talk about full circle.

He has accomplished all of this not because of talent, but because of passion. He is a very talented manager with a tremendous amount of knowledge, but he probably would be nowhere without that passion. Passion will get you more places in life than talent. It will get you where you want to go on a baseball field.

It all starts with that one emotion. When kids are small and starting to play baseball, it should be fun... lots of fun. It should always be fun, but at some point in time, as that child makes his, or her, way through their baseball experience, passion should become a topic of conversation and a mind set. I'm not sure the exact age it should be, but if kids are playing high school baseball competitively, this trait needs to be present. I personally think it can start a lot earlier in kid's lives. I think this is a topic that is far overlooked and yet so important to everyone's mental and emotional health, not just kids. Walk up to anyone you know, and say to them, "Excluding your family and money, tell me your passion in life." As I started writing this book, and this chapter, I have been very surprised to what degree people lack passion. I have asked fourteen adults in the last six months this exact question. I have received the following responses;

Five people didn't answer me, four people said they had none, three people said they "Never thought about it," and two people said, "Let me think about it." I guess they are still thinking....

Not one person out of fourteen has a passion in life! We are a society that has everything; money, power, control, material things, lust. We just have no passion. Fourteen grown up mature adults, not one of them has a passion in life! Where do our kids learn about passion? Who teaches, communicates, and demonstrates passion to our youth? This may be the one most important trait that we could share with our youth, but we seldom hear anyone talking about it.

Passion should be talked about more and certainly demonstrated more. It's a talk that at least each high school coach should have with his ball team every year at some point. It should go something like this:

"If you don't have passion to play this game, you should probably find something else to do. Go play another sport or take up some other hobby. Go find something you're passionate about. You don't belong on a baseball field if that passion for baseball is not there. If you really don't want to be out here, if you really don't have that drive to play baseball, you are wasting my time, your parent's time, and worst of all, your own time."

It may sound harsh, but in reality, it may help lots of kids. Choices need to be made at certain ages. When you are in high school, your next step is college, the military, or the work force. Real life starts and you need to be prepared. Most kids don't have a clue regarding what they want to do or become. Age has a lot to do with this, but I believe the lack of directing our children toward be passionate also has something to do with this. If perhaps we would give passion more emphasis, kids may realize by the age of 16 or 17 something they may really want to do with their lives.

The speech about passion reminds me of a situation my first year of coaching at Gambrills. I had a boy who was a new player on the 13-under team and by looking at his stats from the previous team he played for, it appeared that he was a pretty good ball player. He was small in stature, but he seemed to have this uncanny ability to get on base. His parents were really, really nice. His dad, however, would drive you crazy with his constant pacing. He never stopped pacing. Every practice he would pace and pace and pace. He would stop for a few minutes to "bend my ear," telling me how good of a player his son was, what his average the year before was, and how he led the team with his on base percentage. He would then start pacing again.

He was a very proud and supportive dad. The player, besides having those impressive stats, was cooperative and exhibited good listening skills.

The player had just one small problem that I felt was kind of important.

He didn't really want to be playing baseball.

Despite the lofty statistics and the very supportive parents he had no passion to play baseball. He was doing it for the parents. The funny thing about it is that mom and dad really didn't care if he played baseball or not, but there was this perception that he would disappoint his parents if he didn't play baseball. They didn't realize that all he wanted to do was hit a tennis ball full time. His baseball playing days should have ended much earlier and quieter than they did rather than uncomfortably at a tournament in Richmond, Virginia.

Our team had managed to make the finals in this tournament with three other very good teams. Our pitching, however, was pretty much depleted. This young man was not only a decent hitter, but based on his statistics from the year before also a fairly good pitcher. He hadn't pitched for our team as of yet and I decided to start him in the first playoff game against the Richmond Braves, who happened to be a national showcase team.

It started poorly, and from that point, only got worse

Seven batters into the bottom of the first inning, Richmond had a 5-0 lead, two runners on base and no outs. Our pitcher, who started the game at about 5'2," now appeared to be about 4'2" in size. It looked like he was literally shrinking after every pitch, every base hit, and every walk. I finally went to the mound and took him out of his misery. When you hear the term shell shocked on a baseball field, it should be a picture of this young man at this moment. As I walked toward the mound to replace this player with another pitcher my worst fears were coming true.

He was crying.

I stood at the mound for a few moments, hoping that the sobbing would subside. No such luck. After some insignificant small talk, I asked the pitcher for the ball. He handed me the ball and my attempt to be reassuring to him by saying, "Don't worry about it, you'll get them next time" never made it to his ears. He was crying so hard I don't think he could hear me. We just stood there, neither of us having any chance of erasing this ugly situation. I finally motioned for our next pitcher to come in and we started toward the bench.

If the situation wasn't uncomfortable enough, it was about to get much worse. For the first time in six weeks, from the first practice with our team until this moment, his dad stopped pacing. Now he was standing behind the bench, awaiting our arrival. The young man, without missing a stride and certainly not lifting his head to display his swollen red eyes, walked directly to the end of the bench and parked himself there. The father immediately walked over to him and started to talk to his son. The encouragement and support that I assumed the father would now display never came. I think that I would probably have approached the situation differently with my son, but we all have our way! I guess he was doing what he felt was best.

It was a disaster. You could tell it would not be good by the first words out of the father's mouth.

"Quit crying!"

"What were you doing out there?"

With every comment, the crying was magnified. It was embarrassing. The team finally got three outs and the players came off the field and to the bench area. It was uncomfortable for everyone. The player was crying, dad in his ear, and a bunch of thirteen year olds not knowing real well how to deal with this.

Two hours later the game came to an end. We lost by a score of something like 10-2. It really wasn't much of a game after the first inning. It was kind of going through the motions until you get to the end. It finally came to a merciful end. I talked to the team after the game and sent them on their way. It was getting dark by now and we had a two hour trip back home in front of us. We were all tired and had a long day.

I was ready to get into my car and here came dad and son. They wanted to talk. Actually, based on body language I assumed that they didn't want to talk. Instead, dad wanted to talk and dad wanted to force the son to talk. I opened up my car door and told my wife and son I'd be right back. My wife gave me that "I'm glad it's you and not me" look. I walked the two of them far enough away from the car that just in case the boy started crying again, no one would hear.

That was a good idea.

The dad was standing there across from me and his son was in front of him, head down. Unfortunately, I was correct about the dad wanting to force the son to talk.

He implored his child, "Tell him, tell him what you're supposed to tell him."

The son tried to speak, but nothing came out.

"Look at him when you speak," said the father.

At this point, it would have been nice to have had a 2 × 4 in my hand so I could have cracked the dad over the head with it and possibly shaken up any common sense he had stored in his brain.

He wasn't done, however. He now felt it was necessary to speak for his son.

"I'm not sure he wants to play baseball. I'm not sure he's putting a full effort into this. I'm not sure he belongs on this team."

A few uneasy moments passed.

The boy finally looked up and said, "I'm sorry for how I pitched."

I'm not sure at this point of what made me sadder or angrier.

Was it the fact that the dad was possibly embarrassed by his son's performance?

Was it the fact that the dad was angered by his boy's performance?

Or was it the fact that the dad actually thought an apology was necessary, that in some way as a coach, I was mad because the boy didn't pitch well, that I would actually hold it against the boy?

A few more uneasy moments went by and somehow we managed to end the conversation with me saying to the boy, "Just go home and forget about it. We'll see how you feel in a couple of days."

The passion wasn't there. The boy had no business being out on that ball field. He wanted to be somewhere else. You could tell from the first day of practice (at least I could) that the boy didn't have this burning desire to be out on the baseball field. The conversations were always about his average or his earned run average or some other statistic. It was never about him and how he felt and I never had a really good feeling about him. He was nervous and timid and always being pushed by his dad.

Driving out of that parking lot in Richmond late at night was the last time that I ever saw either one of them. That's my last memory of the boy, a boy so distraught that he pitched poorly that he couldn't stop crying; a thirteen-year-old boy walking to his car in the dark, crying uncontrollably while his dad was still berating him. I felt sick to my stomach.

His dad called me a few times in the next couple of days. I felt more like a therapist than a coach. As the father continued to talk and talk and talk, I realized more and more it was not an issue with the boy. It was an issue with the dad. Dad couldn't say good-bye to baseball and was the one having the problem.

The son just wanted to play tennis.

That was his passion.

All of this could have been avoided by starting with the very core of a player. Does he want to be out on the field? Does he enjoy it? Does he have a passion for it?

Start there.

The rest of the stuff is insignificant. It really is. A good coach will look for passion first, and then he will harvest that passion. He will bring out that strong emotion and that feeling will then be contagious on the team. You will find your passionate players and then build around them. That is your nucleus, your foundation. A kid with lots of talent but no passion is like a candle that will soon burn out. As he is burning out, there is always the fear that he will take a few more players with him. Because of the lack of passion his heart isn't in the game. Others see that and there's always the fear that he will be a negative influence. A high majority of "bad influences" on a team are from kids who do not have a passion for the game. So why are they there? Why even put them on the team? They can hit a ball 375 feet. So what? The problems that they are creating aren't worth the talent they have. Put nine passionate kids out on the field and you will never lose. A true coach would never regret doing that.

You can't get to second base without getting to first base. You can't get to first base without passion. You just can't. If you think you can, you're only a pretender. You may be out there doing well, but you're just going through the motions and taking up space. A good coach recognizes this up front and deals with it.

There is a difference between having a lot of fun doing something and being passionate about it. You learn to tell the difference in people and it's hard to separate unless you as a coach have that passion. You need to have that feeling in your gut.

I've thought a lot about passion and at what age it could be, or should be, important. I believe it can be, and should be, present in kids as young as 9 or 10 years old. A few weeks ago, my thoughts were validated. In the summer of 2007, I ran two baseball camps at Gambrills. Most of the kids were between the ages of 10 and 14, a few were younger. Out of the 60 or so kids who attended there were a few who were a "challenge" for one reason or another. I always like a good challenge. I had two who were really tough to deal with. One was Jake and another was Tyler.

Jake seemed to be a troublemaker, always interrupting, always saying something, always disagreeing. He also appeared to be lazy. This went on all week and I did my best to work with him. I yelled at him a lot and told him constantly that he not only was disruptive, but that he wasn't being a good teammate. When the week was over, I wasn't too worked up that I wouldn't see Jake the next day. He pushed me about as far as I wanted to be pushed. I just hoped he got something out of the camp.

About a month later, Jake's dad e-mailed me and asked if I would work with Jake. He told me that Jake really liked me and thought that we really hit it off well at the camp. Hit it off well! I spent the week reprimanding him! Anyway, I told his dad that I would work with Jake.

I gave him a few lessons and have shared a few e-mails with his dad about Jake's progress. He has improved a lot and both father and son are happy. After one of Jake's fall baseball games, I received an e-mail from his dad that just had to be responded to. It is one of my favorites:

Coach Potter—

No doubt in my mind that you are the best thing since "sliced bread" for Jake.

This was truly a benchmark game for Jake.... not because of his stats but the WAY he played the game—with passion, intensity, focus, and hustle—the WHOLE game. This was the first time since Jake started baseball a year ago. I gave no pep talk on the way to game....only thing I said was remember and ex-ecute the things Coach Potter has been teaching you.

Right from the start at third base he was mov-ing and intense, in left field he jumped as soon as contact was made on the bat (he actually anticipated things!). at shortstop in the last inning he did the same thing. He covered, he backed up, etc. He made the move the way u taught him at third the whole game. He actually anticipated the ball off of the bat.

His stats showed—-one hard line drive over the first basemen to the corner for a clean triple (of course he needed oxygen when he got to third), a double between the left and center fielder, and a single to left field—-all clean hits.

He had two put outs at third and a relay throw to home to get the runner at the plate. BUT it was the way he played that just made my heart burst with pride.

Thanks Coach

Tom

My response:

Tom:

There is nothing... nothing... that I could have heard today that would have made me happier.

One would have to understand what passion is all about to understand how I feel at this moment. As you know, I am not bragging about being passionate... I am only communicating how blessed I feel to find passion in something.... and perhaps on some level.... communicate it to someone else.

You seem to give me a lot of credit for Jake's performance on a ball field. I will take credit for one thing and one thing only.... I have communicated to Jake a little about passion. It is not what I say to him or show him. It is a "feeling" that he has picked up from me. It cannot be faked or pretended.... it is a feeling that is only captured by someone from a person that truly has passion.

We all know that passion is much deeper than showing a kid how to hit or throw. Most coaches don't have it and they try to make up for it in other ways that just don't compare. Kids are incredible. They are so much smarter and in tune than we as parents (and coaches) give them credit for.

They pick up on passion... or lack of it. They tune out people who are coach in name only, who are really pretenders. They want to relate to people who believe in what they are saying and doing ... who have that true excitement and joy in what they are doing. The kids just know the difference ... and we as parents don't really get it sometimes.

Jake is an incredible kid with incredible insight. I've had conversations with him that I treasure. They will never go any further, not even to you. I know that you understand what I am saying. It goes much deeper than giving a kid a lesson. I will share one moment with you that I had with Jake:

About three weeks ago we were in the cage- and I was throwing some batting practice to him. We were talking about "this and that," nothing in particular. He then hit three balls in a row harder than I had ever seen him hit a ball. I must have said something to him that made him feel good. A smile came over his face and he said to me,

"Why are you such a good coach?" Now, me and you both know that his comment probably had very little to do with any technical teaching that I had bestowed upon him... rather it was that "thing" that is hard to explain, and hard to grasp, and hard for most coaches to comprehend.

Jake has come a long way in the few months from the summer camp... in more ways than one, as you know. I am very proud of him.... and I feel very blessed that he has allowed me to work with him.

You have made my day.............

Jeff

Tyler on the other hand was not loud, boisterous, demanding or arrogant. He was shy. When I say shy, I mean extremely shy. Most of the time I couldn't even get him to look at me. He would look down at his feet and not reply. Most of the week there were one or two drills a day that Tyler did not participate in. Again, when the week was over, I had just hoped that Tyler had a good time and the experience was worth it.

I heard from Tyler's dad about the same time as Jake's dad with the same type of message. Do you mind working with Tyler a little, he really liked the camp. Liked the camp! So I also worked with Tyler and had him stop up at the field once a week. He seemed to improve quite a bit and now likes coming to our little workouts. Tyler is eight years old.

Another e-mail, this one from his mom, is another favorite.

Dear Coach Potter,

I just wanted to tell you how much I appreciate you working with Tyler. Jeff (dad) and I are very selective of who we expose are kids to. But we have made the decision that you are someone we want are son to learn from, and most importantly we want Tyler to feel the positive attitude that you bring to learning about the game of baseball and much more important, life. When Jeff tells Tyler he is coming to see you I see something that I don't see in anything else that he does, excitement, even a little nervousness. He wants you to be proud of him. It's one thing for us to tell him that we are proud of him, it's entirely different if it is you. I don't know what that is, not even sure if I will ever know. But I know that it is important. Tyler has had some tough times in this game so far but he has not lost his passion for it, so I think it is important that he keeps up with it. Not all kids have natural talent but I do think there is such a thing as "acquired" talent. That's just hard work and good coaching (you know exactly what I mean). I don't know how to react to 8-year-old emotions sometimes. But I do know how to encourage and stick with it even when he makes me crazy. And obviously you do too. Thank you so much for taking out your valuable time for Ty. We are really grateful and lucky,

Kim Purper

If a player or coach has passion, no matter what age, you'll know immediately. Passion has that hold over you and it becomes a part of you. Everyone needs a passion.

Find yours.

It will change your life.

HARDWORK

Since I am one of those people who buy the inspirational and positive thinking books, I found a saying that I kind of like, which was written by Grantland Rice. He was speaking of baseball players.

You wonder how they do it,
You look to see the knack
You watch the foot in action,
Or the shoulder or the back.
But when you spot the answer
Where the higher glamour's lurk
You'll find …
That most of it is practice,
And the rest of it is work

The year is 2008 and it is a long time since I was a kid and I know that almost everything in life has changed. One thing hasn't changed, however. One thing has stayed constant.

There still is no substitute for hard work.

We take it for granted that people know that they need to work hard to get ahead. Surely, everyone knows that, don't they? The truth is that some kids work hard, some don't. The truth is some coaches work hard and some don't. In general the kids, like parents, who have passion usually work hardest. It starts with passion, and then goes to hard work. Baseball is hard work. It should be. Anything that has value should be difficult to conquer. The beauty of baseball is that the better you get the more you realize the less you know about the game, and the harder you need to work. Baseball is a very humbling sport and a very humbling experience. Coaching baseball when you know nothing about it is easy because you don't know what you're doing wrong. Once you feel that you have a good idea what baseball is all about it becomes harder to coach because you know how much you really don't know.

I go and watch the high school teams practice in the spring. Not too often but enough so it can take me "back in the day".

I like to watch things unfold. At practices, I compare coaches, unfairly, to Coach Spellman. I like to watch the players who are contenders and the ones who are pretenders. You can see them a mile away. The coaches, if they're good, can also pick them out easily.

So I watch, and smile.

In my own distorted manner, I put the kids in three groups in my mind. It has nothing to do with talent, it has everything to do with passion and hard work.

Group 1

The first group is the kids who just don't get it. They should be somewhere else. Either the parent wants him to play or the player thinks the parent wants him to play, or the player just enjoys the social aspect of the situation. If this player has enough talent, he'll start. The coach doesn't care if he has no motivation and he isn't giving 100% and to be honest, the coach doesn't care if he has passion. In most cases, the coach is just looking for the nine kids who can hit the ball the longest distance. The player knows this and will do what he needs to do to get by. This player should be escorted off the field and told to go invest his time in something that he could feel passionate about. He has no burning desire and he really doesn't want to work real hard. He has no business on the baseball field. By being out there, he disrespects the game. These kids are at an age now that sport is more than a social event. There are so many options out there for a kid to do. Why does a kid spend countless hours participating in something that he doesn't have a burning desire to do? At least 80% of these kids will not play college baseball which is okay. Of the small amount that will go on to college ball, their candle will burn out quickly. Usually one out of four kids on a team fit into this category.

Group 2

These are the kids who play real hard, give 100% and want to play. They are out on the field because they have a good work ethic and they enjoy the competition. They are respectful of authority and the coaches. They get as much as they can out of their physical abilities. Most of them have done well on all of their teams growing up and are very serviceable players. They give a full effort while they are out on the field, but during the off season probably find other things to do other than work out religiously. They are stuck between mediocre and good and what they need to get to the next level, they are not prepared to do. They don't have the passion and the drive and the perseverance to get better. They like playing baseball a lot, and the competition. They just lack the drive. This is basically 50% of the team.

Group 3

These kids have the passion for the game. They combine that with whatever talent they possess and they are your players. They never disrespect the coaches and seldom disrespect the game of baseball. They take in the experience every day that they are out on the field. They love baseball. They love the game. Players react three different ways when the pressure is on and the game is on the line. The first player hopes the coach doesn't ask him to go up and hit. The second player hopes the coach DOES ask him to go up and hit. The third type of player, this group, does neither. He goes up and ASKS to hit, ASKS for the ball, ASKS to be the guy to do the job. He doesn't sit back and wait. He wants to pitch against the best teams, and hit against the best pitchers. He feels that he can handle the job and never shies away from the competition. Baseball is going to take him a long way. He doesn't think it, he knows it. He's passionate

When a player has the passion and works hard, he's half way home. He loves the game and he works hard at the game. He doesn't just go through the motions in practice, he goes at it full speed. He does it again and again and again until it's done right. He will work very hard, even if he knows it will get him to be just a little better.

It's the price of success.

Then you may have the right outcome, like the one we did on March 21, 2004.

Gambrills Wins Olney Tournament

The Olney baseball tournament was called the "Mutiny at the Park" and was supposed to be very good competition, a good warm up for the Baltimore-Metro season that would be starting soon.

The highlight of the tournament was the fact that we, the Gambrills Athletics, may play the Maryland Mavericks. They were the cream of the crop, the best team around. Inside the program to this tournament, every team was displayed with their roster and their accomplishments. Some teams had "runner up" in a tournament, some had nothing listed. The Mavericks had the following resume:

Baltimore Metro League Champions
AABC Maryland State Champions
AABC World Series National Champions

They were one of those teams who were well financed (the players didn't have to pay a fee) coaches were paid, and the uniforms were the sharpest around. It's a little easier getting players when everything is paid for. You go to the best tournaments and you already have the best players. The team was coached by Brian Frederick who seemed to have good teams wherever he went. Brian is one of those guys who have a passion for the game of baseball.

The first day of the tournament went as planned. We won our two games easily and the Mavericks did likewise. If we both could get by our first game Sunday, we would play in the championship. Again on Sunday, things went like clockwork as the Mavericks and the Gambrills Athletics won their first games decisively. By the time the preliminary games were over, however, it was getting late in the day and there was talk about not playing the championship contest. Not only was the tournament about 45 minutes behind time, but it was bitter cold. Snow was now falling at the ball park. After a little discussion, we decided to play the game. We kind of said, "We're here …let's play." So both teams took the field.

The game was a great game, the kind that you want to play … win or lose. You would rather be on the short end of one of these contests than to win a game against very little competition. This is the type of game that you look back and said, if this would have happened or if we had executed here, a real learning experience.

We didn't start out real well as we fell behind the Mavericks by a score of 4-1. Their fans were having a good old time as they were accustomed to not only winning, but dismantling teams. And now they knew that we were joining the Baltimore Metro League as a new team and we had a reputation as a pretty good team. They wanted to send a message and they were doing a very good job of it. They were all enjoying the game thus far very much and things looked pretty bleak for us. They were sitting on that lead, with a runner on second base, two outs, and the possibility of making a decent size lead in the game even bigger. Basically, we were getting our butts kicked.

Then it happened.

What occurred in the next ten seconds completely changed the game, probably changed our baseball season, and perhaps solidified my thoughts on certain work ethics forever.

The runner on second base took his lead and the batter promptly stroked a hit to left field. There were two outs so the runner was moving on contact. Our left fielder did not have a strong arm. We're looking squarely at a 5-1 deficit and perhaps this game is realistically out of reach.

But something very strange happened.

The left fielder, Al Shandrowski, came running up a little faster than usual, swooped up the ball a little cleaner than usual, and threw a strike to the cut off man with a little more zip than usual. The cut off man, Matt Pace, happened to be in the right spot. He got his body in perfect position and with seemingly one motion, caught the ball and threw a strike to our catcher. The catcher, Kieran Flannery, took the throw and once again, seemingly with one motion swung his glove around and took a swipe at the runner in an attempt to stop him from scoring. His tag beat the runner's hand to the plate.

The umpire emphatically gestured that the batter was out! It was followed by the actual words, you're out, screamed loudly. It sounded like sweet music.

You could hear a pin drop on the other side of the field. Yelling and screaming became silence in a split second for the stunned Maverick fans. Our team came running off the field, a bunch of high fives, and we knew at that moment we could win the game.

I don't think that our newfound confidence had much to do with throwing a guy out which had happened many times before. It had to do with how it happened, the circumstances of it all. It was a big play that needed to be made. It didn't happen by chance.

It happened nine months before this.
It had to do with hard work.

It was in the month Of June, 2003 and the new 13-u team was just forming. All the players were coming to the first practice with a new team and a new coach. Some of the kids didn't even know each other.

The players warmed up and ran a lap. After a little talking we were ready to start practice.

"This is what we're going to do guys," I said. "We're going to do a drill and we're going to do it until we do it right."

I then told them that I wanted a third baseman, shortstop, two second basemen, two catchers, two first baseman, and three pitchers. The rest of the players were instructed to go to right field.

Then I continued,

"Guys, here's how it's going to work. I'm going to hit balls to the right fielder. The right fielder is going to throw a strike to the cut off man who is going to throw it home. The catcher, after catching it and swiping the imaginary runner trying to score, will throw the ball back to first base, which will be covered by the second baseman. He is covering because that's where he would go on this play in a real game. The second baseman, once he swipes the imaginary runner, will throw the ball to second base, covered by the shortstop. The shortstop, once swiping that imaginary runner, will throw the ball to third base, who will swipe the imaginary runner. The pitcher will begin on the mound like he is actually pitching in the game. Once he sees the ball hit to right field he will back up home plate. If the ball gets by the catcher, the pitcher will get the overthrow and throw it to first base and the ball will go "around the horn" as before. Whether the pitcher gets an overthrow or not he will back up third base once the throw goes to first base because he knows that the throw will eventually go from second base to third base and he needs to back it up. Once the ball goes around the horn to the third baseman, the third baseman will give the ball to the pitcher who will go to the back of the mound and wait for his turn again."

Understand?

There were more than a few puzzled looks by the players, but they had the premise of what we were doing so they went to their positions.

It's a great drill. The right fielder needs to do two things correctly. The first baseman needs to do four things correctly, the catcher three things, the second baseman three things, the shortstop three things, the third baseman two things, and the pitcher two things. That's 19 things that need to be done correctly each time the ball is hit. Doing the drill correctly you can hit a ball every ten seconds. That's 114 things a minute. Do this for 10 minutes … non-stop and correctly, and you can see 1,140 things that can be observed. Do this for an hour; you're up to 6,840 actions. I would say in the first two weeks of practice, I hit 7,000 balls …which if done correctly is about 133,000 actions.

There were 133,000 actions to make one play. Nine months later, it was done perfectly. The left fielder rushing up, third baseman in position, hands in the air; the catcher lining up the third baseman; the left fielder throwing a strike, third baseman getting the body in correct position. Catcher yelling "cut home", the third baseman making a perfect throw, the catcher making the perfect tag. Even the pitcher did the right thing, backing up home. I've never seen better execution by a whole team on a single play.

If nothing else went right that day, even if we had eventually lost 7-1 or 8-1, I would have been happy. I would have felt that all that hard work was for something. More importantly than that, the players perhaps would have understood the importance of proper practice. They worked hard on that play. When they did it wrong I called them all in and talked to them about practicing the right way and practicing hard, and working hard. They did it over and over again.

Well, once this play happened in this particular game in this particular circumstance, everything went right for us. The guys stormed off the field, I stormed out of the dugout. There was passion on that field. All of a sudden we're hitting the ball a little harder, running a little faster, and getting a bunch of luck. Within two innings, the 4-1 deficit became a 6-4 lead. We had them on the ropes.

The Mavericks manage to put a rally up in the bottom of the last inning and with two outs and the score 6-5, they had the tying run on third base. The next batter hit a sharp grounder past the pitcher up the middle. Tyler Hibbs, playing shortstop, went to his left behind second base, scooped up the ball, and threw the runner out by half a step. We won the tournament all because we practiced one play 7,000 times and did it right once.

That's what you need to do to be successful.

You don't get better by doing things once in a while or when it's convenient. It's repetition; over and over and over again. Pitchers go to spring training and they cover first base over and over and over again. Very seldom in a big league game do you see screwups where the pitcher doesn't cover first base on a ground ball to the right side of the diamond? It's not because they are so smart or so alert. It's because they do it thousands of times. It's muscle memory. The ball is hit to the right side and it is a reaction, they don't even think. Go to a high school game and you will see how many times the pitcher doesn't get over to cover first base or the outfielder misses the cut off man or the batter can not put down a sacrifice bunt. They will miss the cut off man over and over and over again. Watch how many times they can't put down a sacrifice bunt.

If you want to be the best you need to put in the extra effort. Do it until you can do it right all the time. Then do it some more. There are no short cuts to success. You need to work hard, not just put in the time. Work hard. Go at it 100% all the time.

It's the price of success.

My mind now goes back to the players on the field, practicing on this cold March afternoon. They are ready to start a scrimmage and the one team just took the field. I picked out a couple of the kids I would consider Group 1 kids in my mind that happened to be on this team in the field. They jogged onto the field. I'm not sure but I think they just made a major mistake. The rest of them ran onto the field. Like clockwork, here comes the coach out of the dugout,

"Get in here."

I have myself a nice chuckle. I know what's coming next. The team runs into meet him by the first base line and nobody is jogging now. They are sprinting. The head coach is going at it with them for what seems like five minutes and then, all of a sudden, they take off for their positions, like caged animals that were just given their freedom. The pace has picked up immensely. It's worth another laugh.

The Group 1 kids are the Group 1 kids; and they just showed why. It has nothing to do with talent. They just don't work as hard as the others and they don't have the passion. They don't get it. Some of these kids are juniors and seniors. They've seen this happen time and time again, and they allowed themselves to be on the wrong side of the wrath of the coach.

I watch for a little longer. I see Tyler Hibbs going out to third base. He's sprinting. Of all the players who need to impress the Coach the most by hustling on to the field, it isn't Tyler. He's the star of the team, but he's not jogging, or running. He's sprinting. He's not driven by a desire to impress the coach. He's driven by passion. I smile and head for the car.

RESPECT

Respect means supporting your teammates and coaches. It means encouraging fellow players, even those kids that are competing with you for a position. It means playing the game the way it should be played, no throwing the helmet or bat, no running a grounder out half speed, no arguing with the umpire. It means not showing up the umpire or showing up a teammate.

Respect means understanding the game, knowing what it's truly all about. You know that every facet of the game is important and serves a purpose. The bunt, the cutoff, the double steal, the pick off all has their significance.

As a coach you need to show the same respect. Having authority over kids doesn't mean that you can disrespect them. It needs to be mutual, respect goes both ways.

Eric is now in his junior year of high school. He is what I would consider a decent pitcher. He has done well for the last couple of years in the summer leagues against competition that is better than high school. I know that he has a lot of potential and he has now started growing. He has always been one of the smaller kids on his teams and always lacked the physical stature that would be necessary to get him to the next level. Now he's growing, though, and that makes me happy.

Nothing in a parent's life is more enjoyable than time shared with their kids, doing something they both love................

He still loves baseball. High school baseball, however, has not been the best of experiences for him. It has been like a seesaw. He would play well in the summer, and then digress during the school year. Then he would go back out in the summer and play well, then once again go backward during the school year. It became a painful pattern. He liked the guys on the high school team, he loved playing the game, but it was difficult for him to understand the lack of opportunity.

When Eric went out for the JV team as a freshman, he got an opportunity to pitch in two league games. He did fairly well, winning both games and pitching decent. His experiences at the plate weren't very good, however. During the entire season, he never had a chance to bat. Not once did the coach allow him to hit. Eric always held his own with the bat, never the top hitter on his team but always near the top. I knew why he never got a chance to hit. He was one of the smallest kids on the team and he didn't "rate out" well during the tryouts. He didn't hit the ball far enough. I said nothing to the coach and my only words to my son were, "Hang in there, summer will be here soon."

I sent a letter to the JV coach, asking for some explanations.

Coach:

I have a few general comments and questions regarding Eric (my son) and his JV baseball playing this year. I am hoping you find the time to respond to my comments and concerns.

1. I would like, as he would, to see his evaluation for this year. He has asked to see an evaluation yet has never received one. I would think that it would be common policy to evaluate the players and communicate to them their strengths and weaknesses. Eric took the initiative to go to you and request to see one. Perhaps other players are not as concerned about an evaluation, but Eric takes these things very serious. If a player isn't getting a lot of playing time, I feel he has the right to know why ...especially if he takes the initiative to ask.

2. I also would like an explanation in regards to why Eric never had an opportunity to (other than pitch) play in any games or bat in any games. Certainly somewhere in a 16 game schedule with many of the games called after five innings because you were killing the other team, a player would have an opportunity to swing the bat or play the field ...just once. If you had a set lineup from last year's spring team, I could certainly see why it would be tough for a new guy to play much, but you had several freshman starting or playing this year that were new to the program. They may have played last fall in the pick-up league and you may have known of them, but I don't feel that a player should be penalized because he played fall ball somewhere else and honed his skills. From the end of July of last year until the end of the year, Eric played in over 60 games and in six tournaments (winning three of them) against some good competition. I understand that the philosophy at many schools is to get the "nine best hitters," the nine guys who can hit the ball 300 feet. I hope there is room on your team for someone who makes contact almost all the time, hits for a decent average, can put a bunt down, can work the pitcher ...On offense...and on defense.. can track a fly ball, scoop a ball at first base, get in position for a cut off, make the proper throw and lead off a base without being picked off.

3. In regards to pitching, Eric had an opportunity to participate which I am thankful for. He pitched in two games. The first one was against Meade (I wasn't present) which I heard he did okay. Not great but okay. He waited for a while to get another chance and it came against Annapolis. Again, I think he pitched pretty well. He managed to get 11 strikeouts, which as the scorekeeper stated set a record for the year. Annapolis or Meade weren't exactly top teams, but to be honest, there were a lot of inferior teams and all in all, I believe Eric pitched okay as did most of your other pitchers. So why would he only get two opportunities when other pitchers were getting five and six starts? He strikes out 11 guys and his reward is to never pitch again.

4. I don't know the extent of how you stay up with the development of players during the off school season, but I would like you to follow Eric's development. He has been playing at Gambrills all year. The Baltimore Metro League that he plays in will be finished the end of June. He will then play in probably three National Tournaments in July and August among other games and then play once again this fall either at Gambrills or with Arundel if there is a decent fall program. our web site ....www.eteamz.com/GAC. From there, you can see our upcoming schedule and individual statistics ... hitting and pitching. Yes, Eric Potter, batting average of .454. He is the top hitter on the team. He has a great swing and he makes contact and he can draw a walk and he doesn't strike out much. I don't understand how a player who is hitting .454 in a much more competitive league than the JV county ball this spring didn't even get a chance to swing a bat once in a game this year. Again, the web site is www. eteamz. com/GAC.

I would appreciate a response at your earliest convenience.

Jeff Potter

Three months later, I had not received a response. I e-mailed again and this time there was a reply. I stopped reading it when it said that Eric "Didn't lift enough weight over his head and wasn't strong enough."

That summer, Eric went back out and played in the summer league, the Baltimore Metro League with the rest of his Gambrills teammates. It was a pretty good team and we had some really good players on the roster. Tyler Hibbs was an awesome hitter. He was the third top hitter on the team with an average of .436. Kieran Flannery was another player and he is a great hitter, one of the best that I've seen. He was the second leading hitter on that team with an average of .458.

Eric was happy being back out on the field with his buddies. He was finally given a chance to not only pitch regularly, but to swing the bat. Despite still being small and not real strong, he did as well as he could with the bat. He led the team that summer with a .482 average.

But he wasn't good enough to swing the bat once in school.

As time went on, I continued doing what I thought I should do to encourage and motivate my son to do the best he could. I would always tell him to "Hang in there, your time will come." I told him to continue to work hard. I also told him to be respect parents, coaches, teammates, and mostly, himself. I relayed to him how important it was to deal with anything and everything that was thrown his way and things have a way of working out.

But there's always an exception to the rule.

There's always a time that someone acts in a way so disrespectful that they don't really deserve anything in return. You hope it never happens, and if it does, it doesn't affect you negatively. I could have never imagined this happening to my son. It did happen though. The date was April, 17, 2006, another day that I will never forget.

Who knew that he would take such a negative and turn it into a positive?

Who knew that this day would change my son forever?

The high school baseball team was hosting their annual tournament over that Easter weekend. A couple of New York teams came down, along with a local team, which made it a nice little four-team weekend get together. Because they were non-league games, Eric would probably pitch a little and perhaps swing the bat once or twice.

Everything started out just fine.

I was 51 years old at the time. I have been around a lot of people and I've heard a lot of things communicated that were not the most complimentary. I've witnessed some really rude behavior in my life. I've been associated with some very shallow people with huge character flaws. I've been involved with baseball and management and sales and customers and family. I think I've had occasion to fight and argue with all of them at some point in time. I'm not proud to say that I have not always taken the high ground when it came to the misunderstandings. I've made more than my share of poor choices of words, and have used some very poor judgment.

But nothing in my life came close to what was communicated to my son on that day. Just a remark, but one I'll never forget. It was just one sentence, but it said volumes about the coach and about the particular program that he was in charge of. It is a remark that will forever be etched in my memory. It joined Joe Sheeler's "Always compare yourself to someone better" and Coach Spellman's words to me in the principal's office, "I think Jeff showed his true character out on the field on Saturday."

It was worse.

The coach took my son Eric and another pitcher, Tyler Lewis, to the side and was explaining to them how they were competing to be the #3 pitcher on the team. He related the fact that they would share pitching duties the first game of their doubleheader that day. Perhaps this was his method of bringing them together and letting the two pitchers know that they were going to slug it out and may the best man win. Both players knew that Tyler Hibbs was the ace of the staff and Joel Roberts was the #2 man in the rotation.

Okay, so far so good. There is absolutely nothing wrong with a little friendly competition as a motivating tool. Matter of fact, all good coaches tries to use these types of mental games all the time when they are trying to get an edge.

I wish he would have stopped there, but he decided to go on with one additional sentence that still rings in my ear today. The next words out of his mouth were,

"Hibbs will be pitching the second game. <u>I want to win that one</u>."

I was at the ball field that day. I am so thankful that this information was not communicated to me during the game. The violent temper that I had somehow hidden away since I was a child surely would have reared its ugly face. Any respect that Eric had for that coach, which probably was not much at the time, I am sure immediately left his body. It had already left me and my wife long before that day. We had already seen enough the first two years of high school to know that this person, at least in our minds, had no business coaching high school baseball. Our job on a daily basis now was to encourage our son despite what he saw and tolerated every day. He had been taught to respect adults. Things don't go exactly your way in life, the coach doesn't give you what you consider a fair shot...these are things you need to deal with. This is life. Bite your lip and go forward and prove him wrong.

But this crossed the line.

I would never even consider saying that to a player. It rings of a pure negative attitude, about as far from respect as you can get. It's nothing more than cold, shallow, and arrogant. There is no way to find any redeeming qualities in this remark, and certainly no team building. This was about as complete opposite of Coach Spellman, and his character, as you could get.

The coach lost a player that day; not physically, but emotionally. Truth be known, that coach over the course of time has lost all of his players. He and his small band of followers just can't see the continuous harm that they inflict on young men.

A coach may have passion and may work hard, but if he has no respect for his players, or cannot show respect, he's stuck on second base. He'll never come around to score.

Just my opinion.

So now Eric was at the crossroads, as I was 35 years prior. The big difference was that I brought my problem upon myself, I disrespected my coach and my teammates and it cost me a lot of playing time. The coach was right, I was wrong and I learned my life lesson. He benched me because he had to show respect to his players. He had to show them (the team) that everyone is treated equally and fairly. If someone can not show respect for their coach and teammates, then they need to be dealt with. This time, Eric was the victim, the coach was wrong. Eric was disrespected, but he managed to continue to show respect, even if it wasn't deserved.

In a very ironic twist this episode probably did more good for Eric than anything that has ever happened to him on a ball field. No credit to the coach but a lot of credit to Eric.

So now he could either put his tail between his legs and crawl into a hole or come out fighting. I think Eric decided to fight. Right there, that day, he decided to fight. He, to his credit, does not have the same temperament that his father had when he was 16. He doesn't get angry too often.

But I think that day changed him forever.

I think he realized that the biggest people can be very small. I think he realized that life isn't fair. There's an old saying, "It's not what happens to you in life that's important, it's how you respond to it." He took the high road. I think this episode motivated him to prove the coach wrong. He took a negative and made it a positive. That day motivated him forever and it gave him one thing I think he was lacking; a little bit of well placed anger. From that day forward, he was possessed.

It's the price of success.

Too many coaches confuse power with respect. They have power and authority, and a few insecure coaches and parents who kiss their feet, and they feel that this gives them the opportunity to treat people like crap. They aren't questioned (everyone is intimidated by them, or concerned about their kid's playing time) so they continue to act in this manner. When they can't motivate or be effective by teaching the right life lessons, they feel they have no recourse other than to be a bully and belittle people.

The conduct displayed that day was at best, pitiful. It was childish, arrogant and condescending. It was the best example of what never to say to a youth or young man. That was not the saddest part of this experience. The part that is truly regrettable is the fact that to this day, he probably does not have a clue in regards to what he did. The many, many times that he has assuredly repeated this behavior over the last couple of years have probably gone on with out a comment made to him by the poor player, or the player's parents, or any coach. They would not have the gumption to question the master. This behavior, however, does not go unnoticed.

We all walk that fine line of balance of what is fair and what isn't fair. When are we spoiling our child and when is he just getting mistreated? When do you say something and when do you just bite your tongue? What I do know is that there just aren't enough good coaches.....like back in the day.

SELFLESSNESS

We finally have made it to third base. We have the passion, we have the hard work ethic, and we also understand and live our lives with the correct respect for each other, and ourselves.

For all of you parents of high school or youth coaches, is your coach still in the game? Has he made it to third base? Think back to all of your kid's coaches…and all of your coaches. Think back to all of your teachers, or your bosses, or someone else. How many of them are still in the game? Are YOU still in the game? Do people look at you and feel you have the passion and hard work and respect?

That respect thing can knock out a bunch of coaches, and players. I was recently talking to a father who has a child who attends a school which has a very successful baseball coach. He told me his son had attended a graduation party of a student who happened to be on the baseball team. His son told him that there were a lot of players at the party and not one of them had anything nice to say about the coach. How can you not have anything nice to say about a successful coach? Not one person respects the coach?

How can that be?

So now we're headed for home and there's only one thing left to do, be selfless. I like to call it "stripping your ego." It is one of the hardest things to do. We're all taught to be confident. Confidence means having a good ego, knowing you can do things and believing in yourself. In a way, stripping your ego brings you back to being a good teammate. You don't have to be the star. As a coach, you don't have to be right.

Sometimes success isn't what you do for yourself; it's what you do for others. It's influencing someone in a positive way. It's knowing you were right about something, but not having to let everyone know that you were right. It's about someone else getting the credit undeservingly, but you being big enough of a man to let it go.

It's talking to the team after the game and telling them what you did wrong as the coach.

It's not about how many victories you have. It's not about the game being about you. It's not grandstanding. It's being the invisible coach. It's acknowledging that the team could probably win as many games without you. It's giving credit to other people. Let the players be known more than you.

As a player, it's also being selfless. It's not about you. It's about the team. It's giving credit to other players even if it's not deserved. It's allowing another kid to have a day in the sun.

It's amazing how much you can accomplish when it doesn't matter who gets the credit.

I sometimes mess with parents, as they mess with me. It's all in fun, but you are still trying to make a subtle point to the other one as you banter back and forth. I usually focus on this area, the selflessness, with a parent. We are all extremely proud of our kids and their accomplishments in baseball. Some of us are prouder. And even though we try to keep our boasting to a minimum, some of us just can't hold ourselves back.

Arundel High School has a tremendous baseball tradition, winning ten state championships. They have a lot of talent that goes in to that school every year. They have a lot of players who are prepared for high school baseball, playing regularly in summer leagues as kids. The school is blessed to usually have the most talent of any school in the county year after year after year. It would be nice if once, just once, the coaches at that school would recognize this fact and give credit where credit is due, instead of pretending that THEY turn these kids in to "real players." Just once, thank the summer coaches and the youth coaches and the parents and the players who have worked so hard. Instead of taking the credit, give the credit. By taking credit yourself, you are actually disrespecting the people that deserve the accolades.

Well, how many of you, or your coaches, or your child's coach, made it around the bases and scored? How many of them had all four qualities? The answer isn't necessarily in the wins compiled or the clippings in the newspaper. The answer is more likely to be in the players who twenty years later talk about their former coach with reverence. They will relay stories of how they learned something from a coach that they now use in their every day lives. Or perhaps the value system that helps them coach a little league team, or even help raise their kids.

I now do three things every morning when I wake up that relate somewhat to baseball; I look at the scar on my hand from that broken bat, I look at a picture of my son on a baseball field, and I think of Coach Spellman. They are all great memories. I think about the good that came out of each memory, and I also think about the sacrifices I needed to make concerning each of the experiences.

Five years ago, I did none of these. I was too busy with life. There were too many errands to run, too much money to make, too many things to bother me. I was running as fast as I could, just not going anywhere. I didn't have ten minutes a day to re-live the past. There was no time for daydreaming.

I discovered the power of being passionate, however, and it has made all the difference. It is something that can clear your mind and put things in perspective real quick. Sometimes being passionate forces you to sacrifice other things.

But it's worth it.

It's the price of success.

CHAPTER 10
THE PERFECT TEAM

"Coming together is a beginning, keeping together is progress, and working together is success."

—Henry Ford

I kind of wish I would have said no to him.

Not that I didn't want my boy to go play in a showcase tournament in Georgia and not that I didn't appreciate the offer. I mean East Cobb is where they play really good baseball. And it felt good that the coach thought Eric could really help his team with his pitching. It was really a great opportunity and I should be happy.

But here I was, standing in this long line at the airport on a Thursday morning, having managed a total of four hours of sleep the night before. My lack of sleep was from the fact that I had just left this same airport about seven hours ago. And of course it was the day of a major terrorist alert. All the airports are now on a "high alert level." I was at the Air Tran terminal at BWI airport in Baltimore with about fifty people in front of me. The line didn't seem to be moving real well. There was not a lot of chipper conversation going on.

Behind me and as far as you could see to my left and right was a line of people which must have been a half-mile long. I felt bad for those people who seemed to have been delayed by something going on in the foreign terminals. I couldn't tell where the line started or finished. At least we weren't in that line!

I was not going on this trip to Georgia. It would have been nice, but we had just got back from Aruba at midnight, last night, and I needed to go back to work. My son Eric was going with my wife. I wanted to make sure they get off okay. Again, I tried to look at the positives; at least we weren't in the long, never ending line!

Our line was unmercifully slow. Every five minutes we moved five feet. Every time we moved we needed to pick up all our bags and move them those few feet. No one seemed to be real happy. Finally, we got to the ticket counter and began the process of using the automated ticket "whatever." Two non-stop tickets to Atlanta were supposed to be waiting for us; we just needed to push the right buttons.

Wrong.

The tickets were not paid for, as promised, and now we needed to shell out over $1,000.00 for two tickets. Out came the trusty master card and I guess we would get this resolved later with the team.

The team was the Maryland Mavericks, a local showcase team. This was the same team who we always played well against, the team who we beat in the Olney tournament three years ago with that one play that we got right after practicing it 7,000 times. Their coach asked me a long time ago if Eric would be available to play with them this particular weekend. The Mavericks were always fun to play. They were good and they were feisty and their parents were feisty. They begrudgingly came to respect our Gambrills team. Over three years, we managed to be the only local team that had played them any amount of games that had a winning record against them. The former coach, Brian Frederick, always reminded me of that fact. It killed him to admit it.

Now my son had joined them.

The representatives of Air Tran were nice enough. Despite a good number of arrogant and obnoxious customers, they managed to hold it together. They helped us get things situated, checked in our baggage, and then informed my wife and son they needed to get to the back of the line.

My wife asked, "What line?"

She pointed to the long, long line of people who I was feeling sorry for.

That line.

We walked to the end of the line which took us to the end of the entire building. Everything now was "code red." No liquids on the plane. People were missing flights left and right, flights were being pushed back. It's was a mess. I needed to leave and go to work. I had no idea if they would make the plane.

Four hours of sleep and back to the airport to fly to Georgia so my son can pitch in perhaps one game. A $500.00 ticket for one wife, along with hotel and food and her expenses may be nearing $1,000.00. All of this to watch our son pitch one game.

We must be crazy.

We, along with thousands of other parents who have joined this silly merry-go-round, must be out of our minds. One can rationalize all one wants about the opportunity and experience. It's still a thousand bucks for one game.

At this age in competitive baseball this happens all the time. Kids are flown all over the country to perhaps pitch a few innings. When I was first approached about Eric playing for this team, I really thought it was quite a compliment to be asked. When I later realized that four or five other guys from across the eastern part of the country were being flown in to pitch a game, it lost some of its luster. As the coach said, "You need at least ten pitchers for these tournaments." Now I wish they would have settled for nine, minus my boy.

Well, they made the flight and everything went relatively smooth at the tournament. Eric pitched one game which we were told he would. He also got a chance to play the field and bat a few times, which we were happy about it and certainly didn't expect.

The coaches and the players couldn't have treated him better and it was a great experience. Because of some bad weather, some contests were cancelled and teams advanced based on a reduced amount of games being played. Unfortunately, Eric's team failed to advance.

My wife, although not knowing anyone, met some nice parents whom she went back and forth to the games with each day. She did her best to figure out what kids belonged to whom.

Sheryl would ask a parent "Who's the boy in right field?"

"We don't know him, he's new."

"Who's the pitcher?"

"I think he's the one from Kentucky", said a parent.

"No, no", said another parent, "That boy is coming in tomorrow."

Perhaps if all these pitchers and other players showed up, they could have what they considered the perfect team. Isn't that what every one is striving for?

The team that Eric went to Georgia with was full of talented ball players, but they were far from perfect. Some players on the team never met because one was flying back home after he pitched before the new teammate was flying in to take his turn on the mound. Other parents were disgruntled with their boy's playing time. Some just didn't like the team makeup. Tens of thousands of dollars were spent on a team who was no more than dysfunctional. They won no tournaments. They came home from that trip and played a few more games. They then cancelled their fall schedule and decided to take the fall off. A few weeks later they decided to basically disband the team.

With all the flying around and showcase teams and picking up star players, they were no more than a shell of a perfect team. They had turmoil and ego problems and players who wanted special treatment. They were well financed, but not well developed. They lacked cohesiveness, teamwork, and passion. There is hundreds of teams like that one out there trying to be perfect. Instead of trying to find more parts to be perfect, perhaps teams should develop the parts they have to strive for that perfection.

Eric wasn't the only player who I knew that was jumping on an airplane that summer to help out a team. Tyler Hibbs was in Venezuela, Jason Patten was in Florida, Kieran Flannery was also headed to Georgia, Matt Pace hooked on with another local team and went to Florida, and Kylin Simms played with Tyler in Florida. Six of my Gambrills guys were flying across the eastern part of the country to play ball. Sometimes the kids paid, sometimes they didn't. Usually teams picked up the player's expenses, parents were on their own.

I guess it's all in the search for the perfect team.

What exactly is the perfect team?

I see and hear about these teams all the time. You get e-mails and letters and phone calls. Guys show up at camps and showcases and hand you their card. You have Perfect Game and Baseball Factory and All-Maryland Teams and this classic and that classic. How can everyone be on a perfect team? If there is a perfect team, then there must only be one team. Everybody can't be perfect!

The main goal of the perfect team, wherever that team is located, seems to have a goal of winning as much as possible. The strategy to winning seems to be to collect the most talented players who you can possibly assemble and put them together on one field.

Then you have perfection.

When my son started playing at Gambrills at the age of 11, they had a pretty good team. There were several really good players and they all meshed together very well. The next year when Eric was 12 years old the coach tried to make the team better.

The coach tried to make the team perfect.

The problem was that his attempt at perfection was not by adding teamwork and chemistry and work ethic, but by adding another player here or there. He had a left fielder who he thought that he could improve on. So he brought in another kid who perhaps could throw harder and further and could hit the ball further and harder. That would get him closer to perfection. By adding this player, however, he then had to deal with the issue of playing time. He tried to make both of the kids and both sets of parents happy by playing both of them half the time. Every game he played the "old starter" half the game and the "new superstar" half the time. He ended up making everyone miserable; the players, the parents, and the teammates.

The original left fielder left the team at the end of the year because the coach told him something to the effect of "You're not good enough, you should really find another team." So although he was a great teammate and a good player, he was forced to leave. A year later, when the coach left the team, the player came back. He still couldn't throw harder and hit the ball further, but he did become a very strong part of that team. Four years later, he's still here. Last year, he led the team in hitting. He's the hardest worker I've ever seen on a ball field and he became part of MY "perfect team."

When my son was playing at Gambrills at the age of 13, the same coach tried to improve the team again by bringing in a "stud pitcher" who had some other issues that the coach didn't want to acknowledge. No need for details, it was another disaster. It helped start the break up of the team. The stud pitcher left after that season and was followed out the door by that coach. His attempts in being perfect were going backwards. He failed to understand that perfection has more to do than how someone "grades out" on their strength and quickness. As coach Spellman made abundantly clear, it also has to do with head and heart.

The coach left without finding perfection. I had my perfect team without looking. It was handed to me.

The team was perfect.

Absolutely perfect.

Over the next few years, a couple of kids dropped off and a couple were added, but this was the "Gambrills Gang of Ten." Some people have the wrong idea about perfection. One of the definitions of perfect is *thoroughly qualified or informed, skilled.* Every one of these kids was qualified, and skilled, in all areas of being a very good baseball player. Put ten qualified kids together, add a pinch of passion and a squirt of hard work, and maybe a half cup of respect and a spoonful of selflessness, and I believe you have a pretty good recipe for success; and perfection.

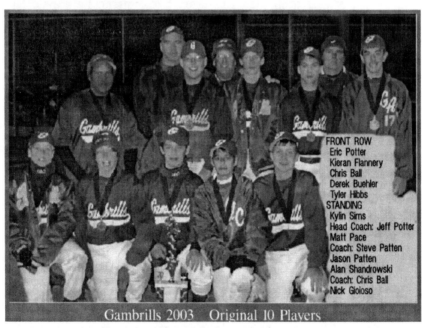

FRONT ROW
Eric Potter
Kieran Flannery
Chris Ball
Derek Buehler
Tyler Hibbs
STANDING
Kylin Sims
Head Coach: Jeff Potter
Matt Pace
Coach: Steve Patten
Jason Patten
Alan Shandrowski
Coach: Chris Ball
Nick Gioioso

Gambrills 2003   Original 10 Players

My Perfect Team

No longer did the Gambrills team try to be perfect by picking up one more really good player. We took another strategy, focusing much more on teamwork, attitude, passion and fairness.

Christopher Ball	Derek Buehler	Kieran Flannery
Nick Gioioso	Tyler Hibbs	Matt Pace
Jason Patten	Eric Potter	Alan Shandrowski
	Kylin Simms	

We stayed the course.
Sometimes that just works much better.

It parallels the story of a woman on a plane.

A middle age lady was nervously squirming in her chair. Although the one thing that passengers dislike the most about flying, the take off, had been completed 15 minutes earlier, she was still quite tense. As a stewardess was walking by, the woman stopped her.

"Excuse me, could you answer a question for me?"

"Yes, of course," said the stewardess

The woman then communicated to the stewardess that she had heard that airplanes are off course a lot while they fly, as much as 75% of the time. She asked the stewardess if that was true.

The stewardess, obviously taken back by such a technical question, said that she really didn't know, but she would try to get her an answer.

About 20 minutes later, the stewardess walked back to the woman, followed closely by the co-pilot. The co-pilot looked at the woman, with a slight smile and said,

"I understand you have a question about the airplane."

The woman, quite surprised by the personal attention that she was receiving, finally managed to get the question out.

"I heard that a plane can be off course a lot, sometimes as much as 75% of the time. Is that true?"

The co-pilot answered.

"That figure of 75% is not correct."

She was visibly relieved to hear the good news.

He continued,

"Actually it's closer to 95% of the time!"

After allowing the passenger to collect herself and catch her breath, he explained.

A plane takes off with an obvious pre-determined ending point. The goal of the pilot is to get the plane to that final destination as safely and quickly as possible. This is done through hundreds of small adjustments. The plane basically is never exactly on course, but the countless number of tiny adjustments allows the plane to arrive at its destination in the most efficient manner.

When the pilot knows that there may be a little turbulence in front of him, he prepares for it and understands that a little inconvenience is a lot more efficient than going 100 miles out of his way to completely miss the turbulence. Although rerouting of the plane may make for a smoother trip, he now has created other problems, such as a delay in getting to his destination and other planes having to be re-routed because of him.

Can you imagine 1,000 airplanes up in the air everyday that are making major changes in their flight pattern to miss a little turbulence? You would have chaos. Those poor air traffic controllers would be re-routing every plane every day. Every plane would be later than usual, every plane would use more gas, every controller would be pulling his hair out, and the chance of an accident would probably be increased.

So what the airline industry does is have flight patterns. In a real emergency (severe storm, possibility of hurricane, emergency mechanical problems) planes are diverted to another area, but small inconveniences are dealt with.

I heard this little story probably 20 years ago or so. I was at a management seminar at the time and the speaker was comparing this little tale to being a good manager. It's not verbatim, but it is close enough to make a good point. You need to understand what your goal is and to acknowledge that achieving your goal won't be exactly a straight line; but if you're a good manager, or good coach, and you don't get too far off the path, you will succeed in attaining your final destination by making adjustments as you go. Not major adjustments, but continuous, small adjustments. That will get you to your final destination.

The more that I thought of this little management tip the more that I realized that my son's youth baseball career should take the same flight as that airplane. Perhaps by all of us continually trying to find that perfect situation or team we are really missing a lot of good things, kind of "not seeing the forest through the trees."

Compare this to playing ball, and playing for an organization. What would happen if everyone with a little issue, a little turbulence, over reacted and decided to re route (change organizations) whenever it wasn't smooth sailing? You would have chaos.

And sometimes you do.

Nobody moves their kid from one organization or school to another to hurt him. Obviously, the parents are trying to improve his baseball experience. Sometimes, however, by making a temporary convenience we make a permanent inconvenience.

We sometimes just need to stay the course.

I don't know all the pros and cons of playing for a lot of organizations vs. a few since I have experienced only two programs. It's obvious that playing for a lot of organizations allows a child to experience more coaches and teammates. More exposure to more people allows you to see a lot of different ways of doing things. If you can pick up a few good things from a lot of different people, that could be advantageous.

It's also apparent to me that playing for a lot of organizations means constantly moving and having to adjust a lot more to new teammates, and every time you move, you're basically the new guy on the team who has to work harder than the others to prove yourself. You don't have the built in favoritism or politics on your side.

What's a parent to do?

There's no real right or wrong answer of course. Every family has a different set of circumstances to consider, and every situation is unique to those people. I can give you my thoughts and opinions, however.

We've all heard about the grass being greener on the other side. In most instances, it is not. It really isn't, but I'm not complaining.

Some of my best friends who I have met are because their kids play baseball, and I was introduced to them because we all were looking for that better opportunity.

My son has played ball now for over ten years and has played for two organizations. We have been extremely lucky to be associated with one of them, The Gambrills Athletic Club. When I think of the other one, I try to remember the saying about "taking lemons and making lemonade." It was definitely lemons; we tried our best to make lemonade.

Sometimes as coaches we should also stay the course. It is so easy to want to change one or two pieces of the puzzle to make a better, stronger team. It seldom works.

I think there are a certain criteria to having the perfect team, and this is a few of mine.

Every player on the team has a passion for the game of baseball.

There's that word again; passion. I truly believe that all of our players on our "perfect team" had a passion for playing baseball and that passion made the difference.

Everybody contributes

In a seven-month period, the Gambrills kids won six tournaments with basically the same players. Five different players was a winning pitcher in a championship game. The nine kids who started each championship game were the nine kids who had played the least in the tournament up to that point. Some of those winning final games had three of the best players on the team sitting on the bench at the beginning of the game. It didn't matter what guys were on the field and what players were waiting their turn. I think it helped humble those players needing humbling. I think it gave confidence to those kids needing confidence. I think it built teamwork.

If your best player gets hurt and that impacts your team a lot, then you're not perfect. Some players were obviously better than others, but you didn't highlight that. You didn't always throw your best pitcher because that gave you a better chance of winning. Maybe you threw your third best pitcher even when your best pitcher was ready. Why? To make him better, to let him know how much better he needs to get.

No player was bigger than the team; not even Tyler Hibbs.

If we ever had a star on our team, it was Tyler. He was always really good and could always throw really hard. Besides that, he could field good, hit good, run good, and play with extreme intensity. That was a combination that you seldom found.

We were playing a tournament in Southern Maryland some years back and were waiting to play in the championship game. Tyler, probably our best pitcher and with out a doubt our most fierce competitor, was slated to start on the mound for us. We managed to get to the finals with our other hurlers and liked very much our chances in the championship game with our ace being the slated pitcher.

I was sitting all by myself watching another ball game, killing some time before our scheduled finale. With a hot dog in one hand and a coke in the other and a nice warm breeze in my face life couldn't have been much better. It was perfect.

Out of the corner of my eye I noticed the tournament director, who I didn't care for much anyway, coming toward me with one of those looks on his face. He was already changing my mood.

"Jeff, I just got a complaint from a spectator. One of your boys threw a battery and it came very close to hitting her."

I couldn't much dispute what he was saying, as he was sticking the evidence in my face. To make matters worse I was still chewing on my hot dog. We were playing at Chancellor's Run in Lexington Park, Maryland, which is a beautiful place to play ball games. At this complex, there are four ball fields with a large building in the center of them which you can go up to the top of and look out over all the fields. That's where the battery came from.

I said the only thing I could say,

"I'll take care of it."

The last two bites of the hot dog were devoured, another swig of the coke, and off I went to investigate the crime. My demeanor had changed quite a bit in the last few minutes. I walked up the steps of the building to the top and as expected no one was present. From that vantage point, however, I looked out and could see that most of my team was on an adjacent field hitting balls. I quickly walked down the stairs and headed toward the field. As I approached the players, you could see their demeanors were changing, probably partly fear and the other part guilt. Kylin Sims, unfortunately for him, was the closest player to me.

Come here, Kylin
Yeah, coach.
Kylin, who threw the battery?
What?
Who threw the battery?
I can't tell you.
Why?
I just can't.

He didn't say he didn't know, he said he couldn't tell me. I respect loyalty, I really do. I think that is a wonderful virtue.

But unfortunately for him in this situation, loyalty was taking a back seat to responsibility. I had a bigger problem here. I could have asked all the other players and hoped that one broke, but that wouldn't really have been fair. I called Kylin back in.

Yeah, coach.

Kylin, I will find out who threw the battery. If you tell me, it will save me some time which I would appreciate a lot. If you don't tell me, I'll find out anyway. Whoever threw it sits at least three innings. If you don't tell me, you're not playing.

It didn't take him long to say "Tyler threw it."

Once Kylin left, I asked a few of the other guys over to where I was standing and had a quick chat with them. I already had my answer, but I didn't want Tyler to know Kylin told me, so this way he really wouldn't know how I found out. All the other guys gave me the same response, "I don't know." I respected their loyalty to their teammate.

I then started walking toward the rest of the players, including Tyler. I got about 30 feet away from him, battery in hand. He turned around and without a question being asked of him said,

"Yeah, I threw it."

I said "You know you're sitting."

Yes, he knew that.

His only question, "How long?"

"I'm not sure yet."

"Okay"

He never argued. He took his punishment.

You would think this would have been something bad, the fact that our star pitcher was not playing. All it did, though, was put me in a no lose situation. If we won the championship game it would show the team that's exactly what they were; a team. Everyone contributed, and when someone didn't play, no matter who it was, you just replaced him with someone else. If you can't, you're certainly not perfect. If we lost the championship, we lost as a team. Your star player knows he's not bigger than the team and he understood the responsibility that he has and how you can let your teammates down. No one was bigger than the team.

The game was played and Tyler sat right on the end of the bench, looking like a caged animal that was ready to be unleashed. He was not in too good of a mood. I felt awful for him but certainly couldn't let him know that. I believe it was the fourth inning when I told him to go warm up. He got in to the game that inning and ended up pitching the rest of the game. We won.

Before the game, I walked up to his dad.

"Hey Tom, Tyler's sitting a few innings."

I got one of those "Tom looks" and then he said,

"What did he do?"

"He threw a battery near a woman and she complained."

Tom said; "Sit him as long as you need to."

During their time at Gambrills, the players all had their "moments" and they were all reprimanded accordingly. It reminded me of the good old days, when I was a kid. Just like my coaches, I would sit a kid for something stupid he did and I never got a hard time from the parents. They would, however, "read the riot act" to their son. When I disciplined a player, he usually heard it twice as much from a parent. Today, you don't see that nearly enough. There is a tremendous lack of discipline by coaches.

By Tyler sitting, it gave another player an opportunity to start, and contribute. Everybody contributed. This goes back to the ad-age, don't have a kid on the team if he doesn't play. If you're keeping a kid on the team just in case you have someone to fill in if kids call off sick or get injured, then you're not perfect. And it really isn't fair. This idea that a kid is a safety valve or emergency player is used by coaches with small minds and large insecurities. Coaches shouldn't be afraid to lose. Coaches should put any kid in any situation. When you put the player in the game in the bottom of the sixth inning when the score is 9-0, you're teaching him nothing. And he's not contributing. There's a difference between getting kids in the game and kids contributing. How exactly will a kid get better batting in a game with the score 9-0? Even if he gets a hit, he won't get better because he's never put in pressure situations.

Everybody gets better

This is development over winning. If kids don't get better, you're not perfect. I love the coaches who win the tournament and do nothing more than play their best nine, who have more talent that the other team.

So what?

I was talking to a mom of a former Gambrills player and she was relaying a story of a coach we both know. He works with younger kids. He took a team to Rehoboth Beach to play in one of those weeks long tournaments, the kind that is copying what Cooper-stown does. My friend asked the woman how it went. The mother said she'll never play for him again. She paid for a week down at the beach, and with all expenses it cost her close to $2,000.00. The boy never got into a game. This is an 11-year-old kid! The team didn't win the tournament, or even come close to winning it. But even if they would have, they don't have anything close to a perfect team. Unfortunately, that coach is still out there running a team.

Parents need to be on board

Parents are just as important as the players. If they don't buy in to what the coach is doing and how the coach is doing it, it will have an adverse effect on the team. Parents need to encourage every player, understand the life lessons being taught, and see past the win at any cost mentality. I know it's hard sometimes, but you need to teach the right lessons out on the field.

Don't coach ... just watch

The perfect team could be on cruise control. They don't need coaching. They understand what needs to be done and they do it without being told. Coaches are over hyped. Egos are way out of control. The best thing that coaches can do is try to make the game fun, motivate the players to give a full effort, and bring out the passion in the kids. The notion that coaches are these Gods is absurd. In the course of a season, I believe very few games are won or lost because of coach's decisions. I do believe, however, that many games can be lost because a coach has "lost his team", can't seem to motivate them or get the best effort out of them.

As a coach, let the team make up the line up a few times and let the team run the game. You may learn something.

Check the kids 5 and 10 years later

The jury is still out. I don't know how perfect my perfect team really was, but I believe that the best litmus test is how they are years later, both as ball players, and as young men. The first check up is very close. Right now they're doing okay. They are all in the midst of their high school campaign or have moved on to college. It's pretty interesting stuff. Of the ten players, there's a good chance that all of them will go to college and most of them will play baseball after high school. There's also a good chance that a few of them could end up playing professional baseball. At least four of them have a shot at it. It may come down to how bad they want it. I don't think the passion will be a problem.

Eric finished his junior year at Arundel High School as a member of the state championship team. He pitched a little, but not much. The teammate that he was competing with to be the #3 starter was also a junior. He was a solid ball player and would have started in the outfield as a senior. He decided to not come out for the team, though. He had enough.

Eric wasn't good enough in the coach's eye to pitch much as a junior. That was his assessment and everyone certainly has a right to their opinion. What was crystal clear at the time was what I had already known. If Eric wanted to play baseball in college, we (Eric, my wife, and I) needed to be proactive. The misconception that I had before Eric entered high school – that high school coaches were so important in the advancement of kids to college baseball, was completely gone.

We went to work.

Three days after the state championship game, he started with the summer Gambrills team. He pitched well his first game out, and by the time he was done in late October, he had compiled a record of 14-0 against competition much better than high school. Fourteen wins in a row against older, better competition, but he wasn't good enough to pitch in high school. One of those wins was against the high school coach's showcase summer team, the Maryland Monarchs.

He had taken the most horrible thing a coach could say to a player and turned it into pure motivation. He was now determined and a bit angry, and with every victory, he had a bit more swagger. Along with this, Eric Potter was no longer little. He was now 6"1" and stronger by the week. His fastball now had some zip on it and he was on top of his game.

Growing up, I'm not sure how perfect any of my teams were. I know that I was usually on a team who won a lot of games, whether it was Little League, Pony League, Colt League, High School, or American Legion baseball. I always had a lot of teammates who seemed to be pretty good. I always had a lot of teammates who seemed to love to play baseball and I always had a coach who seemed to be only interested in teaching us the game of baseball. I seemed to have learned a lot of life lessons out on the ball fields. I seemed to have had a lot of fun playing baseball. I seem to have had a lot of good memories from my playing days.

Perfect, perhaps not, but it was enough.

Last spring, I watched Eric play on his high school team who had all the talent in the world. They had a lot of good ball players who played the game well. I think there was more talent on his team than I ever had on any team that I played for. Unfortunately they did not have the rest of what I had; the fun, the coaching ethic, the discipline. They were far from perfect. They rolled through their weak county schedule undefeated, a glowing 16-0. In their first play-off game in the state tournament, against a team with a losing record, they lost and were eliminated. They were good at rolling over very poor teams. They were terrible at competing against teams who were good, or played well for a game.

They lost that play off game 1-0. Eric was the losing pitcher. He pitched really well; except for one pitch. It was hit over the left field fence in the sixth inning. In the bottom of the seventh and final inning, Eric's team put the first two batters on base. With runners on first and second and nobody out and down one run, they have the batter take a strike. With one strike on him, they finally gave him the bunt sign, which he took for another strike. He eventually struck out and the runners didn't advance. The next two players struck out and the game was over. No runs, no hits, no bunts. Not being able to execute a bunt probably cost them the game. That wasn't being anything close to perfect.

They were great at beating teams 12-0 and 14-3. The close, low scoring games against teams of equal talent were quite different. They went down to Georgia a month earlier and against evenly matched teams, lost all three games. The team was out played, out coached, and out hustled.

They were far from perfect.

Most people, who attempt to put together the perfect team, especially at younger ages, are set up for failure. This is because the perfect team usually consists of a lot of players who have dads coaching the team. In most cases the kids are being protected by their dad and they really are not necessarily good. Therefore, when the coaches try to improve on their team year after year, they are instantly giving their kids a free ride. They are trying to build the perfect house with a structure built in quick sand.

In the early part of last year, sometime in February, I got an e-mail from a friend of mine. She asked if I knew of anyone who could give her 12- year old son some lessons, to perhaps improve his talents enough that he would get decent playing time on his upcoming spring team. A year before this, I would have replied quickly and rattled off a few names. There's a bunch of instructors out there, and I would say that most of them would have been more than happy to take on one more customer. That was then though. A lot has happened since that time.

I started writing a book. I also happened to be working with some kids that had been associated with poor instructors. I was helping start a new team of kids who had moved over from another organization that possessed very poor fundamentals in the game of baseball. I was very disenchanted with a lot of baseball politics. The writing of this book, along with all of these experiences, had brought more to light than I ever imagined.

Now, I felt that I was more responsible in sending kids here and there. My recent experiences with parents, players, and instructors had made me more sensitive to parents just throwing money at lessons. In addition to this, there was another issue gnawing at me. I remembered the experience this young player had with this team the previous year. It was very unpleasant.

The only reason that he was playing for this team again was a last minute "tugging at the heartstrings." The young boy was prepared to go to another team after his lack of playing time the previous year. Although he was not happy with the playing time, he liked some of the kids on the team, the level of competition, and the "nice uniforms." That was enough to have him perhaps lean toward returning to the team. He tried out for the team in the fall of 2006 for the upcoming spring. The coaches told him that he wasn't cut, but they were going to try out some other kids. This was the writing on the wall. His parents presented the options to him, and he decided to play locally. Although the competition would be less and the team would be weaker, he would PLAY... and besides that, it was local. The other team was a Baltimore based travel team.

Every thing was set. Mom, dad, and son had accepted the fact that he would play on a new team and they were all happy with the decision. The only connection to the old team was an end of year banquet. They could have easily just decided to miss it, but the son wanted to go and the parents also wanted him to go for a very special reason. Unknown to the boy, he was to receive a special plaque as "the player with the best attitude." It would be only fair that he had a chance to receive it.

He did go to the banquet with his dad. He did receive his plaque and everyone was happy. He was pumped up, the teammates were glad to see him. Somewhere in all of the clamor and excitement, someone asked him if he was coming back to the team .... because we really want you ... and heart took over head, and his response was, "Yeah, I'm coming back."

His dad was, as one may imagine, taken by surprise. Perhaps everybody was caught up in the moment and things just took off. Or perhaps, this was a cheap trick ... a way to get a young kid back on a team to probably sit the bench once again. I would probably also have given a plaque out to a player who sat on the bench most of the year with a great attitude. That's the last guy who I would want to lose from a team.

To say the least, mom was not thrilled with the news when they came home from that banquet. Weeks and weeks of gentle urging and fine salesmanship down the drain with one tug on his heart.

So now we were going to try to improve his skills so he could play on a team who both parents did not want him on, and truthfully, he did not want to be on. It would probably be like last year ... the sitting on the bench would be okay for a while, and then at some point in time he would become extremely unhappy with the manner in which he was treated.

Now we needed to add to this fine mess the fact that five players on the team happened to be proud sons of the five coaches and yes, you guessed ... they never come out of a game. No, they all weren't really that good. They just always played.

The last part of this perfect picture is the fact that the association that these coaches and players participated for the previous year was not happy with the team's performance. They didn't win enough games. There had to be change and action needed to be taken. So what they did was take the five coaches and made one of the assistants the head coach and the head coach the assistant. They ended up with the same five coaches, only now a couple of them have different titles.

Because his parents are good friends of mine and because his brother played for me for years and because I knew all of this history, I decided that finding an instructor wasn't the answer. Finding a solution to this was the answer. I was intrigued by this situation and what great content for a book about youth baseball. This would be a treasure to investigate.

All this rationale was done in my head in about five minutes. I e-mailed the boy's mom and told her that I would work with him. My motives were deeper, but for the time being I would help him with his baseball skills. She refused to allow me to do this for free so we came up with a nominal fee. I would work with him, assess his abilities, and see what we could do to improve his skills. Based on the conversations that I had with his parents up to now, I had a fairly good idea that he in fact was comparable with most of the kids regarding talent. We just had to get him in the line up some way.

The cards were stacked against him big time. Although the team had picked up several new players who they had never seen play on a field, they had already prepped the player that he would not be a starter. They had no idea the talent on the team, but they knew that he was not good enough to start. The only option that I could see was to work with him and improve him so much that they had no choice but to play him. I knew he was a decent player.

I worked with him for about four weeks and I could see no reason why he was not good enough to start on a 12-u baseball team. He had a decent arm, good hitting, and average fielding. He played third base, catcher, and did some pitching. The only thing left to do to assess how he stacked up against the other players on the team was to go to one of their indoor practices.

So on a cold Monday night in the month of February I went to one of the team's regularly scheduled indoor practices. Although it is difficult to properly evaluate kids by watching them practice only inside hitting in a cage, I had seen enough. The practice was run very poorly, the coaches were non instructors, and it was total confusion. Kids were running around and it was obvious that there was not only a lack of organization, there was no discipline.

I left there that evening and sent his mother a long-winded e-mail. I could have actually cut it down to five words, GET HIM OUT OF THERE. It was awful. The trip up to the work out that night solidified my belief that he would not get a fair opportunity with this team.

About three weeks later this team was playing in their first real games of the spring. It was a tournament at Rehoboth Beach. The boy and his dad went to the tournament which was played over the weekend. Two games were played on Saturday and two games were played on Sunday. In four complete games, he played a total of two innings. He batted three times. Yes, every one of the five coach's sons played every inning of every game. These were the first games of the year, practice games.

If this was the end of the story it could be considered sad and unfair.

It gets better.

The parents had no doubt that this was it for this team. They would not put him through this anymore. They both believe in keeping your commitments, but this was way past the point of being fair. A letter was written to the coach of the team communicating their intention to leave the team and although the reason should have been evident, they also explained in detail why they were leaving.

The coach, upon receiving the letter, couldn't understand why they were so upset. This coach then attempted to convince the parents that he did in fact play 50% of the time. The coach was adamant that hitting three times over the weekend and playing the field a total of two innings was equivalent to playing 50% of the time.

How do organizations let this happen? How does one have a totally dysfunctional team one year that doesn't win, develop kid's talents, or have fun, and turn around and resolve this by putting the same five people in charge the next year? And you act like you have the perfect team.

Eric was blessed to be a member of a team that was perfect, or as perfect as you would ever want to be. He was only 13 and probably didn't know that it would never get better. I coached that team. I certainly thought at the time I could improve on the team and make them "more perfect."

I couldn't.

As time went on, I believe Eric appreciated that one season more and more. His experience in high school was on the other end of the spectrum. One of the saddest things that I have ever seen on or around a baseball field occurred on May 28, 2007. It was the day that my son pitched his final high school baseball game, the 1-0 loss. They were favorites to not only win this game, but to win another state championship.

This wasn't the sad part of the story ....the fact that they lost.

What was sad is what I witnessed in the parking lot 45 minutes after the game had been completed. I went to pick up my son after the typical long talk from the head coach had been completed. I saw Eric talking to a teammate by his car. I stopped and talked for a few minutes. One would think that the best adjective to describe the players would be sorrow, anger, or perhaps humiliation in playing so bad against a team with a losing record. None of these emotions were present.

I saw relief.

Relief that the game was over; relief that the season was over. There was relief that the players did not have to go to one more practice, one more game and deal with the bad attitude and apathy that was present.

I said to my son, and his teammate,

"You guys don't look too upset."

The response from both of them,

"No one is upset."

That was the truth. Guys were running through the parking lot, laughing and giggling, asking each other who was going to Chipotles to eat. The coaches had sapped every ounce of fun and excitement out of the team. As one player told me a few days later,

"I guess we wanted to lose because of the coach more than we wanted to win for us. We were just so tired of it all."

CHAPTER 11

FULL CIRCLE

"It is too bad we can't live life backwards. Wouldn't it be great to have the knowledge as an adult and apply it when we were younger? I see the trivial issues now that were so important to us then. But the innocence was sweet and the picture in my memory of the sparkle in our kid's eyes and the excitement in their voice to each marvelous opportunity still thrills me. I am very honored that you looked at my dad with such warmth. His players were a rare bunch of young men and many times I think you knew him better than I did. He spent so much of his life with his boys that you have your own stories to tell. My dad would love it. He was a very humble man but he would be proud of the fact that his life's lessons to his team was appreciated and incorporated in your own life. This was his legacy."

—Saundra Spellman, daughter of Coach

It's a Saturday night at 6:55 and Sheryl and I had just arrived at the restaurant. Our reservation was for 7:00 and, like usual, we were on time. Conrad and Maria, like usual, were early and they were waiting for us. Steve and Joyce, like usual, had not arrived as of yet. The Pattens have a reputation for never being on time.

The Pattens arrived as expected, about ten minutes late. I wouldn't want it any other way. Steve is always the culprit. At least, he's always blamed. We got our table and ordered. We talked and laughed and compared notes. Jason, Eric, and Derek are no longer on the same field playing on the same team.

Jason had become one of the better pitchers in the area. He blossomed at Spalding High School as a sophomore pitcher as he made the all conference team. As a junior, he didn't miss a beat and put in another solid year and continued to develop. As a senior, he topped off his high school career by being named "Player of the Year" in his conference. His hard work was enough for him to be awarded a scholarship to Radford University in Virginia, a Division I school where he will continue his education and his baseball. He's quite a ball player and he's quite a young man. He's learned a lot of life lessons at an early age.

Eric took a different path, but had arrived like Jason as one of the better pitchers in the area. He started his final year on the high school team again in someone's shadow. After pitching five consecutive shut outs in league play, he was basking in his own sunshine.... for the first time. As nice as it was to see Eric pitch so well, the bigger reward is how many people were happy for him, knowing what he had fought and put up with the last four years.

Derek played ball at Mount St. Joes in Baltimore. Like Jason, he was a senior with dreams of playing college baseball. Interest had been shown by several schools before Frostburg won out. College baseball was also on his agenda.

Sheryl and I stay in touch with the four of them and on occasion enjoy each others company for dinner. On this evening, it was in Gambrills, Maryland, not more than two miles away from where our friendship began at the Gambrills Athletic Club. By the time we were done laughing and talking, we looked around only then to notice that a full restaurant was now nearly empty. The waiters were cleaning off the tables and it was 10:45. It was time to go.

Like so many times on the field, we went back in time, to a better time. We were remembering a tournament in November in Southern Maryland when the kids were 13 years old. It was so cold that Conrad went out and bought 15 pair of green earmuffs. I thought it was a nice gesture, but there's no way I was wearing them. Two hours later, they were on my ears. It was cold! We all laughed.

Steve's favorite story was the one in which I was thrown out of a game. It's only happened to me once. We were playing in Carroll County and the first batter of the game walked. Twice he took leads off of first base and twice the pitcher threw over to first.

Both throws were just "courtesy throws," nothing to attempt to pick off the runner off, only to set up a quicker throw. Sure enough, the third throw over was the pitcher's best move and our runner went back to the base. The play was closer than the first two, but he was definitely back to the base safely. It really wasn't even close. When the throw went over, however, the opponent's coach yelled, "He got him." Upon hearing this, the umpire said, "You're out!"

I was coaching third base and upon seeing what had happened, I yelled out,"Come on, YOU make the call" letting him know that I felt he was persuaded by their coach. He yelled over to me,

"You're out of the game."

I said, "Why?"

"We don't put up with that in Carroll County"

I guess I should have known it would be a long night when their coach was talking to the umpire by his car before the game, calling him by first name and asking him if he would be "coming to the store" tomorrow.

Well, I was out of the game and I needed to leave the area. The field at Carroll County is behind an elementary school. On the third base side, there is a hill where people sit watching the game. Way out in left field is a beautiful view of the whole complex. I decided to make that my home for the next seven innings. Beside a nice view, most of the other team's moms were sitting there as a group. I figured that I could sit there and listen to all the talk about their team. They didn't disappoint me.

Anyway, back to the field. My being given the "heave ho" created a few problems. First, I always coached third base and gave the signals. I had offered for other coaches to do it occasionally, but they always refused. Nobody really feels comfortable being in charge. The second problem was one that I didn't realize at the time. My other coaches didn't know the signals.

Eric and I sharing a great moment in March of 2007 with two other dads who truly enjoyed the Gambrills experience, Steve Patten, right of Eric and Conrad Weibler, far right.

So Steve and Conrad are now running the team and Steve is nominated to coach third base. He went out and started going through these signals that I had never in my life witnessed. I saw several batters looking down at him to get the signals and they all look fairly confused. Although this was an important league game, my once serious disposition gave way to the obvious comedy act given by our new third base coach. I was now laughing non-stop. The funniest part of this whole scenario is that Carroll County is known for a multitude of intricate signals, coaches yelling out code numbers while our batters were batting, and just generally throwing around all kinds of hand signs. They also spent a lot of time trying to steal the other team's signals. So, as Steve gave these signals which had absolutely no relevance to anything, you saw the Carroll County coaches continue looking at Steve and writing down what they thought his signals were. They were trying to break the code for the signals which really weren't signals. After about the third inning, Steve's son Jason told the team, "Don't even look at him, he has no idea what he's doing." It went on and on with the other team's coaches continuing to write furiously, trying to break the code. Finally, about the forth inning Steve called me on my cell phone. He informed me of the obvious, that he didn't know the signals. I told him that I had figured that out.

We went on to win the game 2-0. Eric pitched a shutout and Kylin hit two solo home runs. The same Kylin who was told by that same Carroll County coach when he tried out for his team "If you want to play on this team, you'll need to learn to play the outfield, my son plays first base." It was poetic justice. It was one of the best memories ever at Gambrills.

Every time Steve tells the story, it's funnier. He didn't disappoint us this evening.

We've been to Southern Maryland and Allentown and Richmond and Rehoboth Beach and Orlando and East Cobb and North Carolina and California to watch our kids play ball. We have spoiled them and would have it no other way. Like all other parents, we just want them to have everything that life offers; things we experienced and things we didn't experience growing up.

We wished the night wouldn't end.

There will be another night to go back and remember a bunch of 13- year olds making lifelong memories. Some of the best memories aren't on the field, like Tyler on the go-carts in Allentown, the beaches in California, or all the dinners. The most fun the team probably had was the football game late at night in the pouring rain in Rehoboth Beach. Five years later, Eric still talks about that.

We were playing a game last fall at Arundel High School against a pretty good team. The final score was 4-4. It was a good game to watch. I needed a few players for the game, so I had Eric check in school with some of the former Gambrills players to see if they may be available. He checked with Tyler Hibbs who couldn't play for some reason. But as the game started, there were Tyler's parents, Tom and Tina, sitting up in the stands watching the game. No real reason for them to be there other than their enjoyment of seeing kids they know playing baseball.

Tyler has become quite a ball player, and had quite a summer. He managed to make the Junior Olympic baseball team last year and this team played for ten days in Venezuela. Recently, he made the Pan American team that went to Mexico. Although he plays for a showcase team in the fall that travels on weekends, he occasionally sneaks down to play a game here and there at Gambrills.

Tom is sitting up watching the game talking to one of the parents. They're talking about showcases and competition and tournaments. All of a sudden, Tom says to the parent, "You know, sometimes I just wish we were back in Gambrills."

We all do.

We all want to go back, back to Gambrills, back to little league, to T-ball. Most of all, we want to go back to when everything was innocent and fun. Back to Coach Spellman and Joe Sheeler.

None of us would give up any of the accolades or victories or shining moments that our kids have experienced. We are immensely proud of all of their accomplishments. There isn't a week that goes by now that I do not read in the paper some write-up about a former Gambrills baseball player. They are all in the midst of their high school experience, or have moved on to the collegiate level, and many of them are basking in their own sunshine, their own well-deserved attention.

But in a way, all of us wish we could go back to that time that was related to me in the following e-mail, one which I have printed out and now read every day.

I was talking to a parent of one of my players one night about having a passion for the game. It must have got him thinking, and going back to a better time. He e-mailed me that night, very late at night. I just couldn't delete the message. It's one of my favorites.

Jeff:

You're on point about savoring the passion of the game, the magic, if you will, because in most cases, as you get older, the passion that you hold for baseball is probably your last true connection to the joys of childhood.

Once that baseball connection is severed the harsh realities of adulthood are front and center. As you know, rarely do the adulthood experiences come close to the magic of being a kid, where all things are possible.

You don't appreciate it fully until after it's gone. Sadly our lives are a little less full. We were in Never, Never Land and didn't know until after it was gone.

Jeff, that's why you coach, you want to be close to that magical environment that was Baseball Never Never Land. Where honor, integrity and fair play meant something and were rewarded accordingly. With rare exception, in the confines of the baseball field, your Daddy could have millions but if you couldn't field or hit, the baseball gods relegated you to the bench. If the poor kid was truly the best player the baseball gods rewarded him with playing time and all of the requisite accolades. In many ways, unlike the corrupt adult world, the baseball diamond seems forever pure.

My joy, much as yours, comes from experiencing, vicariously through my son again, the same joys and exhilarations that I experienced as a boy myself. To feel the magic again.

I was fortunate enough, although on a much smaller stage, to have had the game winning hit experience in an important baseball game, to have hit a game winning shot in basketball and scored a big touchdown in football. I will tell you this unashamedly, the feeling of exhilaration that I experienced at the pinnacle of each of those occurrences I have never since reached. At those very select moments no one on the entire planet was more elated or happy than I .... no one!

I want my sons to touch those same experiences, as any father would.

What more could I give them?

Mike

Wednesday, December 20, 2006 started out as just another trip to Pittsburgh. I had done this several times in the last couple of months. It was to see my Uncle Jim. His wife, my Aunt Louise, had passed away a few months earlier and he was suddenly left with an empty house and no one to share it with. He had no children and at 86 years of age, his life had been turned upside down.

No, it wasn't an uncle who I had been extremely close to or we had a lifetime of memories to share. Matter of fact, I had probably seen him three or four times in the last 15 years. It wasn't an uncle who was frail and weak of mind. Matter of fact, he was strong and proud and would rather struggle by himself than ask for help. Something happened to me the day that I attended my aunt's funeral. I still can't quite put it into words but as I left his house that night, something took a hold of me and all I knew was that I needed to make these trips. There was some significance to them that couldn't be explained. Maybe it was the way he grabbed my arm as I passed by him to leave the night of the funeral. He only said three words as he held on to me but they were profound. "stay in touch." Usually these words are said as a nicety, or formality, when you haven't seen someone for a while. The look in his eyes and the tone of his voice said something completely different, almost like a real genuine request from someone who in the last fifty years probably never asked anyone for anything. I just knew I had to come.

This was the week before Christmas and I was anxious to see him. It was always the same ritual. I would leave my house in Odenton, Md. at about 6:30 A.M., drive up and arrive at his house at about 11:00 a.m., engage in some small talk about the trip and my week, go out to lunch, come back and watch him take a nap, go to The Villa for dinner precisely at 5:00 (he would make reservations for exactly 5:00), come back to the house, sit and watch English movies, and see who would fall asleep first. I then would wake up early the next morning and drive back to Maryland before he woke. If I could stay for a while, I would wait until he got up and I would take him to breakfast.

Today my trip to Pennsylvania was a little different – I was going to arrive early. For some reason I woke up and got out of the house by 5:30, way ahead of schedule. My uncle's house is about 25 minutes off of the Pennsylvania Turnpike and I tried to hit that area of my trip by 10:30. Today it was 9:30. Not to worry, there was a nice big mall right off the turnpike and I needed to pick up a few Christmas presents; and of course, my ever present cup of coffee. That's how I would kill my time before I got to his house at 11:00.

As I was writing this book, things started happening that were almost more than a coincidence, kind of things that make you tingle or the hair stand up on your arms. Lots of things were coming together to let me know that this book needed to be written, almost as though it was therapy for me. It was just meant to be. It went way past baseball, it was really about life. Baseball was the comparison to life. Everything that happened out on the field occurred in your life. The key was whether you learned from it.

As I turned into the mall, a Borders bookstore was staring me in the face. This was perfect, a place to pick up a few last minute Christmas gifts. So into Borders I go and immediately head toward the sports section. A book on baseball would be nice, give me perhaps a little inspiration. I had started writing a chapter the night before with the subject matter being passion, how you need passion whether you're playing baseball or in life. As the words and thoughts started coming to me, I zoned in on a subject matter that was going to be my example. It was Jim Leyland, the manager of the Detroit Tigers. Leyland had previously managed the Pittsburgh Pirates, Colorado Rockies and Florida Marlins, where he had won a World Series. Baseball season had just finished two months ago, and once again Jim Leyland had a team in the World Series, the Tigers. He was regarded as one of the best managers in the major league. He was also my first coach when I played some ball in the Tiger's minor league system. Jim Leyland was the perfect person as a specimen for passion.

I also had just re-written some things the night before from some ideas given to me by John Zingaro, who had written the Spellman book and who had been helping me with my writing adventures. I had accomplished a lot the night before, thanks to two people who were clearly on my mind this morning, Leyland and Zingaro.

As I walked into the store, I immediately went to the sports section and zoned in on baseball books. One book stood out like a sore thumb. It was called *Fantasy Camp, Maz and the '60 Pirates*. For those of you who are too young or are not really baseball fans, Maz is Bill Mazeroski, who happened to hit the most renowned home run of all time (Sorry, Bobby Thompson). Mazeroski played for the Pittsburgh Pirates and his bottom of the ninth inning home run against the mighty Yankees in game seven of the 1960 World Series was one of the most dramatic plays in any sport of all time. No one will disagree with that statement. Maz and a bunch of other players from that team run a Fantasy Camp in Bradenton, Florida for anybody who would like to attend. You come up with the $4,000.00 which allows you to spend a week playing ball with all these former Pirates.

I opened the book and started scanning through the pages. I told myself that I am sure there was some inspiration here! I mean I remember these players. I'm from the Pittsburgh area. As I went through the pages, looking mostly at pictures, I stopped on page 108.

It was a picture of Jim Leyland, the same Jim Leyland who I was thinking about as I walked into the store, the same Jim Leyland who took a young Barry Bonds and got the Pirates within one pitch of the World Series. The same Jim Leyland who I took those five and six hour bus trips through the states of Iowa and Wisconsin with as a young minor league player when he was the manager. I fumbled through some other pictures. There was one of Danny Murtaugh, a very popular former manager who was in charge during that magical 1960 season ... the same Danny Murtaugh who came to Ellwood City in 1972 to scout a left-hander who was a pretty good prospect. That left-hander also got his picture taken with Murtaugh after that game and the picture still is in that left-hander's scrapbook.

I was just looking at it the other night.

I then saw a few pictures of Steve Blass, who was very instrumental in putting this camp together. Steve Blass was the star pitcher of the Pittsburgh Pirates in 1971 and he pitched a game-winning effort in game seven of the World Series that year. I have thought of Steve Blass a few times over the years. In that same year, 1971, a young left-hander became the first high school player to pitch in that stadium, on that same mound. That was a great experience!

All of this Pirate history and there was some that I could personally relate to! I grew up with the Pirates and deep inside I guess that maybe in a few of my pensive moments, I imagined myself playing for the Pirates, right there in Pittsburgh.

What a great book this was!

This, as was the case five years earlier with that letter in the mail box from John Zingaro, was without a doubt fate. This was just too many coincidences to not be fate. I thought about this as I was breezing through the rest of the book.

I stopped on page 78.

Fate had now turned to weirdness.

I remember thinking, Coach Spellman, you are certainly having fun with me, aren't you?

Staring at me in this book about the Pirate's Fantasy Camp was a picture of John Zingaro; the same John Zingaro who wrote the Spellman book, the same John Zingaro who attended this Fantasy camp, the same John Zingaro who wrote all those press clippings in my scrapbook. I now remembered John telling me that he had gone to this camp the year before. His church congregation had actually donated the money ($4,000.00) for him to go. It was a dream of his. And now I'm looking at pictures of him. I have been e-mailing him and talking to him for the last four years about this book. Several times, I have wondered what he looks like present day. I haven't seen him since high school.

Now I had my answer.

John as a different type of coach

After I got back from my trip to see my uncle, I dove into this book that I obviously had purchased. I read the whole thing and was extremely motivated. I was really into my chapter on passion.

I got a brainstorm.

I would write a letter to Jim Leyland. I played for him for such a short period of time; he wouldn't even remember my name. But it was something I needed to do, to tell him that some young 18-year-old kid was still affected by him 35 years later. So I wrote him a letter to tell him that, knowing that a response was probably not coming.

It didn't matter.

I also had intentions of sending John Zingaro a note about his write up in this book, but I was holding off. John had e-mailed me a month or so before this and told me that he had colon cancer and had to have surgery. He had bigger things on his mind.

I mailed the letter to Jim Leyland on a Tuesday and the very same day I received mail from none other than John Zingaro. He sent me details of his cancer surgery. He also sent me pictures of him at Fantasy Camp. We had never spoken about this camp, I never had the chance to talk to him about the book I bought, but the very same day I am sending a letter out to Leyland I am getting a letter from Zingaro. This whole scenario was way more than coincidence.

This planet is immense and awesome, but in a way the saying, "It's a small world" is very true. I was born in Freeport, Pa. the place I now go every few weeks to visit my uncle. I had given the Spellman book to all of my former players. One night a mother of one of the players called me and asked where I was born. When I told her, she replied, "So was I." Her family ran a grocery store there in Freeport, my uncle knew the family well (the Giardis) – and shared a few stories with me about them. Their other son went to college to play baseball at Marietta College in Ohio. I told her that my brother went there, that the coach there for years and years, Don Schaly, played his high school baseball in Ellwood City and he was on the first baseball team that Bill Spellman coached. He then went to Marietta to be the coach.

Last year, another father was telling me about this really neat tournament his son had played in the year before – where teams from Japan and the Netherlands came over and played. He said it was a small town outside of Pittsburgh. When I asked what town he said Freeport. I checked with my uncle about that tournament. He laughed and then told me a story. He was in World War II and has the souvenirs to back it up – including a knife that he took off of a Japanese soldier and killed him with – blood still on it. Anyway, he has several other Japanese souvenirs, but has never known what the writing on them meant – until the Japanese came to this tournament. He went down to the field one day during the tournament and the Japanese coach was gracious enough to spend time with him, translating all the writing.

Another dad told me to look into a Perfect Game Showcase that was being played in Florida. I looked it up on the internet and it was being held at Bill Frasier Stadium – the same Bill Frasier who coached at Gulf Coast Community College for many years and was very successful. This is the same Bill Frazier who played his high school ball in Ellwood City for Coach Spellman on his very first team. My brother Rich graduated from Lincoln High and went on to play for Coach Frazier at Gulf Coast – actually babysitting for the coach off and on. Frazier's wife tells the story that they would have to stock up on food before the ball players came over to baby-sit, and when the Fraziers came home, the cupboards were bare. The coach at Gulf Coast Community College became Darren Mazeroski, yes son of Maz, the Pirates Hall-of-Famer.

When Jim Leyland took a break from major league managing, he spent some time coaching a youth league that played out of New Brighton, Pa. –about six miles from where I played high school ball. New Brighton is the hometown of Terry Francona, the manager of the Boston Red Sox. Terry's dad, Tito, is a former major league ball player that scouted me in high school. It was the same New Brighton that was down the road on Rte. 65, where the frozen custard stand was.

It was July 7, 2003, the day of my mother's funeral. I was getting out of the car at the church at the same time my brother Rich had arrived. We hadn't seen each other for a while. From a distance, our eyes met and the first words out of his mouth were, "You look more like dad every time I see you."

I said, "Thank you."

He countered with, "It wasn't a compliment."

We both laughed.

I do look more and more like my father as I grow older. It's actually quite incredible how you cannot seem to have much of a resemblance as a child, and then all of a sudden there it is. I kind of like that. There's nothing wrong with having something of your parents that you can keep with you forever, especially their looks. Eric has turned out to be a good looking young man. He takes after his mother.

I remember as a young boy my dad would help coach teams that my brothers and I played on. I assumed at the time that it was just something a dad should do. Only years later, did I realize the huge commitment it took to coach. As my parents would say, "Money doesn't grow on trees" and growing up, money didn't come easy. Yet my dad managed to fit baseball time into his schedule. He didn't really have the time. He was an electrician by trade and it seemed that he was always doing some sort of side job to compliment his full time job of working in the mill. With six kids, one didn't have a choice. Moms didn't work back then. He worked full time, had a side job, and coached baseball.

It was different back then. You played ball in the summer in your home town. No showcases, no select teams, no high school coach telling you where to play or telling the coach how to play you. There was no fall ball. When the end of August came, you were done. The town then moved all its attention to the football team, and so did the players. Lots of guys played multiple sports. The baseball cleats went away, the football cleats came out. Baseball bats were packed away until March 1. We would go out when we could and still play pick-up games, but nothing really organized.

Our summer baseball coaches loved to coach. There simply was a passion for the game. There was one main field that was used, Sanders Memorial Field. It was named after Frank Sanders, who helped organize many a team in the small town of Ellwood City while coaching the Moose team in the local little league for years. The field was busy Monday through Saturday with a 6:00 p.m. and 8:00 p.m. baseball game. If it wasn't Pony League, it was Colt League, or American Legion ball. On Sunday the field was used in the afternoons. Everyone waited for the schedule to come out at the end of May. It was a big deal to see how many games you played "under the lights." Usually the older guys had the opportunity to play the 8:00 p.m. games, but occasionally a Pony League game (13/14) was slipped in there.

This was the field "over at the park," where Coach Spellman spent his summer nights.

Little League games were scattered throughout the neighborhoods. The older boys would umpire for $2.00 per game. Mr. Belonzi, the coach of the Colt League Reds, was also the baseball commissioner. He set up the umpire's schedule. You would get your schedule for two weeks. After the games were umpired, you would see him at the park the following Monday. Your money would be there in an envelope with your name on it. If Mr. Belonzi wasn't walking around giving out the envelopes, we went to see Charlie Maggi, who ran the concession stand with his wife. He would have the money.

My dad was a good coach. He knew the game. The one thing that stuck with me was that he would always go out of his way to not show favoritism toward me or my brothers. Although I was usually one of the best pitchers and hitters on the team, he would pitch me less than he should have and he would always move me down in the line up further than was necessary. I never complained. I knew what he was doing.

Who knew then that 35 years later I would do the same thing to my son, who I hoped would understand! I made sure he sat as much, or more, as the other players. Not until this moment, writing this book, did I realize that this came from my dad. Another one of those memories locked up that comes out only because I'm involved with baseball. You hear all these stories, and see in person, the player's dad who showcases his boy to always be the clean up leader, always be the pitcher who had to finish the game. "Why can't the rest of you be as good as my son" seems to be to familiar chant. Not back in the day.

Dad coached Little League, Pony League, and Colt League. He wasn't one of these dads who went out there and pretended he knew everything. Matter of fact, back in the day it wasn't about the coaches. There was no grandstanding and showmanship. It was about the kids. There was very little instruction from the coaches. They left that up to Coach Spellman and the high school. Summer ball was all about bragging rights. The coach put a line up out there and the kids played hard. All your games were against kids you went to school with; back to that community thing. We would spend the day at the Ewing Park pool swimming, and playing dodge ball, or playing pick-up games. Then we would go home, dress for the game, and play against each other.

I remember one game that was played "under the lights" at Ewing Park. It was a Colt League game, The Reds against the Cubs. This was big time stuff. I must have been 10 or 11 years old. My brother Jim played for the Reds, so he had to be 15 or 16. There were two teams from Ellwood City in this league and they were playing against each other. These were the same guys who were teammates on the high school team. Brothers played against brothers, best friends against each other. It was brutal. Dave Blazin was on the Cubs, Jeff Blazin, his brother, was on the Reds. These were wars. Somehow my big brother would get me a seat on the bench to watch the game. That was a thrill.

It was late in the game and the score was tied up. My brother Jim was on third base and there was one out. The coach of the Reds team was Chuck Belonzi, who was also coaching third base. All of a sudden Jim took off for home while the pitcher went in to his wind up. Jim was a really good ball player, and at that particular time, my hero. He didn't exactly have world-class speed, though. I mean he was a catcher. Well, here he comes and the pitcher threw the ball to the waiting catcher and he was out at the plate. Not even close. He tried to steal home! On his own!

I was in shock, as was all his teammates. He came in to the dugout and without saying a word, started putting on his catching equipment. All of a sudden I hear this voice from the stands saying to Mr. Belonzi, "Why did you send him?"

It was my dad.

Coach Belonzi just shook his head and said "I didn't send him."

My dad, without hesitating said, "Get him out of there."

Out of the game he came.

I'll never forget that night. Parents very seldom said anything to the coaches and my dad would be the last one to get involved with his son and a coach. These words just came out of his mouth.

Seeing that my big brother Jim obviously made a bonehead play, there was no choice other than to bench him. At least in my dad's mind. This was the rivalry of the year and they were playing for first place. It didn't matter, there was a lesson to be learned. Just like a couple of years earlier with Pete Sheeler and his dad. There was fierce competition, but it always seemed to take a back seat to a life lesson.

Where did those days go?

My dad coached me in Little League and one year in Colt League when I was 15. That was it. I was the last of three baseball brothers. From that time forward, he was a spectator only.

By this time, my brother Jim had attended Marietta College in Marietta, Ohio. He played for Don Schaly, who went on to become one of the most successful college baseball coaches ever. Coach Schaly played his youth baseball right on this field in Ewing Park. He went on to play at Lincoln High School, my high school, on Coach Spellman's very first baseball team. After a stint at Penn State University, he went to Marietta as baseball coach where he compiled at career record of 1,412 -316 (82%). He won three national NCAA Division III titles and was runner up seven times. Twenty of his players reached the major leagues. His favorite saying was, "Nobody will outwork us." At college, Jim's shoulder finally gave out. Years of blocking pitches, throwing out runners and home plate collisions had taken its toll. The dream was over. Any fleeting thought of advancing to the next step in baseball had met the harsh realities of life. It was time to move on.

I never saw Jim play college ball and actually had only witnessed one high school game that I can remember.

But what a game! I was fortunate that this memory was formed, and through Jim it has been engrained in my mind for the last forty years.

Just like it was yesterday.

When Jim was a senior, the baseball team won their division and had a play off game against Riverside, which was a school located extremely close to Ellwood City. Players on both teams knew each other and some were good friends. You couldn't have had a bigger rivalry. In the summer, they all played together, but now they were on a collision course against each other. The two pitchers, Ray Ott of Riverside, and Rich Bartholomeo of Ellwood, were two of the best around. The game was played at Ellwood City … at Ewing Park … and although not yet named it, at Sanders Memorial Field. Bartholomeo (Bart) and Jim were best friends.

I was in attendance at the game and I was a few weeks short of my 12th birthday. I remember being way out in left field about 400 feet away. That's the best view I could get of the game. There were more people there than I had ever seen at a game. To this day, I have never seen so many people at a high school baseball game. There were thousands of people. They were lined up and down both sides of the field from home to well past the poles that were about 330 feet down both foul lines. There were hundreds of other people sitting on chairs up on the road in right field, looking down on the field.

The game started, and expected, was somewhat of a pitching duel. The first few innings went quickly with the game being scoreless.

The game went on into the fourth, then fifth innings, still no score. The sixth inning came and went, still 0-0. The seventh inning also came and went without a run being scored. With every inning was more suspense. The huge crowd who was present at the start of the game had now become larger. No one was leaving.

The game went to extra innings and in the top of the eighth inning, Ellwood City put runners on first and second base with one out. Jim Potter was coming to bat. I remember that I was standing next to Ed Wigton, who happened to be my sixth grade basketball coach. As Jim walked up to hit, he looked at me and said, "I guess it's up to your brother."

I remember saying to him, "He'll get a hit."

The next thing I remember is Jim batting and a sound that, even at my age, well… I knew that sound. It was bat hitting ball the way it was intended to be done. Although as we all know it is round ball and round bat, the connection was made squarely, and the noise it made was heavenly, and the ball flew threw the air as if being shot out of a cannon, and the crowd on the third base side went delirious as the crowd on the first base side lost their breath. The left fielder and center fielder both took off toward the flight of the ball, both knowing there was no chance of catching it, only running it down before Jim could circle the bases. It was a "shot" to left center field that ended up being a triple. Two runs score and Ellwood went on to win 3-0.

Jim was the hero, and to be honest, he was *my* hero. He was my big brother and at that moment, I was so proud to be his little brother. I don't think in the last 40 years we have ever talked about that hit. I know it has to be the one that he'll never forget. Ray Ott, Bart, and Jim all ended up at Marietta College as friends and as teammates.

When I was 15, my brother Rich had just graduated from high school and was ready to enter Gulf Coast Junior College in Panama City, Florida that fall. His college coach would be Bill Frazier who also played on coach Spellman's first baseball team in Ellwood City. By the time Coach Frazier had finished coaching at Gulf Coast College, he had accumulated a record of 888-352 (72%)Today, the stadium is named after him. He also played at Ewing Park, right on this same field as did Richie Allen, Joe Namath, Mike Ditka and a slew of other western Pennsylvania athletes. Right on this field in Ellwood City, in Ewing Park. Rich graduated from Gulf Coast, then attended the University of Alabama to play for the Crimson Tide his junior and senior year. Once again, the hard facts of baseball were staring him in the face. Baseball was good to him, but it was over. Another flame had gone out.

We all grow up too fast. Everybody wants to finish high school and go out and conquer the world and be their own person. That world can have a nasty attitude. Life can get a hold of you and throw you around.

I graduated from high school, went off to conquer the baseball world and I was done in the blink of an eye. My career was over and the baseball memories were locked up for a long time.

Very few players make it to the majors. You need to have a combination of talent and good fortune. Most kids who are lucky enough to be signed by a professional baseball team never make it. They linger in the minor leagues until they are let go, or until they realize on their own that they may still have the desire, but not the necessary talent. So they finally leave the game and move on with their lives. They may stay away from the game for years, or perhaps forever.

Sometimes it takes a son to bring you back, to live your childhood again. That's what most of the dads are doing out there, trying to get that feeling back, the one we all had when we were just a kid.

The spring of 2007 was bitterly cold and baseball fields were not the most pleasant place to spend several hours – at least weather wise. I went out and watched Eric pitch and it warmed my heart. The county league started and Eric got the opportunity to pitch the first game. I told him that this was an honor, considering the fact that two of his teammates who were pitchers were both back from last year. They were both ahead of him in the pitching rotation a year ago and still considered better pitchers, at least in the coach's mind. For whatever reason, the coach decided to give Eric a shot.

He responded by pitching a shutout.

The next time it was Eric's turn to pitch he went out and pitched another shut out.

The third opportunity to go out and pitch in the league, he pitched another shut out.

He pitched three shutouts in a row.

Then it became four, and finally, a fifth consecutive shutout.

By the time he was finished, he had pitched 34 consecutive scoreless innings; no runs, not even an *unearned* run. I know that his "old man" never did anything close to that. I think that's a pretty good feat for any pitcher at any level. Elation and pride couldn't begin to explain how I felt.

By the end of Eric's senior high school baseball season, he managed to make several all county teams, get selected to the prestigious Brooks Robinson High School all-star team, be selected to represent Maryland against seven other states in Oklahoma, and accept a baseball scholarship to the University of Maryland, and go on to play in perhaps the toughest college baseball conference in the country, the ACC.

A year earlier, he wasn't deemed good enough to pitch for the high school team.

Eric Potter has now grown up. He now throws the ball like I used to throw the ball. He loosens up like I used to loosen up, standing 15 or 20 feet behind the mound before he actually gets on the mound. He changed to #13, the number that I always wore, the last year of high school without saying a word to me. He's a lefty like his dad.

**Eric showing his form in the 2007 Brooks Robinson
All-Star Game played at Camden Yards.**

Eric is now 6'2" and the 185 pounds that stretches over his frame consists of quite a bit of muscle. A long, long time ago – when I was in high school – I looked like this.

Those days are long gone.

At one time those memories were also long gone. Now, however, they are here, ever present every day. I can see and touch and smell them constantly — they are that real …that vibrant. I am once again a ball player. I am 17 and I am out on that field, out on that mound. The feeling of being a dominant pitcher has come back. There is no position on any team sport that is as exhilarating as being a pitcher on a baseball team who can dominate with his abilities.

The feeling is back.

I throw batting practice to my team, but it's more than that. When I walk out on the field before a summer game, I am back in high school in a play off game. When Eric now pitches, I can feel what he is feeling. He has given me this treasure to be able to re-live my childhood.

It is a great gift that I have received. It is so wonderful because to receive it, someone must first have it — have that ability to play the game and to be passionate about the game. I am happy for Eric.

Lots of people have called me, e-mailed me, and told me when I ran into them that they were proud of Eric and congratulations. Many added, "No one deserves it more than Eric." That's the part that I will savor. No one does deserve it more than Eric. You would have to know what he's gone through to understand why so many people have told me this. All kids go through a bunch of politics, pressure, egos, favoritism, and just plain bad coaches in their baseball career. Eric has had it more than the average kid.

Now Eric has his time in the sun. It may last a long time, or be over tomorrow. As we all know, there are no guarantees, but for this brief moment in life Eric has exemplified and combined great ball playing and a great amount of character. He is well liked and well respected. He returns these traits and values to others. He is selfless and more than most encourages and roots for his teammates. He gives credit when due and it seems that most people are genuinely pleased to see him do well.

Eric is an excellent baseball player, one that no longer can be denied. The coach who at one time called him "little Eric Potter"

e-mailed him last year with congratulations on his pitching performances. That was nice, but that coach still doesn't get it. The last
time I saw him, he told me that Eric had become a good ball player.
I didn't bother correcting him. I just smiled and said thank you. The
truth is that he was always a good ball player, but that coach, like
many others, couldn't see past their tape measure and jugs gun.
They don't have a clue about real ball players. They would notice a
ball crushed over the left field wall, but they wouldn't notice drive,
passion, and integrity if it bit them in the ass.

Now Eric is getting all the attention in the world. That's what
some coaches do — they cling on to kids that have done it on their
own — and pretend that they brought the kid along and developed
him. I would love to pretend that I had so much to do with Eric's
success, that I worked with him for years, nourished him, encouraged him, taught him and motivated him. I would love to be the
reason that he is such a good ball player and a fine young man.

But although that would certainly boost my ego and give me
that little shot of positive re-enforcement, it would be unfair and
selfish. Every day that Eric looks into the mirror, he sees all he
needs to see. No one should ever take credit away from someone
that deserves it.

Eric has done it all. It's not all about the destination; so much has
to do with the journey. The right life lessons need to be learned.

Perhaps some day I will watch Eric on TV. There's always a
chance. That would be wonderful, to see him make it to the major
leagues. I would be so proud of him and that may be a goal that he
has for himself.

I think, however, that Eric's final mark in baseball may be a little
less public with a little less fanfare.

But I think it may be more rewarding.

Instead of watching him on TV five years from now, perhaps I
will watch him on a ball field. Perhaps it will be the same ball field
that I am still coaching on, the same field that I am trying to motivate, educate and communicate baseball to kids. Perhaps it will be
the same field that I am trying to be effective.

Maybe Eric will feel that passion for baseball, as I do...... the
passion to go out and do the two things that you should do every

day while you're on a ball field coaching – learn something and be grateful that you have the opportunity to work with kids. Perhaps Eric will understand that through others he will get the best gift ever - a chance to re-live his memories- to go back to a better time.

Perhaps he will become a Coach Spellman.

Eric, thank you for the ride………..